€25.00

BRITISH AND IRISH AUTHORS

Introductory Critical Studies

JOHN DRYDEN

BRITISH AND IRISH AUTHORS
Introductory critical studies

In the same series:

JOHN DRYDEN

DAVID HOPKINS

Lecturer in English
University of Bristol

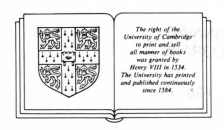

The right of the
University of Cambridge
to print and sell
all manner of books
was granted by
Henry VIII in 1534.
The University has printed
and published continuously
since 1584.

CAMBRIDGE UNIVERSITY PRESS

CAMBRIDGE

LONDON NEW YORK NEW ROCHELLE

MELBOURNE SYDNEY

Published by the Press Syndicate of the University of Cambridge
The Pitt Building, Trumpington Street, Cambridge CB2 1RP
32 East 57th Street, New York, NY 10022, USA
10 Stamford Road, Oakleigh, Melbourne 3166, Australia

© Cambridge University Press 1986

First published 1986

Printed in Great Britain at
the University Press, Cambridge

British Library cataloguing in publication data
Hopkins, David, 1948–
John Dryden. – (British and Irish authors)
1. Dryden, John, 1631–1700 – Criticism and
interpretation
I. Title II. Series
821'.4   PR3424

Library of Congress cataloguing in publication data
Hopkins, David, 1948–
John Dryden.
(British and Irish authors)
Bibliography: p.
Includes index.
1. Dryden, John 1631–1700 – Criticism and interpretation.
I. Title. II. Series.
PR3424.H67   1986   821'.4   85–19007

ISBN 0 521 30914 x hard covers
ISBN 0 521 31379 1 paperback

GG

Contents

v

A note on texts and abbreviations

There is, at the time of writing, no complete, old-spelling edition of Dryden's works, since eight volumes of the University of California Press edition (begun in 1956, and to be completed in 20 volumes) have yet to appear. I have, therefore, been unable to take my quotations for this book from any single edition. I have, wherever possible, used James Kinsley's Oxford English Texts edition of the Poems (4 vols., 1958). Plays (and their associated prefaces and critical essays) which have already appeared in the California Dryden are quoted from that edition. Where appropriate, I have supplied cross-references to George Watson's Everyman's Library edition of the prose, since this edition is easily available and commonly used by students. Dryden's letters are quoted from C. E. Ward's edition (1942; reprinted New York, 1965). A few quotations have had to be taken from other editions.

References for quotations are supplied in the text. Line references for poems and act/scene references for plays are followed by a citation of the relevant edition(s) (by volume and page), using the following abbreviations:

C   *The California Edition of the Works of John Dryden*, ed. E. N. Hooker, H. T. Swedenberg, Jr and others (20 vols., in progress, Berkeley, Los Angeles, London, 1956–)

H   S. Johnson, *Lives of the English Poets*, ed. G. B. Hill (3 vols., Oxford, 1905)

K   *The Poems of John Dryden*, ed. James Kinsley (4 vols., Oxford, 1958)

L   *The Letters of John Dryden*, ed. C. E. Ward (1942; reprinted New York, 1965)

W   John Dryden, *Of Dramatic Poesy and Other Critical Essays*, ed. George Watson, Everyman's Library (2 vols., London, 1962)

Preface

This book has been primarily designed as an introduction to Dryden's work for readers coming to the poet for the first time. I have attempted to give a coherent overall view of the shape and development of Dryden's career, and to discuss some of the pressures and forces, internal and external, which formed his work.

'A Man who is resolv'd to praise an Author, with any appearance of Justice', wrote Dryden in one of his prefaces, 'must be sure to take him on the strongest side; and where he is least liable to Exceptions.' I have tried to direct readers clearly towards those areas of Dryden's work which, in my view, display the poet's genius to its best advantage. Since I have sometimes emphasised areas of Dryden's work and qualities of his mind which differ from those which feature most prominently in modern commentaries, this book might have some interest for experienced readers who have never ventured outside the handful of Dryden poems which are most frequently recommended and anthologised today. Dryden is nowadays often thought of primarily as a commentator on the political and religious ideas, events and personalities of late seventeenth-century England. This book argues that his work is more profound, diverse and wide-ranging than such descriptions would imply. Dryden's verse, I shall suggest, abounds in insights and speculations of general and permanent interest about Man and Nature. He is more accurately described as a 'philosophical poet' than as a 'satirist' or 'public writer'. His best writing has an energy, vigour and liveliness which have seldom been rivalled in English poetry.

My specific debts to previous scholarship are recorded in the notes. I should like to acknowledge here the more general help I have had in thinking about Dryden and writing this book. My longest-standing debt is to Mr H. A. Mason, who, when I was an undergraduate at Cambridge, first kindled my interest in Dryden and showed me the importance of translation in the history of English poetry. His teaching and published work have been a continuing source of inspiration. Dr Lois Potter gave me help and encouragement in the early stages of my work. I have enjoyed and profited from many hours' conversation about Dryden, and literature generally, with Dr Richard Bates. I have had encouraging and enjoyable discussions with another fellow Dryden-enthusiast, Professor Charles Tomlinson. During the preparation of the book, Mrs Sandra Hopkins has read my drafts and made many suggestions for improvements. Ms Katy Koralek has also made useful comments. Dr Andrew Brown of Cambridge University Press has advised me on organisation and presentation. Dr Paul Hammond provided an invaluable critique of my final draft. My greatest debt is to my colleague, Dr Tom Mason, with whom I have had the opportunity to discuss each part of the book, and who has been unstintingly generous with his time and learning in commenting on my drafts.

I should like to thank the University of Bristol Publications Committee for granting me a loan towards typing expenses.

Introduction

Dryden: then and now

How much real poetic force there is in Dryden! His genius was acute, argumentative, comprehensive and sublime. He seems to take thoughts that are not by nature poetical but under a living force like fire they are all powerfully changed and incandescent. His chariot wheels *get* hot by driving fast. His style and rhythms lay the strongest stress of all our literature on the naked thew and sinew of the English language. Not only did the stronger feelings of the heart in all its dark or violent workings, but the face of natural objects, and their operation upon the human mind, pass promptly in review at his command. His figures and landscapes are presented to the mind with the same vivacity as the flow of his reasoning, or the acute metaphysical discrimination of his characters. Dryden's poetical power appears most of all, perhaps, in his translations. They are stamped beyond the others, with the skilled ease, the flow as of original composition, the sustained spirit and force, and fervour – in short, by the mastery, and keen zest of writing.

This chorus of praise for Dryden has been assembled from the remarks of six of the poet's most distinguished admirers. They include Coleridge, Tennyson and Gerard Manley Hopkins. Such enthusiasm for Dryden's work was commonly expressed during the eighteenth century and for most of the nineteenth. For a period of a hundred and fifty years after his death, Dryden was widely considered to be a poet with large and penetrating thoughts of general interest about Man and the world he inhabits. Few English poets, it was often said, could rival Dryden in the acuteness of his depictions of human behaviour, or of Man's relation to the animal world, to inanimate Nature, or to the workings of the gods. Dryden's best verse, it was thought, was remarkable for its variety, vigour, metaphorical vitality and imaginative fertility. Dryden had established imaginative links with great minds of other ages and other civilisations. He had improved as a poet as he grew older. Though marks of his genius were visible somewhere in practically everything he wrote, they showed most clearly and consistently in the translations which he composed in the last fifteen years of his life.

Though Dryden's work had been adversely criticised by a number of individuals in the early nineteenth century (Southey, for example, and Leigh Hunt[1]) it was not until the late Victorian period that sympathy for Dryden withered away extensively, and a consensus about his work began to emerge which (to judge from

1

popular textbooks and the attitude of most readers coming to Dryden for the first time) is still substantially the current one.

Dryden's talents, according to this view, were significantly different in kind from those of the other great English poets. Rather than having challenged or transformed the normal assumptions, modes of feeling and styles of writing current in his day, Dryden was said to have been peculiarly at home in the cultural and historical climate in which he lived. Dryden's work was seen as something very much of its own age, addressed to its own age, concerned with its own age. Dryden was thought of as the exemplar *par excellence* of Restoration culture – of an ethos which was rationalistic, prosaic, worldly-wise, complacent, urban, and essentially masculine and secular in temper. Consequently, the story went on, one could not expect from his work much depth of emotion, strength of religious feeling, breadth of human or cultural sympathy, or sensitivity to non-human Nature. Nor could one expect from him poetic language which exploited the resonance and nuances of words as well as their purely denotative properties.

Dryden, it was pointed out, was, in a very literal sense, the spokesman of his age. He occupied the posts of Poet Laureate and Historiographer Royal to two of the later Stuart kings, and wrote both prose and verse in support of the monarchy and of royal policies. He was also a member of the Royal Society. His works made use of the influential ideas of Hobbes and Descartes. Hobbes's philosophy, it was pointed out, was materialist. He was widely suspected of atheism. He advocated an absolutist state as the only way of controlling men's competing self-interests. Descartes believed in a dualistic separation of mind and body and in a universe whose motions could be explained by mathematical laws. The work of both philosophers was widely considered to have been crucial in the spread of a pervasive spirit of rationalism and scepticism in the later seventeenth century. Dryden's use of Hobbes and Descartes was thought to reveal his implication in and complicity with that ethos.

Finally, it was pointed out that Dryden provided entertainment for the substantially court-based audiences of the new Restoration theatres. His prose and verse often lauded the achievements of his age in literature, science, commerce and manners.

The present book can be seen as a plea for a return to the older spirit of enthusiastic but discriminating generosity towards Dryden. The post-Victorian received view, I shall suggest, has its basis in an overconcentration on a handful of Dryden's works (and those not always of the best), and on oversimplifications and misrepresentations both of Dryden's age itself and of the poet's relations with and attitudes towards it. Once one has jettisoned the oversimplifications and turned the main beam of one's attentions onto Dryden's best work, most of the modern objections fade away, and it becomes easy to recapture the infectious enthusiasm of Dryden's earlier critics for the vigour, fire, penetration, and imaginative fertility of his writing.

Like Dryden's earlier critics, I shall suggest that much of Dryden's best work is to be found in the translations of the last years. These are nowadays usually only read by specialists. But the qualities of Dryden's translations are such that they might win the immediate sympathy of readers new to Dryden, and also interest others who have not been attracted by those aspects of his work most often stressed by critics and anthologists today.

But to emphasise the attractiveness of the later work is also to cast new light on some of the (nowadays) more familiar poems of the earlier years. Many readers, accustomed to view Dryden's satirical and controversial poems narrowly in relation to the historical ideas, events and personalities to which they refer, miss the larger interests which they offer. When set beside and viewed in the light of the later work, the satires and public poems can be seen to contain, sporadically, penetrating general speculations about Man and Nature of the kind which are so clearly evident in the best poems of the last years, and thus to hold more interest for the ordinary poetry-reader than they would if merely regarded as topical and party-polemical documents.

The concerns of a true poet, Dryden and his early critics believed, can never, even when he is writing public or topical verse, be exclusively with the world in which he actually lives, moves, eats and talks. The necessary focus of any true poet's interest, they thought, is 'general nature' – the set of permanent unchanging conditions governing life on this planet which persist through the most momentous changes in society, language and manners. It is his hold on general nature which makes it possible for the poet to amuse, delight, impress and move men and women whose life, times and assumptions might seem in every way dissimilar to his own.

But, they believed, the poet can rarely write about general nature directly. For while nature's laws may be constant, the details of their working-out are continually and completely changing. 'Mankind is ever the same', wrote Dryden in the Preface to *Fables*, 'and nothing lost out of nature, though every thing is alter'd' (K4 1455; W2 215).

The poet penetrates to general nature by observing the workings of nature's laws *in* the precise details of the particular local world in which he lives. But the poet's observation of the world around him is entirely transformed by being brought into contact with other worlds which he has encountered in his reading and in his imagination. The poet is prompted by the world around him to ask again the great questions which have always been of concern to humans. What is man? How is man like and unlike the animals and 'inanimate' nature? In what ways is civilisation a hindrance or a help to him? How does man stand in relation to the great processes which seem to govern the workings of the universe?

Establishing the 'context' of Dryden's work amounts to far more than being attentive to the events, personalities, conditions and ideas which surrounded the poet at the time of writing. We must also be sensitive to the subtle ways in which the world before the poet's eyes is being brought into imaginative contact with the inner worlds of reading and reflection.

It is customary to distinguish, when reading topical poems of the past, between two broad types of writing. In the first type we feel that, once we have done some initial homework on the commentary in a good annotated edition, the footnotes seem on subsequent readings to fall quite naturally into the background of our minds. The poem or passage seems after a while to come (in Coleridge's words) to 'contain in itself the reason it is so and not otherwise'. Within what seemed at first to be a merely topical observation there was an insight which was not, after all, narrowly dependent for its life or truth on one particular, immediate, point of reference.

Other works never seem to take on this independence of existence and largeness of implication. On each re-reading the commentary has to be mugged up again from scratch. The poetry never becomes free-standing, with a life of its own.

The modern emphasis on 'Dryden the public poet' has perhaps encouraged readers to discriminate less than they should between those parts of Dryden's work which are narrowly tied to their original circumstances (and whose primary interest is therefore for the historian or the chronicler of changing literary taste), and those in which a leap from propaganda, documentary or fashion into the imaginative independence of art has taken place.

Dryden and translation

The suggestion that some of Dryden's most attractive and

impressive verse might be found among his translations often meets with a basic objection: How is it possible to include Dryden's translations among his best work when one can never be sure how many of their qualities are to be attributed to Dryden and how many to the authors he is translating? How can one legitimately praise Dryden for characters, descriptions and narratives which are not really his?

The objection rests, I believe, on a confusion about what constitutes originality in a poem. Dryden and his early admirers thought that a poet's originality does not reside in his ability to present ideas, feelings and situations which have *never* occurred to any other human being before or since; if poets did that, they would be unintelligible. Poets, it was considered, are gifted with the ability to formulate thoughts and to describe feelings and situations which seem to have been lurking within their readers' minds in an embryonic or confused form all along. An important part of the pleasure of reading any poem is, therefore, a feeling of recognition and assent. The reader's reaction to a poem is paradoxical: on the one hand, he feels that he is being told something entirely fresh and new in an entirely fresh and new way. But he also feels that he is being reminded of something which, in a sense, he has known all along – though without the poet's help he would never have realised it. Originality might, therefore, be more usefully thought of as a term to describe the effect which a poem has on its readers than as a term to describe the circumstances of that poem's composition. In the act of poetical composition, a very distinctive individual genius has brought to bear the full force of his art to produce a work which seems to allow its readers to experience, as if for the first time, thoughts and feelings which are simultaneously recognised as the common property of humanity.

If, therefore, a poet were to find himself just as fully engaged when he was inhabiting, imaginatively, the mind and character of an earlier poet as when he was reworking 'raw' experience or events, there would be nothing to cause us to relegate his translated work to a second-class status, or to regard it as any less his work than his other poems.

Translation, for Dryden, was an activity far removed from the mechanical hackwork which the word often implies today. So great was the bond of imaginative sympathy which Dryden felt to have existed between himself and each of the authors he chose to translate, that the translating process seemed to him as much a matter of discovering hitherto unrecognised elements in his own artistic character as it was of attending to the thoughts of another mind in another language. Often Dryden found that his originals gave him new perspectives on interests and problems which had already been preoccupying and fascinating him in other contexts. One can consequently see many anticipations, resemblances and continuities when one moves from his original to his translated verse and back again. So, while much interest and profit can be gained by exploring the precise nature of Dryden's relation to each of the poets whom he rendered, the translations can also be treated quite properly as an integral part of Dryden's own poetry, continuous with and inseparable from the rest of his work.

The Age of Dryden

Many of the prejudices which modern readers often have against Dryden seem to stem from prejudices against the Age of which he was the alleged spokesman and representative. I have already intimated that I do not think that Dryden can, in his best work, be rightly thought of as 'the voice of his Age' at all. But there are also reasons to believe that the Age itself has often been misrepresented in the popular imagination. Recent scholarship in several disciplines has cast in doubt many of the older generalisations about the political and intellectual history of post-Restoration England. Since the findings of this scholarship have sometimes been slow to reach the general reader it may be helpful to give some indication of their broad outline.

The Restoration has often been described as the beginning of an entirely new phase in English history, civilisation and culture. There are good reasons why to a Londoner of the time it might indeed have seemed so. Samuel Pepys gives eloquent testimony in his Diary to the feelings of relief and joy which were widely shared by Englishmen on the re-instatement of the monarchy, and to the hopes which many sustained that the new reign would usher in a period of unprecedented peace and prosperity for the nation. At his coronation, King Charles's procession passed through a series of triumphal arches. These were explicitly designed on the Roman model to reinforce the parallel between his accession and that of Augustus, renewer of peace after the Roman Civil Wars, genius behind the expansion of Roman dominion and empire, and patron of the Golden Age of Roman literature. The Puritanism of the Interregnum was now subjected to scornful abuse. Samuel Butler's *Hudibras*, a long burlesque poem pillorying the Presbyterians, became a best-seller. The life of the new king's court was in marked contrast to that of the Lord Protector's. Charles was surrounded by a group of young noblemen whose extravagant dress, flamboyantly licentious life-style and scurrilous lampooning soon became notorious. Charles freely indulged tastes which he had acquired during his exile on the continent. The theatres were re-opened, employing actresses for the first time in England.[2] Instrumental music, played by a band closely modelled on that which the king had heard at the court of Louis XIV, was heard in court and Chapel Royal.[3] Charles encouraged his royal musicians to study abroad. Pelham Humfrey, one of the most talented of the new Children of the Chapel Royal, returned from his studies in France, wrote Pepys, 'an absolute Monsieur'. The royalists' sojourn on the continent was also associated with the 'libertine' attitudes advocated by some members of the court circle.[4]

But the tendency of historians to stress the ways in which the England of the 1660s and 70s was a markedly different place from the England of the earlier seventeenth century has led to certain important distortions of the period.

Politics and the court

Earlier accounts of the political history of the Restoration period were often coloured by a set of assumptions which have been recently wittily caricatured by Professor J. P. Kenyon:

The later Stuarts, the sons of Charles I, soon showed that they had learned nothing from their father's fate. True, Charles II was clever and adaptable; after all, he was credited with the invention of the British Empire, the Army and the Navy, not to mention Science and the Theatre. But he was cynical and dissolute; he wasted money on women, just as his father had wasted it on paintings and his grandfather on boys. He managed to evade an enlightened and patriotic parliamentary opposition led by the great Earl of Shaftesbury, with the even greater John Locke as his ideas man, but the event proved Locke and Shaftesbury right. James II, not only an autocrat but a Catholic to boot, showed the Stuarts up in their true colours again, and he was painlessly removed by William of Orange, who was called in by the Whigs, assisted by a few unusually enlightened Tories. It was they and he who established a form of government which proceeded, subject to various trifling adjustments, down to the present day, and which not only made the nation Free and Rich but showed it to be Great and Right.[5]

Such a view, 'a distillation of nearly two hundred years of Whiggism, topped up with Liberalism', saw the Restoration as one phase in a continuing conflict between a crypto-Catholic and crypto-absolutist monarchy and 'the parliamentary gentry, fearless upholders of personal liberty and constitutional government',[6] true English Protestants whose eventual triumph in the 'glorious and bloodless revolution' of 1688 was crucial in establishing the modern system of parliamentary democracy and constitutional monarchy. And the generation of Marxist historians who set themselves against the Whig–Liberal orthodoxy saw the period as a temporary lull in an alternative drama whose heroes were the religious sectaries of the Interregnum and the Jacobins and anarchists of the French Revolutionary period. It is easy to see why neither view of the period would be likely to encourage or support a favourable view of Dryden – Poet Laureate to two of the detested later Stuart monarchs, controversial opponent of Shaftesbury and the Whigs, writer of theatrical parts for the most famous of Charles II's women, later a Roman Catholic convert, and, in his last years, a passive but unrepentant Jacobite.

Lately, however, historians have been disposed to take a less teleological view of the late seventeenth century than their Whig or Marxist forebears. Recent analysts of seventeenth-century political history have been less concerned with the partisan apportioning of praise or blame to Whigs or Tories than with exploring the complex power-struggles and clashes of personality and vested interest which can be seen to underlie the events of the period.[7] New work has established the gulf which lies between the paranoid fear of 'Popery' which prevailed in the period and the actual ambitions and desires of the majority of the small English Catholic community in the reigns of Charles II and James II.[8] Historians are now 'much less inclined to view Parliament and all its works with the awestruck veneration of their fathers and grandfathers'.[9] They are more appreciative of Charles II's genuine political skills. And they have been more inclined to emphasise the rôle played by incompetence, stupidity and pure chance rather than that of absolutist ambition in creating the various problems which beset the later Stuart monarchy.[10]

A distinctive feature of the older accounts of the Restoration period was an abhorrence of the life and values of Charles II's court. Commentators stressed the dissoluteness, profligacy and viciousness of the 'Court Wits' whose conduct brought disgrace on the country abroad and was resented at home. The Earl of Rochester had, after all, once admitted to having been 'for five years together . . . continually Drunk'.[11] And there was the famous story of Sir Charles Sedley and his cronies who once, after a heavy drinking

bout 'at a cook's house at the signe of the Cock in Bow-street near
Covent-Garden . . . being all inflam'd with strong liquors . . . went
in the balcony joyning to their chamber-windows, and putting
down their breaches . . . excrementized in the street'.[12]

The king, it was stressed, was little better. Sir John Coventry,
wrote Pepys in July 1667, 'tells me that the King and Court were
never in the world so bad as they are now for gaming, swearing,
whoring and drinking, and the most abominable vices that ever
were in the world'.[13] Charles, reported Pepys, 'is at the command
of any woman like a slave . . . he . . . cannot command himself in the
presence of a woman he likes'.[14] Rochester put the point less
diplomatically:

> Peace is his aim, his gentleness is such,
> And love he loves, for he loves fucking much.
> Nor are his high desires above his strength,
> His sceptre and his prick are of a length,
> And she may sway the one who plays with th'other,
> And make him little wiser than his brother.
> Restless he rolls about from whore to whore,
> A merry monarch, scandalous and poor.[15]

Taking their cue partly from such evidence, literary historians often
remarked on the falling-off which Restoration court life represented
in comparison with its Jacobean and Caroline antecedents. The
degeneracy of the Restoration court, it was suggested, was both
symptom and cause of the diminished position which the monarchy
was coming to hold in the life of the nation:

If the old monarchy had permeated the social organism from roots to crown,
the restored court sat uneasily on top of a flourishing and self-sufficient body
of merchants, who in the very principles of their ethics and religion were
diametrically opposed to the conceptions which the Court wanted to
perpetuate. This body of hard-working and enterprising citizenry had
solidified and extended its position independently through the many years
of the King's absence, and were in financial control of the country upon his
return. The Court recognized its old enemies, and cocked a snook at them at
every opportunity by flaunting its own licence and privilege, but this did the
Court little good and only provoked a showdown before the century was out
which fairly well quenched their by then flagging spirits. But in addition to
this bellicose obligation to offend the standards of the solid bourgeoisie, it
was natural that the court should really go rotten in and of itself, since its
position was so superficial and dependent that it was more like a bad appen-
dix than that combination of head and heart which it could once lay claim
to.[16]

The contrast in aura and spiritual values between the Restoration
court and the old regime was suggested by others:

Royalty returned, but never again would men feel for it as they had before the deluge: one was 'loyal' to Charles II – aggressively, heartily, alcoholically loyal – but nobody felt for him the mystical reverence that had been felt for his father and grandfather. The Court and courtiers returned, and so did poets to flatter them; but nobility and magnificence would never be what they had been to Shakespeare and Donne.[17]

But such views, later scholarship has maintained, often underestimated the degree of tension which had always existed when men of intelligence had attempted to conceive of the court and king as divinely sanctioned cornerstones in the spiritual and cultural life of the nation. The person of James I, we are reminded, with his seedy homosexuality, his penchant for worthless favourites, his revolting appearance and unsavoury personal habits, cannot have made it always easy for thinkers and observers to sustain the traditional concept of the king as God's minister on earth and the centre of a divinely appointed social order. King James's tongue, reported one witness, was 'too large for his mouth, and made him drink very uncomely, as if eating his drink, which came out into the cup of each side of his mouth . . . his walke was ever circular, his fingers were ever in that walke fidling about his cod-piece'.[18] Shakespeare's creation of the benign and saintly King Duncan, it might be felt, could not easily be based on models to hand. The ideal vision of king and body politic to be found in the best Elizabethan and Jacobean writers was one which had to be created by strenuous (and often precarious) imaginative effort. H. A. Mason has pinpointed the dilemma which faced intelligent men from the reign of Henry VIII onwards when they contemplated the court:

The Humanist . . . found the Court setting him the most serious of his life-problems . . . For it was clear that if civilisation were to return to Europe, it could only spread by taking root in the centres of each society. In semi-feudal countries, such as England, it was the court or nothing. When the Humanists came to court, as come they must, if they wanted responsible posts, they contrived a sort of civilised community among themselves, but they did not set the tone at court. It is remarkable to find how More and Erasmus, men fond of company, hated the life of the court and avoided it as much as possible. It did not provide them with a fit setting for their social lives, for it offended their practical morality at every step. This problem, of course, was never solved: there is little difference in Erasmus' picture of the court and that we find in Donne's Satires: 'I do hate/Perfectly all this towne.'[19]

Dryden had very good reasons for his continued support of the Stuart monarchy. His political conservatism was always closely bound up with a horror (shared by many of his contemporaries) that the chaos of the Civil War could easily return. At no time was this fear more acute than in the early 1680s, when Dryden's activity as a political propagandist was at its height. The Civil War of the 1640s had been preceded by talk of a popish plot, and by a widening breach between Parliament and what was regarded as a crypto-Catholic and francophile court. The parallels between 1641 and 1681 were obvious and ominous to many observers.

But Dryden's conservative royalism was always a complex phenomenon. In some of his best poetry he voiced criticisms of the Restoration court which are every bit as severe as any to be found in the writings of the nineteenth- and twentieth-century historians.

Literature and ideas

Just as older generalisations about the political history of the Restoration period have been questioned by recent scholarship, so have older accounts of the 'ideas' of the age. Prominently stressed in earlier accounts of Restoration intellectual life was the rôle of the Royal Society, the institution for the development and propagation of scientific knowledge which was granted its Royal Charter by King Charles in 1662. In his *History of the Royal Society* Thomas Sprat described the style of prose recommended by the Royal Society for its members' use:

They have exacted from all their members, a close, naked, natural way of speaking; positive expressions; clear senses; a native easiness: bringing all things as near the Mathematical plainness, as they can: and preferring the language of Artizans, Countrymen, and Merchants, before that, of Wits, or Scholars.[20]

This style, it was often suggested, was symptomatic of the rationalistic matter-of-factness of the new age: it was the style of the Age of Reason, and the desire for order, clarity and ease expressed by Sprat was closely akin to that felt by the poets and literary prose writers of the period and implemented in their work.

But recent work on late seventeenth-century science has demonstrated that the scientific advances of the period cannot be simply identified with the work of the Royal Society. Nor can the work of Restoration scientists be straightforwardly associated with the advance of sceptical, secularist, materialist and anti-supernaturalist attitudes in the larger community.[21] More specifically, it has been shown that Sprat's remarks on the Royal Society style cannot be afforded the significance which they were given in older accounts of the literature of the period. Indeed, it has been demonstrated, they have been seriously misrepresented by being taken out of context:

> Sprat rejects equally the sophisticated language of academy, commonwealth and court as unsuitable for the purpose of science. Academic language was verbose and satiated with out-worn terms; the language of the commonwealth was too rhetorical, seeking to sway opinions by plausibility; that of courts too ornamental and poetical. The mode the Royal Society adopted was . . . not a literary form, and the Royal Society knew this. In the *History* Sprat says that experimental philosophy will not impair 'the usual *Arts*, whereby we are taught the Purity, and Elegance of *Languages* . . . the same words, and the same waies of Expression will remain'. The only effect on the language, he said, would be an addition to its vocabulary and imagery . . . The prose form which did emerge triumphantly during the second half of the seventeenth century, the style of which Dryden was the great exponent, was not characterized by scientific starkness. Its outstanding quality was not plainness but flexibility . . . That new style was the one through which the main-stream of modern English prose was to flow, the style to which Samuel Johnson paid tribute for its clarity, vigour, variety, lightness of touch, ease and grace. . . . Sprat himself in the Royal Society's *History* did not employ the style which he recommended to scientists, for the obvious reason that he was writing history, not science.[22]

Dryden made use of modern scientific discovery as a source for vocabulary and imagery in just the manner that Sprat envisaged. But the passage just quoted indicates some of the reasons why it is quite mistaken to look in Dryden's style, in prose or verse, for any more pervasive influence of the 'Royal Society manner' described by Sprat.

Modern research has made similarly short shrift of earlier accounts which sought to attribute the supposedly universal scepticism and rationalism of the later seventeenth century to the philosophical thought of Hobbes and Descartes. The reception of both philosophers' work, it has been shown, was (like the work itself) a far more complex phenomenon than was often previously supposed. And the opportunistic use of Cartesian phrasing or Hobbist sentiment in a play by Dryden or one of his contemporaries cannot be used to demonstrate that the Mind of the Age was being steadily diseased by Cartesian or Hobbist assumptions.[23] Dryden, anyway, usually gives his Hobbist sentiments to his villains.[24]

Labels for the Age of Dryden

Various titles have been used by literary historians to characterise the period which is thought to have been inaugurated at the Restoration. It has been variously described as the Age of Reason, the Age of Science, the Neoclassical period, the Age of Satire and the Augustan Age. Each of these labels, recent scholarship has suggested, is seriously misleading.

The designation of the period as an Age of Reason rested on the misconceptions about the importance of the Royal Society and Descartes already mentioned. The period's literature is, in fact, often characterised by a marked *distrust* of reason.[25] The very term 'reason' was, in fact, hardly ever used by the best writers of the age as if it had a fixed or absolute meaning. And Dryden, as we shall see, stressed the crucial rôle of inspiration in the creative process: for him, poetic composition simply could not be effected by a mind operating at ordinary room temperature. We are told that a friend, visiting Dryden the morning after he had been up all night composing *Alexander's Feast*, found the poet 'in an unusual agitation of spirits, even to a trembling'.[26]

I have already alluded to some of the oversimplifications which are involved in calling the Restoration an Age of Science. To call it a 'Neoclassical' age is equally misleading, since it implies both that the writers of the period thought of their works as derivative, and that what they were derivative *from* was exclusively the literature of ancient Greece and Rome. But

Like all great artists, Dryden and Swift and Pope did not think of themselves as 'neo'-anything: they were attempting to do something new, something that had not been done before; and it is Johnson (whose own ways of writing and thinking are utterly unlike anything that had been done before or was to be done afterward) who most loudly applauds their originality, their invention, as an indispensable element of their genius.[27]

When Dryden and his followers drew on the classics for inspiration (as they frequently did), it was in the full confidence that they could make use of the Greek and Roman poets because they were their modern peers. And it was not only to the classics that they went. (The term 'classical' itself, anyway, covers over a thousand years of writing in two languages, from Homer in the seventh century B.C. to the Christian Boethius in the fifth century A.D.) Dryden and his disciples drew on Renaissance Italian epic, Elizabethan poetry and drama, contemporary French literature, the Bible, medieval romance, and Miltonic epic as well as on the poets of Greece and Rome.

The title 'Augustan' for the post-Restoration period of English literature has commonly been used in two senses. Sometimes it suggests that it was to the Roman writers who flourished under the reign of the Emperor Augustus (Horace, Virgil, and Ovid) that the writers of Dryden's period looked for particular inspiration. But even within Roman literature, Dryden's sympathies and interests extended beyond these poets to pre- and post-Augustan writers: Lucretius, Juvenal, Persius, Tacitus. The second use of the title 'Augustan' suggests that the writers of Dryden's time saw their own period as a modern equivalent of the reign of Augustus: a period of peace, prosperity and imperial expansion, in which old factions were reconciled and the arts might be expected to flourish under the beneficent patronage of the king and his attendant aristocracy. This suggestion is borne out by some of the evidence. But important qualifications must also be made. It has recently been pointed out that analogies between the present and the reign of Augustus were constantly made by English writers from the Middle Ages to the Regency: nothing special marks off the post-Restoration period in this respect from those which preceded and succeeded it.[28] And while Dryden and his contemporaries could sometimes write as if they thought their own age had arrived at a pitch of artistic perfection which rivalled that of the Golden Age of ancient Rome, they also, in their better moments, were able to respond generously to the genius of writers (such as Homer, Chaucer and Shakespeare) whose work, it might be thought, should have seemed inimical to men who were convinced of the transcendent refinement and polish of their own times.

The 'Age of Satire' label for Dryden's period is, like the others, misleading, and, again, has been both a cause and symptom of the post-Victorian contraction of sympathy for Dryden. It is, of course, true that much satirical poetry was written during the period. But to stress satire involves overlooking the many other kinds of writing which flourished at the time. In Dryden's own *oeuvre*, satire as such occupies a very small place – less than one volume of the twenty which comprise his complete works.

Perhaps the most misleading of all the blanket titles for the literature of Dryden's period is the label 'Restoration' itself. For the almost universal habit of regarding 1660 as a Great Divide has done as much as anything else to inhibit appreciation of the best work of the period. Milton is generally thought of as a 'pre-Restoration' author. But *Paradise Lost* did not reach its final form until 1674, when Dryden was forty-three and the Restoration already fourteen years in the past. Dryden, Milton and Marvell worked together in the same government office. The careers of most writers who published works in the years after 1660 – Cowley, Milton, Marvell, Cotton, Davenant, Waller, Evelyn, Hobbes, Isaak Walton and Bunyan, for example – had already been established before the Restoration. Many revivals of Jacobean and Caroline plays were presented on the Restoration stage. Many older literary works (those, for example, of Spenser, Donne, Herbert, and Shakespeare) were reprinted after 1660. The careers of many of the writers of Dryden's circle continued well into the eighteenth century. None of the major verse forms of the Restoration are new. There is a direct continuity of diction, phrasing and rhythm between the couplets of Dryden and those of Chaucer, Spenser, Jonson, Sandys and Denham, just as there is a direct continuity between Dryden's blank verse and that of Shakespeare, and between his Pindarics and those of Jonson and the pre-Restoration Cowley. Just as the stress on the 1660 divide has caused many continuities between the Restoration and the periods which preceded and succeeded it to be obscured, so it has caused new developments within the Restoration period to be overlooked. A notable instance is the important influx of new French ideas in the 1670s and 80s associated with the names of Thomas Rymer and John Oldham. This movement represents a quite different kind of 'French influence' from that which was brought home by the exiles in 1660.[29]

The cumulative effect, therefore, of recent scholarly work on the Age of Dryden is to encourage extreme scepticism about older generalisations about the period and its effects on literature, and to see it both as more diverse within itself and more continuous with the Ages which preceded and succeeded it than had been commonly supposed.

1

Dryden's verse

Reading couplets: a lost art?

It is never possible when discussing any poet's work, to separate 'manner' from 'matter', 'form' from 'content', 'style' from 'substance'. A chapter offering to discuss Dryden's verse before discussion of the works in which that verse is used therefore needs a few preliminary words of apology and explanation.[1]

Such a chapter might be useful for two related reasons. The first is that reading 'heroic couplets' (the verse-form which Dryden uses in nearly all his most famous poems) seems to have become something of a lost art. Readers new to Dryden often find it difficult to hear his verse, and consequently are unable to read it out, whether aloud or to the inner ear, with anything like the required range of tones and expressiveness of movement. Because they don't feel comfortable with couplet verse beginners often tend to reduce it to a uniform sing-song, with a lurch towards the rhyme-word at the end of each line, whatever the sense of the passage might seem to demand, thus:

diDUM diDUM diDUM diDUM di*DUM*
diDUM diDUM diDUM diDUM di*DUM*

It is, I believe, often because, though their eyes may have passed over many pages of couplet verse, readers have never really listened to it, that they are so willing to believe the worst of the form and are so easily bored by it.

A reader of verse in an unfamiliar form faces problems similar to those faced by a musician coming to study a piece written in an idiom new to him. When sight-reading the piece through, the musician will stumble over technical difficulties and his phrasing and articulation will be insensitive to many of the composer's demands. Many hours of thoughtful, attentive and patient practice will be necessary before he can play the piece with both proficiency and understanding. But he might find that while practising he is given some help and confidence by written commentary on the general features of the new composer's style. It is help of an analogous kind which the present chapter attempts to offer a reader new to Dryden's verse.

Dryden's couplets: discipline and freedom

Dryden, like all great poets, believed that there can be no art without discipline and artifice. The poet's art, he thought, controls, shapes, moulds and adorns the inchoate, vague and ugly mess of language which we use in everyday life, so that it becomes in his hands something far more precise, expressive, beautiful, and truthful. Through the exercise of his art, therefore, the poet produces something which is the very opposite of being restrictive or restricting.

A large part of the pleasure in reading Dryden's couplet verse derives from that paradoxical combination of predictableness and surprise which is part of the experience of reading all good verse written in a regular metre. The effectiveness of Dryden's couplets as an expressive medium depends on the reader's recognition that a particular combination of stressed and unstressed syllables constitutes what we might call the metrical norm of each line. The rhyme constitutes another element in that norm, linking each pair of lines into a larger metrical unit, the couplet. For expository purposes, the metrical norm of Dryden's verse can be represented diagrammatically as

diDUM diDUM diDUM diDUM di*DUM*
diDUM diDUM diDUM diDUM di*DUM*

Here the italics indicate the rhyme word. But it must immediately be pointed out that this is a norm to which no actual heroic couplet ever entirely conforms. For no set of English words, even if their pattern of stressed and unstressed syllables seemed at first sight to correspond exactly with the paradigm, could be read with the impassive evenness of its nonsense syllables. Even lines like Dryden's

They drank, they laugh'd, they lov'd, and then 'twas Night

or Donne's famous

Before, behind, between, above, below

would never be read with exact mechanical evenness by any reader who was really thinking about what he was reading. Even in such regular lines, the resonances, force and colourings of the constituent words ensure that the reader departs subtly from the norm.

17

For many people, the epitome of the 'Augustan' heroic couplet is to be found in the self-contained epigram, such as Pope's

> You beat your Pate, and fancy Wit will come:
> Knock as you please, there's no body at home

or the string of end-stopped antitheses, as in this passage from Pope's *Eloisa to Abelard*:

> I ought to grieve, but cannot what I ought;
> I mourn the lover, not lament the fault;
> I view the crime, but kindle at the view,
> Repent old pleasures, and sollicit new:
> Now turn'd to heav'n, I weep my past offence,
> Now think of thee, and curse my innocence.

It was this second pattern which the young John Keats seems to have had in mind when he wrote that the poets of Dryden's school

> . . . swayed about upon a rocking horse
> And thought it Pegasus . . . [2]

Dryden's best couplet verse, however, does not run regularly into epigram or antithesis, or indeed into any predictable set of shapes or formulae. Even when his couplets are technically end-stopped, they seldom in fact stand alone as separate entities, but usually form an integral part of a larger block of sense. Two of Dryden's most famous lines are often quoted as if they comprised a self-contained epigram:

> Great Wits are sure to Madness near ally'd;
> And thin Partitions do their Bounds divide:

but the final punctuation mark of this couplet is a colon, not a full stop. For the unit of thought to be completed, we have to wait another eight lines:

> Great Wits are sure to Madness near ally'd;
> And thin Partitions do their Bounds divide:
> Else, why should he, with Wealth and Honour blest,
> Refuse his Age the needful hours of Rest?
> Punish a Body which he could not please;
> Bankrupt of Life, yet Prodigal of Ease?
> And all to leave, what with his Toyl he won,
> To that unfeather'd, two Leg'd thing, a Son:
> Got, while his Soul did hudled Notions try;
> And born a shapeless Lump, like Anarchy.

The eighteenth-century prosodists sometimes spoke as if all heroic lines must have a pause, a temporary resting-place for the voice which can only come at certain points in the line, and which divides each line into two 'hemistichs' or half-lines.[3] But Dryden's subdivision of his couplet lines is nothing like as regular, restricted, or mechanical as such descriptions might imply. Sometimes his lines have no internal division whatsoever:

> The Priesthood grossly cheat us with Free-will.

Sometimes there is a central break, dividing the line into two equal, or nearly equal halves, and producing a neat antithesis:

> Bankrupt of Life, yet Prodigal of Ease?

Sometimes a line is broken up with three or more pauses:

> Wrath, Terror, Treason, Tumult, and Despair.

As well as Dryden's pauses varying in number, they can come at any point within the heroic line, from after the first syllable:

> No; I have Cur'd my Self of that Disease;

to the ninth:

> The King . . .
> Thus answer'd stern! Go, at thy Pleasure, go.

When reading Dryden, therefore, the voice may have a pause at any point between each of the twenty syllables which make up an heroic couplet. The rhythmic units which form a Drydenian couplet line are often not peculiar to the iambic pentameter at all. Dryden can form an heroic line out of component parts which are equally in place as short lines in a non-couplet poem. In *Alexander's Feast*, for example, a short line occurs –

> He sung Darius Great and Good,
> *By too severe a Fate,*
> Fallen,

which had previously formed the 'hemistich' of a couplet line in *The Third Book of the Aeneis*:

> And Priam's Throne, *by too severe a Fate.*

A Dryden couplet line, moreover, can contain as many as ten words:

> By Love his want of Words, and Wit he found

or as few as four:

> Expos'd upon unhospitable Earth.

19

Dryden's couplet verse therefore has great flexibility both (on the level of individual lines and couplets) in the variety of phrase-lengths which can be accommodated, and (on a larger scale) in the number of lines which it takes to complete the unit of sense. Pregnant aphorism and sweeping verse-paragraph are equally possible, and so are numerous intermediary stages between the two. This, combined with the fact that the 'iamb' (diDUM) is a predominant rhythmic pattern in most ordinary spoken and written English, allows Dryden to accommodate an immense variety of utterance within his couplet form without either violating natural English word-order or straying so far from the metrical norm that the reader is left uncertain about the metre in which the lines are written. 'Varying the pauses' (as the eighteenth-century prosodists would have put it) is thus for Dryden, an organising, patterning, and controlling of the natural rhythmic elements of the English language.

Dryden can, if he wishes, enjamb his couplets, compelling the voice to read over the line-endings for several lines on end, in a manner which is more usually associated with the blank verse of Milton or Shakespeare:

> For backward if you look, on that long space
> Of Ages past, and view the changing face
> Of Matter, tost and variously combin'd
> In sundry shapes, 'tis easie for the mind
> From thence t'infer, that Seeds of things have been
> In the same order as they now are seen:
> Which yet our dark remembrance cannot trace,
> Because a pause of Life, a gaping space
> Has come betwixt, where memory lies dead,
> And all the wandring motions from the sence are fled.

From this example it can easily be seen that the rhyme words in Dryden's couplets are by no means always designed to 'clinch' an epigrammatic point. Their main function in the passage above seems to be to remind the reader, subtly but constantly, of the metrical pattern against which the units of sense are working so powerfully, and to reinforce our realisation that we are being invited to attend to a strenuously connected chain of thoughts.

Speed

Another element in the variety of Dryden's couplet artistry is his ability to control the speed at which his verse needs to be read, both within individual lines and couplets, and on a larger scale from

group of lines to group of lines. Dryden's verse can accommodate a
large number of different *tempi*, and can make rapid transitions
between them. The speed can sometimes become breakneck:

> Stiff in Opinions, always in the wrong;
> Was every thing by starts, and nothing long:
> But, in the course of one revolving Moon,
> Was Chymist, Fidler, States-Man, and Buffoon:
> Then all for Women, Painting, Rhiming, Drinking;
> Besides ten thousand freaks that dy'd in thinking.

It is sometimes briskly businesslike:

> The Midnight Parson posting o'er the Green,
> With Gown tuck'd up to Wakes; for Sunday next,
> With humming Ale encouraging his Text;

sometimes slowly and steadily majestic:

> The Monarch Oak, the Patriarch of the Trees,
> Shoots rising up, and spreads by slow Degrees:
> Three Centuries he grows, and three he stays,
> Supreme in State; and in three more decays:
> So wears the paving Pebble in the Street,
> And Towns and Tow'rs their fatal Periods meet.
> So Rivers, rapid once, now naked lie,
> Forsaken of their Springs; and leave their Channels dry.

The final line of this example shows Dryden varying his verse
by departing from his ten-syllable couplet norm. He does this
frequently, and in two main ways: either a third ten-syllable line is
added to form a 'triplet' (marked in the right-hand margin for the
reader's convenience by a curly bracket), or a longer line, such as a
twelve-syllable 'Alexandrine' (as in this example), or a fourteen-
syllable 'fourteener', is substituted for one of the heroic lines. These
substitutions can have different effects in different contexts. In his
Essay on Criticism, Pope offered a witty description of the slow,
laboured movement which is associated with the Alexandrine in the
hands of a hack poet:

> Then, at the last, and only Couplet fraught
> With some unmeaning Thing they call a Thought,
> A needless Alexandrine ends the Song,
> That like a wounded Snake, drags its slow length along.

Dryden can sometimes use an Alexandrine deliberately to evoke a
feeling of laboured effort:

> He courts the giddy Crowd to make him great,
> And sweats and toils, in vain, to mount the Sovereign Seat.

But his Alexandrines can, on other occasions, be light and mercurial (in this example we have the common combination of triplet and Alexandrine):

> Nor darkling did they dance, the Silver Light
> Of Phoebe serv'd to guide their Steps aright,
> And, with their Tripping pleas'd, prolong'd the Night.

Dryden's ability to effect rapid changes of *tempi* can be seen to good advantage in this movement from ponderous effort to headlong motion:

> What is it, but in reasons true account
> To heave the Stone against the rising Mount;
> Which urg'd, and labour'd, and forc'd up with pain,
> Recoils and rowls impetuous down, and smoaks along the plain.

Here the couplets are again varied, this time with a final fourteener.

Harmony and rhythm

It is impossible for a reader of any verse to say whether he responds first to its sound or to its sense. For no reader can feel clear in his own mind whether he enunciates a passage of verse in a particular way because he has first determined its meaning, or whether his very sense of its meaning is partly created by the way it sounds. The reader feels himself to be responding to two inseparable elements, sound and meaning, which seem, as it were, to influence one another simultaneously.

Just as the rhythmic patterns which pervade the ordinary spoken and written language can be organised and rendered more expressive and precise when disciplined and controlled by a poet's metrical organisation, so the sounds of vowels and consonants and the intonations and inflexions which form an equally important part of ordinary English utterance can be deployed by a poet in a way that renders them less hit-and-miss, more consistently expressive and therefore more pleasurable than they usually appear.

Dryden's repertoire of 'tunes' can encompass a wide variety of expressive effects. His control over particular combinations of vowels and consonants is a crucial ingredient in his being able to evoke with equal skill drunken rotundity:

> Round as a Globe, and Liquor'd ev'ry chink,

sharp-eared, nervous expectation:

> The fiery Courser, when he hears from far,
> The sprightly Trumpets, and the Shouts of War,
> Pricks up his Ears; and trembling with Delight,
> Shifts place, and paws; and hopes the promis'd Fight

hard bone and taut muscle:

> Dauntless at empty Noises; lofty neck'd;
> Sharp headed, Barrel belly'd, broadly back'd

moist fecundity:

> And mixing his large Limbs with hers, he feeds
> Her Births with kindly Juice, and fosters teeming Seeds

but in none of these cases are Dryden's sound-effects simply mimetic. The sound suggests and evokes but never simply imitates or echoes the object being presented.

Dryden's control over his verse-music plays an equally important rôle at those moments in his verse where he is attempting to epitomise a particular attitude or state of feeling in a tone of voice. Sometimes the tone is one of jeering contempt:

> A monstrous mess of foul corrupted matter,
> As all the Devils had spew'd to make the batter.

On other occasions Dryden conveys a defiant self-possession (this and the next-but-one example are taken from Dryden's non-couplet verse):

> I can enjoy her when she's kind;
> But when she dances in the wind,
> And shakes her wings, and will not stay,
> I puff the Prostitute away

or a tone of stately and extensive survey:

> Heav'ns Pow'r is Infinite: Earth, Air and Sea
> The Manufacture Mass, the making Pow'r obey

or a jauntiness in contemplating (apparent) catastrophes:

> Thy Wars brought nothing about;
> Thy Lovers were all untrue.
> 'Tis well an Old Age is out,
> And time to begin a New.

So aptly (Dryden seems to have thought) did certain of his combinations of rhythms and sound convey the essential nature of a particular action, attitude, personality or emotion, that they often recur in his verse, either *verbatim* or in a very similar form, when that subject is being once again evoked.

When translating Lucretius's third book, Dryden hit on a verbal formulation to convey the heady intoxication of the demagogue:

> Drunk with the Fumes of popular applause,

to which his mind returned when describing how the 'Doves' (the Anglican clergy in *The Hind and the Panther*) turned against their king and appealed to popular sentiment:

> Now made the Champions of a cruel Cause,
> And drunk with Fumes of Popular Applause.

When writing *The State of Innocence*, his stage adaptation of Milton's *Paradise Lost*, Dryden remembered a phrase from Spenser's *Faerie Queene* which must have struck him as epitomising the tone of ardent, insistent adoration in which a mortal might properly address a great goddess. In Spenser's poem a lover had included the following line as part of a hymn in praise of Venus:

> Thee, goddesse, thee the winds, the clouds doe feare.

Dryden gives the same phrase to Adam, when addressing Eve:

> Thee, Goddess, thee th'Eternal did ordain
> His softer Substitute on Earth to reign.

In his lover's hymn, Spenser had in fact been silently translating from the Roman poet Lucretius's invocation to Venus at the beginning of his *De Rerum Natura*:

> te, dea, te fugiunt venti, te nubila caeli
> adventumque tuum

[From you, O goddess, from you the winds flee, and the clouds of the sky flee from you and your coming.]

When Dryden came himself to translate this Lucretian passage in 1685, he retained the Spenserian phrasing:

> Thee, Goddess thee, the clouds and tempests fear,
> And at thy pleasing presence disappear.

And he remembered it again fifteen years later when adapting Palamon's hymn to the love-goddess in Chaucer's *Knight's Tale*:

> Thee, Goddess, thee the storms of Winter fly.

One of the most interesting of all Dryden's recurrent patterns of wording is the phrase which he used on several occasions to epitomise an attitude of what might be called 'reasoned decision': in several poems Dryden, or one of his characters, has reached an impasse or crisis and stops in his tracks to ask himself: 'Where do we go from here?' There then follows an extended piece of reflection. In *Religio Laici*, Dryden presents his sense of how a man might pick his way through the various kinds of religious confusion and dilemma which have been presented in the body of the poem:

> What then remains, but, waving each Extreme,
> The Tides of Ignorance, and Pride to stem?
> Neither so rich a Treasure to forgo;
> Nor proudly seek beyond our pow'r to know.

In *The Tenth Satyr of Juvenal*, the satirist, having systematically revealed the ludicrousness of every human striving and aspiration, presents his own sense of how it might after all be possible to live one's life in contentment:

> What then remains? Are we deprived of Will?
> Must we not Wish, for fear of wishing Ill?
> Receive my Counsel, and securely move;
> Intrust thy Fortune to the Pow'rs above.

And the same question, 'What then remains?', is on the lips of Theseus in *Palamon and Arcite*, when, in his speech at the end of the poem, he reminds the assembled company of the conditions under which, despite the catastrophes of the past and the uncertainty of the future, life must be lived:

> What then remains, but after past Annoy,
> To take the good Vicissitude of joy?
> To thank the gracious Gods for what they give,
> Possess our Souls, and while we live, to live?

Stress and emphasis

A reader of any verse has to decide on the word or words which need especially emphasising in order that he might convey the poet's meaning most fully and clearly. While it is true that no two readings of the same poem or passage (even by the same reader) will or should ever be *precisely* the same, it does seem to be the case with many poets that there is one particular way in which any given line or group of lines are intended to 'go'. It may take a reader a little time and thought before he hits on this way, but once it is established, it seems broadly right, and is subsequently never abandoned.

Many of Dryden's lines (and in this respect his couplet verse differs markedly from that of Pope), can be read in several different ways, each of them perfectly legitimate, each one stressing a slightly different dimension of Dryden's thought and giving the verse a subtly different direction.

The point can be neatly demonstrated with reference to two of the most famous lines in all Dryden's work, the opening couplet of *Absalom and Achitophel*:

> In pious times, e'r Priest-craft did begin,
> Before Polygamy was made a sin.

If one puts the main stress when reading the first line on 'pious':

> In *pious* times, e'r Priest-craft did begin,

the main point of the line becomes the contrast between the piety of former times and the *impiety* of the present. If one stresses, with a contemptuous edge in the voice, the words 'Priest-craft':

> In pious times, e'r *Priest-craft* did begin,

the main implication of the couplet is that it is the doings of priests which have caused all the trouble. A point which might be emphasised further in reading by bringing it out in one's intonation is the fact that 'Priest-craft' can mean, quite neutrally, 'the profession of the priesthood', but also could suggest 'the *pseudo*-profession of the priesthood' and 'the cunning schemings of priests'.

In the second line, if one stresses the word 'Polygamy':

> Before *Polygamy* was made a sin;

one might provoke a snigger from a reader of the poem who, knowing the context, would be aware that what was in question was not Charles II's 'polygamy' but his adulterous fornication. If one stressed 'made':

> Before Polygamy was *made* a sin;

one might provoke the reader to ask (and perhaps to wonder whether the question was merely rhetorical): 'Well, *isn't* polygamy necessarily a sin?' If one stressed 'sin':

> Before Polygamy was made a *sin*;

one might provoke the reaction: 'Well, if it's not a sin, what *is* it?'

In none of these imagined readings, would one be conveying an implication which cannot be legitimately deduced from Dryden's words. Nor are the different readings in any way contradictory or mutually exclusive. But, though the mind can happily entertain the various possibilities, it is difficult to see how they could all be brought out in any single vocal rendering. The reader's dilemma as to how the verses should be read aloud does not derive from any uncertainty about their meaning or implications. The problem is, rather, one of an *embarras de richesses*, a genuine abundance of possibilities resulting from the fertility of the play of mind in the lines.

Vocabulary and diction

Dryden draws in his verse not just on the language of the court and city in which he spent most of his professional life, but on that of a wide range of activities and strata of society. His vocabulary can encompass the technical jargon of many professions – sailors, musicians, scientists (both of the old and new persuasions), husband-men, wine-makers, theologians. He can adopt the idiom of a rustic yokel as well as that of a rakish gallant. On occasions he will even use a dialect form from his native Northamptonshire.[4] And he can, when required, command a whole vocabulary for the depiction of cottage life. In the fable of *Baucis and Philemon* Dryden writes of the 'Brush wood' and 'Chips' which go to make the cottage fire, the 'little Seether' (the kettle in which 'the good old huswife' boils her water), the 'Trivet table' on which the cottagers eat their meal, the 'Autumnal cornels' ('In Lees of Wine well pickl'd and preserv'd'), 'Endive', 'Radishes' and 'succory' which form the basis of the cottage feast, and the 'Chine of Bacon' which the cottager seizes 'with a Prong', and from which he cuts a slice for his guests – 'A sav'ry Bit, that serv'd to rellish Wine.'

Dryden's early admirers frequently remarked on the daring and novelty of his use of language. This daring can take widely different forms. Dryden will sometimes use a word which (since his is the first recorded instance in the *OED*) was either very rare at the time of writing, or a coinage of the poet's own:

> If you *tralineate* from your Father's Mind,
> What are you else but of a Bastard-kind?

Sometimes, Dryden's verbal surprises take the form of the introduction of a rare cant term:

> There will I be, and there we cannot miss,
> Perhaps to *Grubble*, or at least to kiss

or a throwaway colloquialism:

> Come, *give thy Soul a loose*, and taste the pleasures of the poor

a deliberately 'low' term:

> Form'd in the Forge, the Pliant Brass is laid ⎫
> On Anvils; and of Head and Limbs are made, ⎬
> Pans, Cans, and *Pispots*, a whole Kitchin Trade ⎭

a daring pun:

> Then, round her slender Waste he [i.e. Jove] curl'd,
> And stamp'd an Image of himself, a *Sov'raign* of the World

a whole line composed of repetitions of a single word or phrase (a skill perhaps learnt from Ben Jonson):

> *Fallen, fallen, fallen, fallen*
> Fallen from his high Estate
> And weltring in his Blood.

In one of his most famous critical essays, T. S. Eliot wrote that 'when a poet's mind is perfectly equipped for its work, it is constantly amalgamating disparate experience'.[5] The poet, Eliot suggests, brings together in his figurative language and strokes of wit areas of experience which might never otherwise be thought of in conjunction with one another, and of them forms 'new wholes'.

Dryden's verse abounds in such imaginative fusions. Spring rain, for example, is assimilated to a mother's milk:

> Spring first, like Infancy, shoots out her Head,
> With milky Juice requiring to be fed

the sap of young plants to the blood pulsing through the human body:

> ... the tender Blades of Grass appear,
> And Buds that yet the blast of Eurus fear,
> Stand at the door of Life; and doubt to cloath the Year;
> Till gentle Heat and soft repeated Rains,
> Make the green Blood to dance within their Veins

clouds to a sponge gorged with water:

> Still as he swept along, with his clench't fist
> He squeez'd the Clouds, th'imprison'd Clouds resist.

The language of Dryden's verse, like that of all our great poets, has a substantial element which is inherited from the work of his predecessors. Just as he takes words and idioms from all aspects of life, so he takes over or adapts words and phrases which had been charged or coloured in various ways by the uses to which earlier poets had put them.

Dryden draws on the diction and rhythms of the full range of English poetry from Chaucer to his own day. This fact is often overlooked because readers tend to regard as specifically 'Augustan', features of Dryden's diction which are actually part of the mainstream common property of English verse. The essential phrasing and rhythm of a line like

> Along the sandy Margin of the Sea

for example, are to be found long before Dryden, in Shakespeare's *A Midsummer Night's Dream*:

> Or in the beached margent of the sea,

and long after him in Book Ten of Wordsworth's *The Prelude*:

> Along the margin of the moonlight sea –

A line in one of Dryden's Chaucer translations contains a striking Latinism:

> The Temple stood of Mars Armipotent

which is not a piece of 'neo-classical' diction, but has been taken over straight from his Chaucerian original:

> There stode the temple of Mars armipotent

Dryden's Chaucerian translations show most vividly his ability to make contact with the distant English poetic past. They are fully fledged rethinkings and reworkings of Chaucer in Dryden's own seventeenth-century idiom. And yet, when he came upon a line, phrase, or rhythm in Chaucer which he thought could not be bettered (because its inevitable rightness, to his ears, meant that it did not seem at all 'dated') he felt free to incorporate it unchanged into his version. A reader coming across:

> Black was his Beard, and manly was his Face

might suspect the stock Augustan couplet-antithesis. But the line is Chaucer's:

> Blacke was his berd, and manly was his Face.

Dryden can take from Chaucer diction and rhythms which do not at all accord with what are normally thought to be the Augustan canons of propriety and decorum. His line:

> Now up, now down, as Buckets in a Well

is, like the other examples, a direct borrowing from his edition of Chaucer:

> Now up, now doune, as boket in a well.[6]

Dryden also draws many words and rhythms from the Elizabethan, Jacobean and Caroline poets. In the passage referred to earlier from *Baucis and Philemon*, he combined his own first-hand experience of English rural life with his reminiscences of the translations of the same episode in Ovid's *Metamorphoses* which had been made by Arthur Golding in 1567 and George Sandys in 1626 and 1632. He drew elsewhere on Spenser, Donne, Jonson, Fairfax. Sylvester, Chapman, Marvell, Waller and Denham as well as a host of less well-known figures.

Dryden's borrowings from the language of Shakespeare and Milton often reveal a thoughtful remembrance of the context from which the borrowed word or phrase is drawn. For example, in making the goddess Iris (in his translation of Ovid's story of *Ceyx and Alcyone*) refer to sleep thus:

> O Peace of Mind, repairer of Decay,
> Whose Balm renews the Limbs to Labour of the Day,

Dryden clearly remembered Macbeth's poignant yearning for sleep:

> Balme of hurt Mindes, great Natures second Course,
> Chiefe nourisher in Life's Feast.

In his own descriptions of the creation of the world, Dryden constantly remembered Milton's grand evocation of the earth and the heavenly bodies. In describing the lofty arch of the sky as

> Heav'ns high Canopy, that covers all,

Dryden remembered Milton's description of

> the circling Canopie
> Of Nights extended shade . . .
> (*Paradise Lost*, III. 556–7)

(which, Milton's editors suggest, might itself owe something to Hamlet's celebration of this most excellent Canopy the Ayre . . . this brave or-hanging, this Majesticall Roofe, fretted with golden fire).

As well as drawing on Milton's sonorous grandeur, Dryden is also drawn to what might be called the more intimate regions of Milton's poetic language. When he makes Diomedes (in the *Aeneis*) lament:

> The Gods have envy'd me the sweets of Life,
> My much lov'd Country, and my more lov'd Wife:
> Banish'd from both, I mourn

he draws on the very special charge of meaning which Milton had given to the phrase 'the sweet of life' by associating it with all that Adam and Eve particularly valued about their life together in Eden. In Book VIII of *Paradise Lost*, Adam tells the angel how he had taught him

> to live,
> The easiest way, nor with perplexing thoughts
> To interrupt the sweet of Life, from which
> God hath bid dwell farr off all anxious cares.

Dryden's echoes of the language of the Bible similarly show his consciousness of the nuances with which that language had been invested in its original context. When Dryden's Pythagoras, for example, hymns the flux of Nature:

> Thus in successive Course the Minutes run,
> And urge their Predecessor Minutes on,
> Still moving, ever new: For former Things
> Are set aside, like abdicated kings:

his words are imbued with the apocalyptic significance which the phrase 'former things' had acquired in the Book of Revelation:

And God shall wipe away all teares from their eyes: and there shall bee no more death, neither sorrow, nor crying, neither shall there bee any more paine: for the former things are passed away.[7]

To incorporate material from a wide number of areas of life and literature into one's own work is in itself no guarantee of success. But Dryden's earlier critics felt that he had formed from diverse sources a style which appeared to have a distinctive living quality of its own. It was the *vitality* of Dryden's style that, above all, these critics noted. They constantly remark on its 'fire' and 'energy'. 'Of Genius', wrote Dr Johnson (comparing Dryden with Pope), 'that power which constitutes a poet; that quality without which judgment is cold and knowledge is inert; that energy which collects, combines, amplifies, and animates – the superiority must, with some hesitation, be allowed to Dryden' (H3 222). It was the animating power of Dryden's poetic genius, Johnson felt, which had enabled him to make something new and permanently lively out of all the collecting, combining and technical dexterity which had gone into the making of his verse. Dryden was as conscious of the essential role of inspiration in poetic composition as any Romantic poet. 'We who are the Priests of *Apollo*', he wrote

> have not the Inspiration when we please; but must wait till the God comes rushing on us, and invades us with a fury, which we are not able to resist: which gives us double strength while the fit continues, and leaves us languishing and spent, at its departure.
>
> (Dedication to *Eleonora*; K2 582; W2 61)

It was the presence of such a white heat of inspiration when Dryden was composing which, the poet Gray thought, made the effect of his best poems one of 'Thoughts that breathe, and words that burn'.[8] Wordsworth's friend and champion, John Wilson, described the effect of Dryden's verse in terms which vividly convey his sense of its tumultuous excitement and constant variety:

> sinewy, flexible, well-knit, agile, stately-stepping, gracefully-bending, stern, stalwarth – or sitting his horse, 'erect and fair', in careering, and carrying his steel-headed lance of true stuff, level and steady to its aim, and impetuous as a thunderbolt.[9]

It is still often said that Dryden's couplets are inflexible, end-stopped, and monotonous, and that they fall into predictable patterns; that his words have few nuances or overtones; that the harmony and music which earlier critics admired in Dryden's verse is merely a matter of external refinement and polish; that his diction is largely limited to the Latinate, the artificially decorous, and the plain; that he had no gift for amalgamating disparate experience in metaphor; that he was cut off, by his age's demand for 'politeness', from the expressive richness of earlier periods of English literature; that his vocabulary reveals his insulation from imaginative contact with modes of English life outside the narrow confines of the Restoration Court and City; that his verse is a prosaic 'poetry of statement'.

The evidence presented in this chapter, I believe, points in precisely the opposite direction. Dryden, the record shows, can create, in verse which is simultaneously tightly disciplined and flexibly free, a wide variety of moods, tones and tempi. Our appreciation of the rhythms and harmony of Dryden's verse and of the nuances of his words is inseparable from our understanding of that verse's meaning. His vocabulary is wide and diverse, both in its nature and origin. He displays in many places an ability to fuse disparate experience in figurative language. His choice of diction shows him to have been in imaginative contact with a very wide range of English life and literature. The qualities of his best verse are such that it can never be confused with prose or ordinary statement.

2

Disappointment and promise: Dryden's early career

To the Restoration

Of all the English poets, Dryden best deserves the title of 'late developer'. He did not begin writing in earnest until he was thirty. And if he had died just before he was fifty (an age to which Spenser, Keats, Shelley and Byron did not survive, and by which Shakespeare, Wordsworth and Coleridge had completed the work for which they are best remembered) he would certainly not have enjoyed anything like his subsequent reputation. For Dryden published nothing in the twenty years following the Restoration of Charles II which attains more than intermittently the quality of the best work of his last two decades.

Dryden's reputation among his contemporaries was quickly established. By the mid 1670s, the most discerning critics were certain that he was the leading literary figure of the day. We are even told that the distinguished French critic, René Rapin, learned English especially to read his work.[1] But if Dryden had died in 1680, the enthusiasm of his contemporaries would almost certainly seem, from a later vantage-point, puzzlingly excessive. Dryden, it is true, had in his first twenty years of writing acquired technical mastery of most of the main English verse forms. He had provided copious and diverse entertainment for the new theatrical audiences. He had composed eloquent and readable discourses about literature of a kind hitherto unknown in England. But none of his works of these years (the judgement might go on) justifies his contemporaries' verdict that they had a major genius in their midst. Without the work of the last two decades, Dryden could easily be mistaken for the Dryden of the modern received picture: a 'man of his age' producing the kinds of writing which the age demanded. But without the work of the last two decades it would be equally easy to overlook the touches of real promise and potential which can be seen to exist in the work of the 1660s and 70s.

Dryden's family were minor gentry of Puritan sympathies. He was born in 1631 at Aldwinckle, a village near the small Northamptonshire town of Oundle. We know next to nothing about his early life. He may have received his first education locally, but was soon sent to London, to study at Westminster School, then under the celebrated headmastership of the severe and learned classical scholar, Dr Richard Busby. At Westminster in the 1640s Dryden received a thorough grounding in the classical languages. He tells us that he was once set by his headmaster to translate into English verse the Third Satire of the notoriously difficult Latin poet Persius, as one of many 'Thursday night's exercises'. While still at Westminster, Dryden published, in 1649 (the year of Charles I's execution) his first extant poem, a not-very-distinguished contribution in the 'metaphysical' manner to a series of elegies by various hands on the death of an aristocratic Westminster pupil, Henry Lord Hastings. The following year, Dryden was admitted to Trinity College, Cambridge, graduating in 1654.

In the same year as Dryden's graduation, his father died. We know little about the poet's life at this period, but one fact of significance is clear. Dryden had evidently decided shortly after leaving Cambridge that his future lay in London rather than in the provinces. For we find him in the mid 1650s employed by the Cromwellian administration in the same office as two distinguished literary seniors, John Milton and Andrew Marvell.[2]

We can be certain that Dryden spent the years of the Interregnum in profitable self-education. The work of the 1660s offers proof that by that period he had acquired an impressive first-hand acquaintance with a wide range of literature in English, French, Spanish and Italian, as well as Latin and Greek. The poetry, plays and prose of these years show him able to make easy and informed reference to (among others) the plays of Aeschylus, Terence, Plautus, Quinault, both Corneilles, Molière, Calderón, Shakespeare, and Fletcher, the poetry of Ovid, Horace, Statius, Ariosto, Spenser, Waller, Cleveland, and the prose writings of Macrobius, Descartes and Hobbes. But apart from an elegy on the death of Cromwell and a short commendatory poem to a book of epigrams by an obscure young poet, John Hoddesdon, Dryden published nothing in the 1650s. His first sustained poetic activity followed the Restoration of Charles II in 1660. Dryden was now in his early thirties.

Dryden at the Restoration

In the introduction to this book I advocated scepticism about received views of the Age of Dryden and about Dryden's rôle as a representative of that Age. Many of the weaknesses in Dryden's work of the 1660s and 1670s, however, are to a large extent attributable to the times and circumstances in which those works were written. Dryden's output in the post-Restoration years falls into three main categories: occasional poetry, drama, and literary criticism. The first works he published after 1660 were five poems addressed to the king and to three other prominent public figures of the day. These, like the dedicatory epistles which accompanied the printed texts of Dryden's plays, were designed to attract, or give thanks for, patronage and to bring the poet's work to the attention of men of influence.[3] In *To my Honored Friend, Sir Robert Howard*, Dryden praised the aristocrat and amateur poet who would shortly become both his artistic collaborator and his brother-in-law (Dryden married Lady Elizabeth Howard in 1663). Dryden complimented Howard on the 'native sweetnesse' of his verse, and, in particular, on the elegance and learning of his translations from classical poets. In *Astraea Redux. A Poem on the Happy Restoration and Return of His Sacred Majesty Charles II*, Dryden welcomed the peace brought about by the Restoration after the violence and extremism of the Interregnum, and looked forward to a period of English naval power and imperial expansion. In *To His Sacred Majesty, A Panegyrick on His Coronation*, published the following year (1661), he again celebrated Charles as a bringer of peace, this time stressing the king's clemency and his paternal regard for his people. In *To my Lord Chancellor, Presented on New-years-day* (1662) he greeted Charles's chief minister, the Earl of Clarendon, hailing him as a potential patron of poetry, and, like his royal master, an agent of justice and mercy. In *To my Honour'd Friend Dr Charleton* (1663), he praised the recent growth in England of intellectual enquiry, and in particular the pioneer archaeological work on the antiquities of Stonehenge by Dr Walter Charleton, the scholar who had been responsible for recommending him for membership of the Royal Society in 1662.

Dryden's main source of income in the 1660s and 70s, however, was to be derived not from occasional poetry but from his writing for the stage. The estate which he had inherited from his father brought him a small income, but it was insufficient to allow him to live comfortably as a gentleman and to bring up his family (his three sons were born in 1666, 1668 and 1669) with ease. So Dryden became a playwright. Nineteen plays written in whole or part by Dryden were performed in one or other of the two London theatres between 1663 and 1680. A twentieth, *The State of Innocence*, an operatic adaptation of Milton's *Paradise Lost* made with the older poet's permission, was never performed, but the text was published in 1677. From 1668 to 1678 Dryden was a shareholder in the King's Company, drawing a proportion of the profits in return for a regular and exclusive supply of plays to the Company.

The conditions of the theatre for which Dryden wrote amply bear out Dr Johnson's judgement that

> The drama's laws, the drama's patrons give,
> For we that live to please, must please to live.

The Restoration theatrical world was one of sharp competition and of rapidly evolving trends and fashions, which the dramatists (not unlike the film and television writers of today) set themselves to manipulate and follow with all the dexterity they could muster. Two companies – the King's, managed by Thomas Killigrew, and the Duke's, managed by Sir William Davenant – had been granted the monopoly of theatrical entertainment by Charles on his return in 1660. They vied with each other for customers, each attempting to come up with a new 'formula' (whether in terms of stage spectacle, acting talent or dramatic genre) which would please their audience. 'Fickle breezes of fashion and sudden gusts of fad were of enormous importance to any Restoration playwright who wanted to eat.'[4] Numerous types of play were tried out in rapid succession: 'heroic' dramas (in which the central characters were overreaching colossi, spouting extravagant rhetoric), 'tragi-comedies' (in which two separate plots, one comic, one serious, alternated), bawdy farces, comedies of manners, operas, moral romances, adaptations of older plays by such writers as Shakespeare, Fletcher and Brome. Playwrights frequently stole, parodied or adapted each other's ideas in the perpetual search for box-office success. Runs were very short (the average play was on for three nights only) so both composition and rehearsal were often hasty. Parts were tailored to the special talents of particular actors. Some plays were particularly designed to show off the scenic splendours of a particular theatre. The audience, though not quite the exclusive coterie of courtiers, rakes and whores described in the older textbooks, was heavily influenced, particularly in the early years of the Restoration, by the taste of courtiers used to the French and Spanish plays which they had seen in exile. The king took a personal interest in the theatre, on some occasions even commissioning plays of a type which had taken his fancy.

Dryden's dramatic career shows how fully he immersed himself in this theatrical world during the first twenty years of his writing life. Though his plays met with varying commercial success, he was often in the van in creating new trends, finding successful new formulae, deftly reviving elements from older plays and combining ingredients from the work of his contemporaries in a way that appealed to an audience constantly seeking novelty. Sometimes he was content to fall in with an existing trend. His first play, *The Wild Gallant* (1663), was a comedy in the manner of Richard Brome.[5] *The Rival Ladies* (1664) was a Spanish romance of the kind made popular by Sir Samuel Tuke's *Adventures of Three Hours* (1663). In *Sir Martin Mar-All* (1667), Dryden attempted to cash in on the current vogues for Molière-adaptations and for coarse colloquial farce. *An Evening's Love* (1668) is a low 'Spanish' comedy of the kind popular in the later 1660s. *The Kind Keeper* (1678) is a sex comedy written, we are told, at the express command of the king in imitation of Thomas Durfey's *A Fond Husband* (1677).

In other plays, Dryden tried to set, rather than merely follow, new trends. In *Marriage A-la-Mode* (1672) and *The Assignation* (1672), he took it upon himself to raise the tone of comedy (after a boom in low farce) by offering models of social grace and wit explicitly based on the language of the court and aristocracy. In *Aureng-Zebe* (1675) and the adaptation from Shakespeare's *Troilus and Cressida* (1679), he responded to the current interest in French drama and dramatic criticism by attempting to combine the virtues of the 'regular' French drama and the more 'diverse' English tradition. In the anti-puritan sub-plot of another of his Shakespearian adaptations, *The Tempest* (1670), and in *Amboyna* (1673) and *The Spanish Fryar* (1680), he indulged in direct political propaganda. In *The Rival Ladies* (1664), *The Indian Queen* (1665), *The Indian Emperour* (1665), *Tyrannick Love* (1669) and *The Conquest of Granada* (1670–1), he contributed substantially to the vogue for plays which offered models of exemplary, or extravagantly exuberant, 'heroic' conduct. In *Secret Love* (1667) he designed the parts of the lovers Celadon and Florimel specifically for two talented actors, Charles Hart and Nell Gwyn, who were beginning to specialise in the portrayal of 'gay couples' locked in exchanges of witty banter.

Dryden's critical work of the 1660s and 70s is closely related to his writing for the stage. Most of it takes the form of prefaces written to accompany the printed texts which were usually issued shortly after a play's first performance. Jonathan Swift's motives were no doubt none too pure when he wrote that Dryden's prefaces were 'merely writ at first for filling / To raise the volume's price, a shilling',[6] but there is some point in the quip. In these prefaces Restoration theatre-goers could find discussion of theatrical matters which appeared to raise the activity above the level of mere entertainment and fashion and to invest it with some intellectual dignity and ambition. In his prefaces and separately published critical essays Dryden addressed himself to the critical issues which seemed at the time to be important. Is blank verse preferable to rhyme as a dramatic medium? How does the sprawling 'variety' of English renaissance drama compare with the decorous regularity of French? or with classical? Is 'tragi-comedy' an acceptable dramatic form, or do the two halves of such plays fight against one another? Should plays always show the triumph of the virtuous and the punishment of the wicked? Should heroes have faults? Can hyperbolic language and exaggerated figures of speech be used in serious drama? What rules govern the acceptable use of supernatural agents in epic and drama? All these issues are discussed by Dryden with flexibility and with a wealth of illustration, his discussions showing acquaintance with the latest continental criticism, as well as with older Italian and classical writings. In these prefaces Dryden had created the first substantial body of literary-critical discussion in the English language.

Limitations of Dryden's Restoration work

The foregoing descriptions of the nature of Dryden's work in the two decades after the Restoration, and of the conditions under which it was produced, themselves suggest many of its limitations. The early occasional poems, it must be conceded, cannot be written off as the mere toadyism they might at first seem. They touch on what would become one of Dryden's abiding preoccupations – the horror of war, and the need to preserve, at all costs, the peace and stability which had been reinstated at the Restoration. And scholars rightly point out that the poems to the king, as well as being acts of courtly flattery, perform one of the traditional functions of panegyric, advising the ruler and formulating an ideal pattern which his reign might follow, rather than merely offering bland praise of the status quo.[7] The poems' weaknesses, however, have always been recognised. Dr Johnson pointed out the difficulties which Dryden had, in these first poems, in disciplining 'the extravagance of his fictions and hyperboles' and in avoiding 'forced conceits' (H1 426–7). Panegyric, moreover, only gave Dryden very limited scope to develop and express his deepest intuitions about Man and Society. The imaginative visions of Man and Nature which came increasingly to appeal to him as a poet could not, as we shall see, be easily harnessed to the celebration of any particular social, political or administrative order, however sincerely Dryden may have supported that order as a citizen.

In his plays Dryden was able to touch on most of the issues which were to preoccupy him in his greatest poetic period. But the mere presence of an idea in a work is no guarantee that that idea had found adequate artistic expression or embodiment. And the inadequate expression or embodiment of an intrinsically interesting idea may lead one to question the security of the artist's focus on that idea at the time of writing. In the plays, Dryden's hold on matters which would be of the greatest concern to him in his later years remains at best intermittent and at worst precarious.

This is no doubt partly due to the temperamental unsuitability for stage-writing of which Dryden himself was, in his better moments, acutely aware. Dryden's plays seldom have that intrinsically dramatic quality which Dr Johnson noted as a particular feature of Shakespeare's art – of making us 'anxious for the event'. Where Shakespeare's instinctively dramatic genius allows him to 'approximate the remote and familiarize the wonderful', by making his personages 'act and speak as the reader thinks that he should have spoken or acted on the same occasion', the characters in Dryden's 'serious' plays often speak in a way that makes the remote seem incredible and the wonderful merely ludicrous, thus making it difficult for the audience to become involved with the characters or care about their fate. And his comic scenes lack even that adroit professionalism of construction and timing which marks the comic writing of dramatists like Congreve and Sheridan – to say nothing of the infinite variety of human interplay to be found in Shakespeare's best comic scenes.

But though the awkwardnesses of Dryden's plays may be attributable in part to the poet's inherent unsuitability for dramatic writing, much of the blame for their failure must be put down to the constraints which writing for the theatre imposed on Dryden's imagination. For rather than being able to follow through and develop the promptings of his deepest imaginative perceptions, Dryden had always, when writing for the stage, to consider the demands and tastes of his audience. The weaknesses of Dryden's dramatic work show up most clearly when one considers moments in the plays which deal with matters also handled in the later non-dramatic poetry. Two examples among many must suffice here to illustrate the point.

In his essay *Of Heroic Plays*, prefixed to *The Conquest of Granada*,

Dryden claimed that he had modelled the character of his hero Almanzor on that of Achilles in Homer's *Iliad*. In particular, he says, he had tried to imitate the Homeric Achilles' fiery impetuosity and his proud sense of honour. Near the beginning of the play, Almanzor declares his heroic credo to Boabdelin, King of Granada:

> Obey'd as Soveraign by thy Subjects be,
> But know, that I alone am King of me.
> I am as free as Nature first made man ⎫
> 'Ere the base Laws of Servitude began   ⎬
> When wild in woods the noble Savage ran. ⎭
>
> (I.i. 205–9; C11 30)

There is, as Dr Johnson noted, a certain appeal in such swashbuckling declarations. But the absurdity of the play as a whole, with its consistently diagrammatic characterisation, improbable reversals of fortune and sustained rhetorical afflatus, prevent our ever being able to take as more than a swaggering stage-boast Almanzor's main claim in this speech that he represents a potent force of Nature: what Heroic Man might have been without the trammelling constraints of civilisation. When, later, Almanzor falls in love, this is how he speaks:

> I'me pleas'd and pain'd since first her eyes I saw,
> As I were stung with some *Tarantula*:
> Arms and the dusty field I less admire;
> And soften strangely in some new desire.
> Honour burns in me, not so fiercely bright;
> But pale, as fires when master'd by the light.
> Ev'n while I speak and look, I change yet more;
> And now am nothing that I was before.
> I'm numm'd, and fix'd, and scarce my eyeballs move;
> I fear it is the Lethargy of Love!
>
> (III.i. 328–37; C11 56)

Commentators have remarked on the clumsiness and uncertain decorum of much of Dryden's dramatic verse when it is compared with non-dramatic poetry written by him at the same period.[8] The monotonous movement, clichéd diction and awkward lurches into unintentional (or, at any rate, uncontrolled) comedy in passages like the one just quoted prevent us from having any fellow-feeling for the speaker, or from being moved or impressed by his predicament. In the second part of the same play Almanzor declares, in characteristic manner, his intention of rescuing Granada:

> I'le stop at nothing that appears so brave;
> I'le do't: and know I no Reward will have.

You've given my Honour such an ample Field
That I may dye, but that shall never yield.
Spight of my self I'le Stay, Fight, Love, Despair;
And I can do all this, because I dare.

(Part 2, II.iii. 101–6; C11 134)

Melodramatic posturing like this removes all possibility of Almanzor's heroism being taken seriously, whether the play is being seen
as psychological drama or 'theatre of ideas'. A contemporary pamphleteer quipped that, while Dryden might have thought of Almanzor as a latter-day Achilles, audiences might be forgiven for thinking
that he was based on Ancient Pistol, the swaggering braggart of
Shakespeare's *2 Henry IV* and *Henry V*.[9] The passage just quoted
was pounced upon by the authors of *The Rehearsal* (a popular contemporary skit on heroic plays), who made their hero 'Drawcansir'
declare:

I drink, I huff, I strut, look big and stare,
And all this I can do, because I dare.[10]

Johnson thought that the extravagances of *The Conquest of Granada*
were only partly attributable to the base demands of a modish
audience:

There is surely reason to suspect that he pleased himself as well as his
audience; and that these, like the harlots of other men, had his love, though
not his approbation.

(H1 462)

In the heroic plays, Dryden's depiction of human behaviour at the
very extreme of the emotional range is consistently marred by the
presence of an outrageous ingenuity of argument and imagery
which, because it is not controlled and contained within an un-
equivocally comic overall design, is always teetering awkwardly on
the border of burlesque and self-parody.[11] One can well imagine
that while composing these pieces Dryden may, indeed, have
enjoyed the opportunity to indulge his natural inclinations towards
argument and extravagantly incongruous wit without the obligation to discipline and temper them which a more serious artistic
endeavour would have imposed upon him.

But, at the very end of his life, Dryden was able to return to the
portrayal of heroically proud conduct, this time with far more convincing artistic success. In his last volume, the *Fables*, he published a
rendering of the same Homeric portrayal of Achilles which he said
had been the model for his Almanzor twenty years before. Dryden's

Homeric Achilles is, like Almanzor, an assertive and wilful figure who spurns the constraints of monarchical rule, as is witnessed by his response to his overlord Agamemnon's rebuke:

> My Worth allow'd in Words, is in effect deny'd.
> For who but a Poltron, possess'd with Fear,
> Such haughty Insolence, can tamely bear?
> Command thy Slaves: My freeborn Soul disdains
> A Tyrant's Curb; and restiff breaks the Reins.
>
> (412–16; K4 1594)

In place of the posturing rhetoric which characterises much of the presentation of Almanzor, Achilles speaks, in Dryden's rendering of Homer, with a vehement flow and rhythmic flexibility and energy which make the 'freeborn Soul' which he claims for himself something, this time, which we can believe in. Dryden has, through the discipline of translation, succeeded in meeting Johnson's criterion of 'approximating the remote'. The self-indulgent extravagance of the heroic play has been transformed into a convincing portrayal of a terrifying natural force, as Achilles launches into his contemptuous denunciation of his king:

> Dastard, and Drunkard, Mean and Insolent:
> Tongue-valiant Hero, Vaunter of thy Might,
> In Threats the foremost, but the lag in Fight;
> When did'st thou thrust amid the mingled Preace,
> Content to bid the War aloof in Peace?
> Arms are the Trade of each *Plebeyan* Soul;
> 'Tis Death to Fight; but Kingly to controul.
> Lord-like at ease, with arbitrary Pow'r,
> To peel the Chiefs, the People to devour.
> These, Traitor, are thy Tallents; safer far
> Than to contend in Fields, and Toils of War.
> Nor could'st thou thus have dar'd the common Hate,
> Were not their Souls as abject as their State.
>
> (335–47; K4 1592)

The same differences in artistic control and in imaginative involvement and depth which emerge when one compares the early 'serious' drama with the best of the later non-dramatic verse are evident when one sets the comic scenes in the early plays beside later, non-dramatic presentations of similar subjects.

Marriage A-la-Mode (1672) is often thought of as one of Dryden's most successful comedies. The main plot of the play concerns two young courtiers, Rhodophil and Palamede. Palamede falls in love with Doralice, Rhodophil's wife, of whom Rhodophil himself has grown weary. Rhodophil, in turn, falls in love with Melantha, a fashionable Frenchified lady, whose marriage with Palamede has been arranged by Palamede's father, but whom Palamede himself disdains. After many intrigues, each discovers the truth about the focus of the other's affections, and concludes that his own wife/fiancée must, after all, have substantial attractions. They first quarrel, then decide to return to their own, and to refrain in future from poaching on one another's preserves.

The play touches at various points on some of the serious questions about love and marriage which were to continue to interest Dryden for the rest of his life: are sexual passion and marriage incompatible? Is love merely a delusion? Or is it a great power which overrides all other human ties, however precious? What are we to make of women's apparently boundless ingenuity and resource in affairs of the heart? But in this play Dryden is prevented by the nature of his enterprise from exploring these issues at any more than a trivialising and superficial level. Though a retelling of the plot of *Marriage A-la-Mode* might lead one to suppose that Dryden's intention might have been to expose the folly of Palamede's and Rhodophil's constant pursuit of 'novelty' in their amatory affairs (the two men, after all, end up with the partners to whom they were originally affianced), the handling of events leaves us, and the characters, with no greater understanding than we or they had at the outset either of the worth of marriage or of the power of the forces which might exist to disrupt or undermine the institution. The lovers' final *volte-face* occurs on the same level of smart intrigue as most of the other events in the play:

Dor. Hold, hold; are not you two a couple of mad fighting fools, to cut one another's throats for nothing?
Pal. How for nothing? he courts the woman I must marry.
Rho. And he courts you whom I have marri'd.
Dor. But you can neither of you be jealous of what you love not.
Rho. Faith I am jealous, and that makes me partly suspect that I love you better than I thought.
Dor. Pish! a meer jealousie of honour.
Rho. Gad I am afraid there's something else in't; for *Palamede* has wit and if he loves you, there's something more in ye then I have found: some rich Mine, for ought I know, that I have not yet discover'd.
Pal. 'S life, what's this? here's an argument for me to love *Melantha*; for he has lov'd her, and he has wit too, and, for ought I know, there may be a Mine: but, if there be, I am resolv'd I'll dig for't.
Dor. (*To* Rhod.) Then I have found my account in raising your jealousie: O!

'tis the most delicate sharp sawce to a cloy'd stomach; it will give you a new edge *Rhodophil.*

(V.i. 314–33; C11 307–8)

Here, as elsewhere in the play, Dryden displays an uncomfortable degree of complicity with the attitudes he is apparently exposing. It is only by allowing the key words employed by the speakers ('wit', 'jealousy', 'love', 'honour') to have as little significance or resonance for us as they do for the characters themselves (and apparently did to the author when composing the scene) that we can be free to smile, as we are intended to, at the neatness of their turn-about. The lovers' 'discovery' happens on a level of plot-contrivance which depends upon a tacit conspiracy between audience and author not to think too hard about the precise issues which are at stake. It is imagined with as little fullness of understanding as their initial ennui. We might note that the smutty innuendo in Rhodophil's remark that Palamede must have found 'some rich Mine' in his wife has the effect of preventing the imagination from exploring the way in which human beings can, indeed, be blinded by habit or expectation from seeing the hidden riches in their loved ones. Similarly, Doralice's suggestion that Rhodophil's 'cloy'd stomach' can be given a 'new edge' by the 'sharp sawce' of jealousy has the effect of preventing us from dwelling on the ways in which both love and jealousy are forces with a real power to confound and disturb, and of encouraging us to see love as a trivial appetite which can be easily aroused or assuaged.

It is for reasons like these that none of the potentially interesting subjects which the play raises are engaged with at more than the trivial or notional level. It was not until Dryden had abandoned the desire to write 'smartly' that he could allow his imagination to dwell on the realities of human life – both comic and painful – which are simply papered over in this kind of stage comedy. The wonder and agony of sexual love (topics which would be so central to Dryden's later verse) are no more vividly present in the courtly manoeuvrings and amorous protestations of the comic scenes of *Marriage A-la-Mode* than they are in the feebly declamatory sentimentalities of the play's 'serious' parts.

Most of Dryden's plays of the 1660s and 70s suffer, to a greater or lesser degree, from the kinds of imaginative limitation which are so clearly visible in *The Conquest of Granada* and *Marriage A-la-Mode*, so that it is difficult to regard any of them, taken as a whole, as an artistic success, or to include any of them in a short-list of Dryden's greatest achievements. Even *All for Love*, the reworking of the Antony and Cleopatra story which Dryden said was the only play he had ever written 'for himself' is disappointingly dull when set beside the best of Dryden's non-dramatic work. It is, to be sure, written with considerable care and skill, and lacks the tumid extravagance of the earlier heroic plays. But Dryden's fundamental lack of dramatic instinct shows through. His anxiety to tidy up Shakespeare's rambling structure and write a play which preserves the Unities, as they were thought to have been defined by Aristotle, leads him to write a drama with much talk but little tension, and his hero and heroine, particularly when set beside Shakespeare's, are conspicuously lacking in vividness and vitality. We consequently have (as Dryden himself might have said) 'little concernment' for them.

The limitations of Dryden's early critical essays are related to those of the plays with which they are so closely associated. Much of Dryden's early criticism is designed, directly or indirectly, to defend or justify his own dramatic practice and that of his contemporaries. Since that practice was itself usually prompted by the need to follow and create fashion rather than by more artistic motives, it is perhaps not surprising that a great deal of the criticism associated with it seems, from a later vantage-point to have dated badly. Whereas the best critical writing of Pope, Johnson or Coleridge, for all the initial unfamiliarity of its idiom, can be seen on closer inspection to bear on those central questions which inevitably recur to readers of literature in all periods, Dryden's early criticism seems, for all the attractiveness of its manner, for the most part narrowly of its time, its best insights coming in incidental observations (which often bear on the general workings of the human mind) rather than in the main body of its literary judgements.

Indeed, even later, when Dryden had abandoned stage-writing and dramatic criticism, he was never able to explain fully in prose the insights which he had achieved in the act of poetical composition. His discoveries, for example, when translating authors, often far transcend what he says about those authors in prose. And sometimes his translating practice straightforwardly contradicts his stated theory. Thus even Dryden's best critical essays only give a partial picture of the poet's thought on the literary issues which we know, from the evidence of his poetry, most interested him.

Some brief sense of the limitations of Dryden's early criticism can be derived from a comparison of a passage from one of the prose prefaces with a passage on a similar subject from Dr Johnson's Preface to his edition of Shakespeare. In the Dedication to *The Spanish Fryar*, Dryden defended his decision to write 'tragi-comedy':

> There are evidently two Actions in it: But it will be clear to any judicious man, that with half the pains I could have rais'd a Play from either of them: for this time I satisfied my own humour, which was to tack two Plays together; and to break a rule for the pleasure of variety. The truth is, the Audience are grown weary of continu'd melancholy Scenes: and I dare venture to prophesie, that few Tragedies except those in Verse shall succeed in this Age, if they are not lighten'd with a course of mirth. For the Feast is too dull and solemn without the Fiddles.
>
> (1681 text; W1 279)

In his passage, Johnson is explaining why the categories 'tragedy' and 'comedy' seem to him more of a hindrance than a help when considering the qualities of Shakespearian drama:

> Shakespeare's plays are not in the rigorous and critical sense either tragedies or comedies, but compositions of a distinct kind; exhibiting the real state of sublunary nature, which partakes of good and evil, joy and sorrow, mingled with endless variety of proportion and innumerable modes of combination; and expressing the course of the world, in which the loss of one is the gain of another; in which, at the same time, the reveller is hasting to his wine, and the mourner burying his friend; in which the malignity of one is sometimes defeated by the frolick of another; and many mischiefs and many benefits are done and hindered without design . . . Shakespeare has united the powers of exciting laughter and sorrow not only in one mind, but in one composition . . . That the mingled drama may convey all the instruction of tragedy or comedy cannot be denied, because it includes both in its alterations of exhibition, and approaches nearer than either to the appearance of life, by shewing how great machinations and slender designs may promote or obviate one another, and the high and low co-operate in the general system by unavoidable concatenation . . . The inter-changes of mingled scenes seldom fail to produce the intended vicissitudes of passion. Fiction cannot move so much but that the attention must be easily transferred; and though it must be allowed that pleasing melancholy is sometimes interrupted by unwelcome levity, yet let it be considered likewise, that melancholy is often not pleasing, and that the disturbance of one man may be the relief of another; that different auditors have different habitudes; and that, upon the whole, all pleasure consists in variety.[12]

Both writers are defending a kind of drama in which elements which might normally be considered the exclusive preserve of either tragedy or comedy are both present in the same work, and please by the variety of response which they provoke in the audience or reader. But their manner of proceeding, it will be noted, is quite different. Dryden's defence against the charge that he has broken the

47

rules of dramatic composition (which say that tragedy and comedy must be kept distinct) is that he can, by so doing, produce an effect which will please the audience of 'judicious men', 'in this age'. Tragi-comedy is justified on the grounds that it produces the 'light relief' without which an audience will 'grow weary'. The comic element is likened to a dessert, or a musical entertainment, which lightens a meal which would otherwise satiate the stomach with an excess of richness.

Johnson, by contrast, argues his case for the rightness of Shakespeare's mingling of comic and tragic elements not (at least in the first instance) on the pleasing effect which such a mingling will produce, but on the profound capacity which the Shakespearian 'mingled drama' has to convey truth about life. Its capacity to please, Johnson argues, will derive from *that*, since it is only on the stability of truth that the human mind can properly repose. Shakespeare's mingling of comedy and tragedy in one work, Johnson argues, makes the conventional parcelling of scenes into one or other of the two categories seem arbitrary and academic. Art which so compartmentalises experience, Johnson suggests, is fundamentally inadequate to the complexities of reality. Where Dryden's concern is to defend the kind of drama which will hold the attentions of an easily bored late-seventeenth-century audience, Johnson's is to pinpoint the qualities in Shakespearian drama which make most other plays seem stiffly decorum-bound. Johnson's closing demand for 'variety' is in part a demand for necessary relief from the painfully vivid presentation of life's sorrows. Dryden's is the much less serious demand for 'light relief'. Johnson's discussion transcends its original context to become a permanently relevant meditation on the comprehensiveness of great art. Dryden's is an elegant piece of sales promotion.

The promise of the early years

Despite its limitations, however, Dryden's work in the Restoration years also displays sporadically a promise which explains the conviction of the more discerning of his contemporaries that he was the greatest poetic genius of the age.

Two main styles of writing can be singled out in which Dryden established a mastery during the first twenty years of his writing career which looks forward to the triumphs to come. The first may be called *poetry and prose of general speculation*.

In one of the notes to his edition of Shakespeare, Dr Johnson described Dryden's genius as 'acute, argumentative, comprehensive and sublime'.[13] In his *Life of Dryden*, published twelve years later, Johnson alighted on four lines from the early poem, *To My Lord Chancellor* –

> Let envy then those crimes within you see
> From which the happy never must be free;
> Envy that does with misery reside,
> The joy and the revenge of ruin'd pride.

– and commented that they 'perhaps afford Dryden's first attempt at those penetrating remarks on human nature, for which he seems to have been peculiarly formed' (H1 429). Elsewhere in the same work Johnson describes Dryden as having had 'a mind very comprehensive by nature' (H1 457). And in his famous comparison of Dryden's poetical genius with that of his greatest disciple, Pope, Johnson included the following remarks:

Dryden knew more of man in his general nature, and Pope in his local manners. The notions of Dryden were formed by comprehensive speculation, and those of Pope by minute attention. There is more dignity in the knowledge of Dryden, and more certainty in that of Pope.   (H3 222)

Johnson clearly intended these remarks as praise of a very high order. In using the words 'penetrating', 'comprehensive' and 'dignity' to describe the kind of generality which, he considered, was characteristic of Dryden's poetic thought, he was at pains to avoid any suggestion that Dryden's kind of general speculation is cold, stiff, abstract or vague. In using the word 'sublime', he makes it clear that he did not consider the 'penetrating' and 'acute' aspects of Dryden's genius to be merely the razor-sharp shrewdness of an accomplished debater. For Johnson, also, there was no contradiction between calling Dryden's genius 'sublime' and saying that the 'favourite exercise of his mind was ratiocination' (H1 459).

Dryden's characteristic way of working, Johnson thought, was to distil or quintessentialise the numerous impressions of life which he had derived from his observations, reading and reflection, into propositions, arguments, meditations and speculations which have large and general implications, and which excitingly extend the reader's perception of the world about him, the excitement coming from the way the verse allows the mind to pass beyond particular circumstance, character and situation to perceive the general conditions and principles which are manifested *in* those particular circumstances. Because of the power, penetration and precision of thought which has gone into their making, and the beauty and eloquence of their expression and the compelling rightness of their rhythms, these large reflections strike the reader not merely as sententious platitudes or stiff philosophising, but as genuinely poetic creations which are not only sharp and intelligent but exhilarating and pleasurable. Dryden's, Johnson thought, is no tepid 'poetry of statement'. It speaks, like all great verse, as much to the nerves and senses and emotions of the reader as to his intellectual faculties.

The best writing in Dryden's plays occurs at those (not infrequent) moments where he is trying out one or other of his general reflective and speculative styles of writing, often with only the loosest relation to the dramatic context. Here, for example, is the most famous speech from his last heroic play, *Aureng-Zebe*:

> When I consider Life, 'tis all a cheat;
> Yet, fool'd with hope, men favour the deceit;
> Trust on, and think tomorrow will repay:
> Tomorrow's falser than the former day;
> Lies worse; and while it says, We shall be blest
> With some new joys, cuts off what we possest.
> Strange couzenage! none would live past years again,
> Yet all hope pleasure in what yet remain;
> And, from the dregs of Life, think to receive
> What the first sprightly running could not give.
> I'm tir'd with waiting for this Chymic Gold,
> Which fools us young, and beggars us when old.
>
> (IV.i; 1676 text)

Dryden is touching on one of the subjects to which he would constantly return: the malign harshness of the conditions of life, as they appear from the perspective of suffering humanity. 'Hope springs eternal in the human breast' is given a bitter turn. Life is imagined as a dishonest trickster cheating Man with deceiving hopes, Man as a willing dupe in the enterprise, constantly buoyed up with hopes for the future despite the disasters of the past, a prospecter doomed for ever to impoverish himself digging for fool's gold. In speeches like this (as in the more lightweight Prologues and Epilogues) one can see the advantages which Dryden had derived from hearing thousands of his lines spoken aloud by the most accomplished actors and actresses of the day. The scornful edge in the tone conveys the inexorableness (to the speaker) of the processes which he describes. The thought runs in one continuous and exasperated burst through to the final clinching couplet.

Many of Dryden's passages of general reflection in the plays bear, in one way or another, on Man's seemingly boundless capacity to frustrate his own happiness by vain strivings. The following passage, this time in blank verse, comes from *All for Love*:

> Men are but Children of a larger growth;
> Our appetites as apt to change as theirs,
> And full as craving too, and full as vain;
> And yet the Soul, shut up in her dark room,
> Viewing so clear abroad, at home sees nothing;
> But, like a Mole in Earth, busie and blind,
> Works all her folly up, and casts it outward
> To the Worlds open view
>
> (IV.i; 1678 text)

Again, the general speculation is clinched in a few, carefully chosen, pungent images. The simile of the mole, casting up the detritus of its own blind burrowings, conveys with a memorable sharpness the myopic 'business' of Man, incapable of diagnosing the faults in his own affairs with the clarity with which he describes things outside himself. The images both suggest the hectic activity and the paltry ludicrousness of so much human striving and (even more strikingly) the mysterious propensity of the individual soul to insulate itself from its environment and from reality.

At other times Dryden will touch in the plays with a pithy trenchancy on those thorny perennial questions bearing on Man's relations with God or the gods. One such question is the issue of Free Will. Given the power of the forces which daily disrupt and disturb his life, Dryden asks on several occasions, can Man be said to have control over his actions? The question forms the focus of a memorable scene in *The State of Innocence*. It is also touched upon with an urgency reinforced by insistent antithesis and pungent clinching rhymes, in a passage in Dryden's reworking of *The Tempest*:

> If Fate be not, then what can we foresee,
> Or how can we avoid it, if it be?
> If by free-will in our own paths we move,
> How are we bounded by Decrees above?
> Whether we drive, or whether we are driven,
> If ill 'tis ours, if good the act of Heaven.
>
> (III.iv. 157–62; C10 64)

Dryden's capacity to formulate impressive general propositions and speculations is not restricted to his verse. Much of the essay in dialogue form, *Of Dramatick Poesie* (published separately in 1668), in which four interlocutors discuss the respective merits of English, French and classical drama, can be described not too unfairly in the terms used earlier of the shorter critical prefaces. But one passage in the *Essay* has deservedly become a classic – the celebrated paragraph on Shakespeare:

To begin then with *Shakespeare*; he was the man who of all Modern, and perhaps Ancient Poets, had the largest and most comprehensive soul. All the Images of Nature were still present to him, and he drew them not laboriously, but luckily: when he describes any thing, you more than see it, you feel it too. Those who accuse him to have wanted learning, give him the greater commendation: he was naturally learn'd; he needed not the spectacles of Books to read Nature; he look'd inwards, and found her there. I cannot say he is every where alike; were he so, I should do him injury to compare him with the greatest of Mankind. He is many times flat, insipid; his Comick wit degenerating into clenches, his serious swelling into Bombast. But he is always great, when some great occasion is presented to him: no man can say he ever had a fit subject for his wit, and did not then raise himself as high above the rest of Poets,

    Quantum lenta solent inter viburna cupressi.

['As high as cypress trees do among the bending osiers']

(C17 55–6; W1 67)

Dr Johnson's comments on this passage make clear the particular nature of its excellence. He calls it 'a perpetual model of encomiastick criticism; exact without minuteness, and lofty without exaggeration', and continues:

In a few lines is exhibited a character, so extensive in its comprehension, and so curious in its limitations, that nothing can be added, diminished, or reformed; nor can the editors and admirers of Shakespeare, in all their emulation of reverence, boast of much more than of having diffused and paraphrased this epitome of excellence, of having changed Dryden's gold for baser metal, of lower value though of greater bulk.

(H1 412)

Dryden, Johnson suggests, has captured with such effortless ease the main constituents of Shakespeare's genius that he makes everyone else who has ever written on the subject (including Johnson himself) seem, by comparison, fussy, academic and otiose. In just a few sentences, Dryden has summoned up, and epitomised the main drift of the thousands of fragmentary and miscellaneous impressions of Shakespeare's work that might occur to a thoughtful reader over a lifetime's reading. And he has done so with perfect precision and proportion. There is thus a profound pleasure in reading a passage which allows one (in a way that is usually impossible) to survey its subject steadily and whole. While most generalisations seem less true the more you inspect the evidence on which they are based, Dryden's praise of Shakespeare, Johnson suggests, takes on more implications, and seems juster and truer the more one reads and thinks about Shakespeare's plays. To set a series of passages by Shakespeare on any given subject beside passages on the same subject by other poets is to be reminded of the extraordinary animating power of Shakespeare's imagination ('when he describes any thing, you more than see it, you feel it too'). To contemplate the range of human situations and types which Shakespeare could imagine and recreate convincingly is to remind oneself of the breadth of his human insight and sympathies ('he was the Man who of all Modern, and perhaps Ancient Poets, had the largest and most comprehensive Soul'). Where Milton or Pope needed to draw constantly on a life-time's reading in many languages to assure themselves that their presentation of human nature was not eccentric, lopsided, or purely personal, Shakespeare could achieve his comprehensive truthfulness on the strength of the smallest hints from his 'sources', plus a direct extrapolation from his own experience and imagination ('he needed not the spectacles of Books to read Nature; he look'd inwards and found her there'). Where other poets have, necessarily, been obliged to reassemble, remodel and recreate, Shakespeare new-created all he saw. Dryden's encomium yields more sense the more it is applied to the facts of the case. The same largeness of view which is evident in the speculative passages in the verse is here informing his vision in prose.

In a speech from *The Conquest of Granada*, Dryden imagined the rise and fall of empires in terms which see them as closely analogous to the processes of human growth and childhood:

> When Empire in its Childhood first appears,
> A watchful Fate o'resees its tender years;
> Till, grown more strong, it thrusts, and stretches out,
> And Elbows all the Kingdoms round about:
> The place thus made for its first breathing free,
> It moves again for ease and Luxury:
> Till, swelling by degrees, it has possest
> The greater space, and now crowds up the rest.
> When from behind, there starts some petty State;
> And pushes on its now unweildy fate:
> Then, down the precipice of time it goes,
> And sinks in Minutes, which in Ages rose.
>
> (Part 2, I.i. 5–16; C11 105–6)

Here we have an example of a kind of writing which is not much appreciated nowadays. We have no adjective in our critical vocabulary which describes it accurately – 'fanciful' or 'playful' might be the nearest approximations – though the style of writing is familiar to modern readers from some of the nature-poetry of Ted Hughes and from 'poetic' passages in the novels of Dickens. The style is in fact used somewhere or other by almost all our great poets. In the ancient world the great master of 'fanciful' poetry was Ovid, and its greatest exponent in Dryden's day was Abraham Cowley.

Fanciful poetry works in some ways like the witty writing of the 'metaphysical' poets. The writer is struck by a strange resemblance between two objects, phenomena or processes, which would normally be thought to have nothing whatever in common. But where 'fanciful' wit differs from much 'metaphysical' wit is that it recognises, and exploits, the element of *comedy* which is almost inevitably involved when the human mind yokes heterogeneous ideas together. If the reader's reaction to the best metaphysical conceits is something along the lines of 'how strange, yet true' (and his reaction to the less satisfactory staple of metaphysical verse is merely 'how strange'), his reaction to a stroke of fanciful wit might be, rather, 'how strange, yet comically delightful, and, yes, in some ways, I can see, true'. Such verse is always in danger of seeming merely whimsical. The poet can get so carried away with his own amusement at his far-fetched comparisons that he simply ceases to think hard about his subject. Successful Poetry of Fancy is always reminding us that an element of truth and precise thought or observation underlies the poet's discovery of hidden resemblances between different areas of nature. Sometimes this verse can take the form of what can be called 'animism' – the imputing or attributing to animals or even inanimate objects of human thoughts, feelings and susceptibilities. Animism always runs the risk of falling into sentimentality, but, in the hands of a master, can amount to a celebration of the strange and wonderful unity which can be observed running through the apparent diversity, randomness and miscellaneity of nature. This is the note which Dryden manages in his best 'fanciful' verse. In the speech on Empire it is the precision of the thought which underpins the humour of the imaginings which makes the verse so delightful. Each stage in the rise and fall of a great empire – its early luck, its growing ambition and confidence, its 'expansionism' for the sake of its own safety, its final cumbersome vulnerability to the more vigorous younger power, the rapidity of its fall once it is on the way out – has its precisely and delightfully imagined equivalent in the history of a man's life. The pleasure of the passage resides in our being allowed, momentarily, to contemplate the ways in which the same laws of nature which governed the grandeur that was Rome can be seen to apply to the playground bully. We are allowed the rare privilege of being able to contemplate the grandest of human endeavours from the view-point of a smiling god.

In his famous description of Night from *The Indian Emperour* Dryden imagined the mountains like snoozing giants and the birds talking (or, rather, singing) in their sleep, to suggest the delightful tranquillity of the hour:

> All things are hush'd, as Natures self lay dead,
> The Mountains seem to nod their drowsie head;
> The little Birds in Dreams their Songs repeat,
> And sleeping Flowers, beneath the night-dew sweat;
>
> (III.ii. 1–4; C9 64)

In *The Conquest of Granada* a girl in a veil is imagined, with beautiful delicacy, as a tulip closing its petals against the blasts of a storm:

> As some fair tulip, by a storm opprest,
> Shrinks up; and folds its silken arms to rest;
> Bends to the blast, all pale and almost dead,
> While the loud wind sings round its drooping head:
> So, shrowded up your beauty disappears.
>
> (Part I, V.i. 298–302; C11 91)

Dryden's most extensive use in his early work of the Poetry of Fancy is to be found in the most ambitious work of the first two decades, the historical poem *Annus Mirabilis, the Year of Wonders, 1666*. In this poem of over 1200 lines Dryden abandoned his usual heroic couplet for a quatrain form which had been employed by Sir William Davenant in his historical romance *Gondibert* (1651). *Annus Mirabilis* was immensely popular, and there can be little doubt that it was a crucial factor in gaining Dryden the prestigious post of Poet Laureate on Davenant's death in 1668. The poem deals with events and issues of topical interest, principally the sea-battles against the Dutch of 1665–6 which culminated in the English victory at North Foreland, and with the Great Fire of London of September 1666. Dryden looks forward to a period of prosperous trade and imperial expansion for the British nation after the defeat of its principal rivals and its merciful release from the twin disasters of plague and fire. Charles II's clemency, his concern for the victims of the fire, his prudence, and his military astuteness are stressed, and the poem makes an implicit appeal for loyalty to such a monarch, in the interests of the continued peace, and financial and cultural prosperity of the nation.

Annus Mirabilis is a boldly and exuberantly experimental *tour de force*. Dryden pulls out every stop to display his learning and his mastery of a variety of poetic styles. He alludes ostentatiously to the poets on whom he has drawn: Statius, Virgil, Terence, Petronius. Footnotes are supplied to identify contemporary events and persons, and to illuminate the more recondite lore with which the poem is packed. *Annus Mirabilis* abounds in a variety of moods and idioms – boyish jingoism, solemn vows, sailors' jargon, extravagant images, illustrations and digressions.

It is difficult, even at this distance in time, not to sense and share some of the feeling of *élan* which struck men like Pepys when they first read this showy celebration of England's state of expectant vibrancy after the disasters which had beset the newly restored monarchy. And the poem's stance is not merely propagandist. At one point Dryden shows an impressive awareness of the tragic plight of the ordinary Dutch combatants (see Stanzas 33–6).

But readers have generally agreed that Dryden did not entirely successfully integrate the poem's diverse elements. Some parts have seemed too crudely jingoistic. Some of the similes have sometimes seemed unacceptably far-fetched, and parts of the poem have seemed rather dully devoted to the mere cataloguing of details of the sea-battles. Some of the extravagances which impressed Dryden's contemporaries have seemed, with the advantage of hindsight, more concerned to impress by their brilliance than to bring their subject home vividly to the reader's imagination. Consequently, it has often been felt that the poem's disparate elements fail to form a satisfactory whole in a reader's mind. Yet it contains several passages which are not only intrinsically excellent but which look directly forward to the more secure successes of the poet's later years.

Particularly striking are the various similes which draw on animal nature. One of the best, imitated from Ovid's *Metamorphoses*, depicts a dog pursuing a hare:

131

So have I seen some fearful Hare maintain
A Course, till tir'd before the Dog she lay:
Who, stretch'd behind her, pants upon the plain,
Past pow'r to kill as she to get away.

132

With his loll'd tongue he faintly licks his prey,
His warm breath blows her flix up as she lies:

She, trembling, creeps upon the ground away,
And looks back to him with beseeching eyes.

(521–8; K1 75–6)

Dryden imbues both animals with something of a human consciousness. But the simile offers something more interesting than
mere sentimental anthropomorphism. Dryden's imagination has
been struck by the similarity between the look of terror in the
hare's eyes and that on the face of a threatened girl. But he is, at
the same time, struck by the humorous potential of the situation.
The dog is utterly exhausted by the chase, unable even to control
the movements of his breath and 'lolling' tongue. The poet's
attitude is thus delicately poised between sympathetic involvement
and distanced amusement, as he contemplates this moment of
strange calm in the midst of nature's violence, and conveys
something of its essence to the reader. As well as being able to convey the near-humorous pathos of nature, Dryden can also thrill to
its violence:

180

So the false Spider, when her Nets are spread,
Deep ambush'd in her silent den does lie:
And feels, far off, the trembling of her thread,
Whose filmy cord should bind the strugling Fly.

181

Then, if at last, she finds him fast beset,
She issues forth, and runs along her Loom:
She joys to touch the Captive in her Net,
And drags the little wretch in triumph home.

(717–24; K1 84)

The description reveals something closer to a delighted appreciation of the spider's deception than to disapproval of her
'falseness'. The reader is made, via the comedy (which seems
temporarily to put to sleep our 'normal' moral sense), to share
the spider's joy at her own cleverness and speed, and to take
momentary delight in a nature which can contain such marvels,
recognising, moreover, as he does so, that they are continuous
with impulses in the human breast.

The most extended piece of fanciful description in *Annus Mirabilis*
occurs in the lengthy account of the growth and progress of the
Great Fire of London, of which this is a tiny sample:

217

In this deep quiet, from what source unknown,
    Those seeds of fire their fatal birth disclose:
And first, few scatt'ring sparks about were blown,
    Big with the flames that to our ruine rose.

218

Then, in some close-pent room it crept along,
    And, smouldring as it went, in silence fed:
Till th'infant monster, with devouring strong,
    Walk'd boldly upright with exalted head.

219

Now, like some rich or mighty Murderer,
    Too great for prison, which he breaks with gold:
Who fresher for new mischiefs does appear,
    And dares the world to tax him with the old:

220

So scapes th'insulting fire his narrow Jail,
    And makes small out-lets into open air:
There the fierce winds his tender force assail,
    And beat him down-ward to his first repair.

221

The winds, like crafty Courtezans, with-held
    His flames from burning, but to blow them more:
And, every fresh attempt, he is repell'd
    With faint denials, weaker then before.

222

And now, no longer letted of his prey,
    He leaps up at it with inrag'd desire:
O'r-looks the neighbours with a wide survey,
    And nods at every house his threatning fire.

(865–88; K1 90–1)

Dryden's fanciful animism is this time applied to an inanimate object. The Great Fire is given the life of other, quite different, beings. The sparks are pregnant ('big') with the fire. It then grows in the buildings like a foetus in the womb. Then it becomes, in quick succession, a crawling baby, a monstrous toddler, a murderous desperado, the client of a whore who is playing 'hard to get' and thereby increasing his desires, a giant confident of his power to dispose of the opposition with the merest flick of his little finger. The pleasure of the passage comes from the way our minds are allowed to play rapidly through the stages of a human life, applying each to the fire and seeing how its growth can be seen as uncannily like our own. The technique here is perhaps riskier than in the animal similes. The description rests on a tacit agreement between poet and reader to forget, temporarily, the more unpalatable aspects of the situation. When we are taking such exclusive delight in the behaviour of the flames, we have not time, for example, to entertain any pity for the victims of the fire. This has to wait for later, separate, treatment. And such is the pleasure which the poet invites us to take in his description that we exclude from our minds any fuller sense of the horrific destructiveness of a large conflagration.

It was, perhaps, considerations like these which led Dr Johnson to remark of the passage:

His description of the Fire is painted by resolute meditation, out of a mind better formed to reason than to feel. The conflagration of a city, with all its tumults of concomitant distress, is one of the most dreadful spectacles which this world can offer to human eyes; yet it seems to raise little emotion in the breast of the poet: he watches the flame coolly from street to street, with now a reflection and now a simile, till at last he meets the king, for whom he makes a speech, rather tedious in a time so busy, and then follows again the progress of the fire.

(H1 434)

Dryden's propensity to view the workings of Nature with breadth and detachment could, Johnson reminds us, sometimes lead him in the direction of an impassive coldness. Yet the passage, like the speech on Empire, escapes the charge of being simply irresponsible, frivolous or whimsical by the precision and felicity of the hidden resemblances between such apparently totally different realms of experience. The pleasure which we derive is, therefore, grounded on truth, even if we recognise that it is only half- or partial-truth.

Dryden's work of the 1660s and 70s, we have seen, was seriously vitiated by its preoccupation with ephemeral concerns. But intermittently present in the poetry, drama and criticism of the first two decades, there is also a body of much more serious interests. These are of a kind which might broadly be called philosophical and speculative. Dryden is interested in asking large questions about the permanent conditions under which man must live his life on this

planet. He is fascinated by the strange resemblances and continuities which the artist's eye can discern between apparently
discrete areas of created nature. These preoccupations find their
expression in verse and prose which is vigorous, vital, penetrating
and delightful. But it was not until Dryden had rejected the lure of
modishness that such preoccupations could come to occupy the
centre of his work rather than remaining an undercurrent which
surfaced only occasionally.

3

Poems of controversy: *Mac Flecknoe* and *Absalom and Achitophel*

The organisation of the two poems

The two satirical poems which form the subject of this chapter seem at first sight to have little in common. *Mac Flecknoe* is a brief squib of just over two hundred lines. *Absalom and Achitophel* is a full-dress poem of over a thousand. The subject-matter of the two works is quite different. And they are separated chronologically by a larger gap than their dates of publication might suggest. *Absalom and Achitophel* was written and published in 1681. *Mac Flecknoe* was probably written as early as 1676, six years before the pirated first edition of 1682 which prompted Dryden to produce his own 'authorised' edition in 1684.[1]

But there are several reasons why it is appropriate to consider *Mac Flecknoe* and *Absalom and Achitophel* together. First, they are the only poems of any length which Dryden wrote for a period of fourteen years after *Annus Mirabilis*. Second, they are currently Dryden's two best-known works. Today, *Absalom and Achitophel* is almost universally assumed to be Dryden's best poem, and topical satire to have been the perfect vehicle for his particular talents.

It is always a problem for a poet seeking to pillory his contemporaries (individually or collectively), to make his attacks seem more than a miscellaneous array of personal or partisan abuse. Dryden attempted to solve the problem in both *Mac Flecknoe* and *Absalom and Achitophel* by organising each poem around a carefully chosen metaphor or parallel which carries with it an implicit set of standards or ideals whereby the victims of his satire are to be judged. The intention of these metaphors is to make Dryden's attacks on his victims seem more than merely a display of animus or *parti-pris*. Rather than censuring his victims purely on his own say-so, the poet is implicitly appealing to the reader to join him in condemnation of persons who are threatening institutions or offending against values which must at all costs be preserved.

In *Mac Flecknoe*, the organising metaphors are those of classical poetry and empire. The poem's subject is Thomas Shadwell, a minor dramatist who had been employed, like Dryden, in the

Cromwellian government service, and with whom Dryden had been engaged in literary disputes since the late 1660s.[2] Shadwell and Dryden had, for nearly a decade before the composition of the poem, been airing in print their disagreements about a number of critical questions, such as the stature of Ben Jonson as a playwright and the relative merits of comedy based on displays of wit and repartee, as against the type of comic play which is devoted to the delineation of 'humours' (extravagances of habit or personality which differentiate a particular character from his fellows). They had also exchanged views about the ultimate purpose of comedy, about the value of rhyme in dramatic verse, and about the nature of literary plagiarism.

In the course of these exchanges, Shadwell had rashly portrayed himself as the champion and dramatic heir of Ben Jonson. In *Mac Flecknoe* Dryden responded to these boasts by imagining a grotesque coronation ceremony, in which Richard Flecknoe, a notoriously bad Irish poet and current monarch of 'all the Realms of *Non-sense*', hands over the throne of his kingdom to Shadwell. Shadwell is solemnly enjoined by Flecknoe always to uphold the sacred traditions of Dullness which have been so lovingly cherished during his own reign.

The poem is written in the style which has come to be known as 'mock-heroic'. The object of this type of poetry is not to ridicule the classical epic (in the manner of burlesque), but rather to bring out the paltriness of the figures and events being satirised by employing an epic style and register which is felt to be ludicrously inappropriate to its subject. Thus Shadwell progresses up the Thames to his coronation just as Virgil's Aeneas had sailed in stately dignity up the Tiber. Flecknoe entrusts power to Shadwell, just as Aeneas had entrusted the future of Rome to his son Ascanius. Shadwell's temples are crowned with poppies, just as the heads of the Roman emperors had been wreathed with laurels on their accession. In this way the discrepancy between Shadwell's Jonsonian, and thus classical aspirations (for Jonson had thought of himself as the dramatic heir of the Ancients) is exposed. Through his mock-heroic strategy Dryden brings home the difference between True Wit and its opposite, Dullness.

In *Absalom and Achitophel* the organising metaphors of Dryden's satire are biblical, and the satire is political. Dryden is contributing to the pamphlet war which accompanied the so-called 'Exclusion Crisis' of the late 1670s and early 80s. The events of this period are so fully documented in the editions of Dryden and in the standard historical works that only a brief summary is necessary here.[3] During the later 1670s, the government of Charles II was meeting with growing opposition under the leadership of one of Charles's former ministers, Anthony Ashley Cooper, first Earl of Shaftesbury. This opposition became concentrated on attempts to pass a bill through parliament which would exclude James, Duke of York, the king's Roman Catholic brother, from succeeding to the throne in the likely event of Charles's dying without a legitimate male heir. Shaftesbury's intention was to instate as heir-designate James, Duke of Monmouth, Charles's illegitimate, but Protestant, son.

The campaign of the exclusionists (or 'Whigs' as they came to be known) received impetus from the supposed discovery in 1678 of a popish plot to murder Charles, instate the Duke of York as king, and restore Catholicism as England's official religion. The tissue of lies and half-truths put about by Titus Oates, a shady renegade priest who claimed detailed knowledge of the plot, whipped up a ferment of hysteria and anti-Catholic feeling in London during 1679 and 1680 which was fully exploited by Shaftesbury's faction.

The first Exclusion Bill, which proposed that the crown should fall, on Charles's death, not to James, but to his Protestant heirs, was passed by the Commons in May 1679. Charles promptly dissolved parliament, but was obliged for financial reasons to summon it again in October 1680, when the Exclusion Bill was passed for a second time. It was, however, rejected by the Lords. Charles again dissolved parliament, ordering it to meet again at Oxford (in March 1681) to avoid the City mobs. As soon as the House began once again to debate Exclusion, Charles (who had by this time secured the financial aid he needed by doing a private deal with the French) dissolved parliament for a third and final time. The king justified his action in a *Declaration* which he commanded to be read out from all the pulpits in the land. Dryden defended the king's declaration against the Whig criticisms which inevitably ensued in a prose pamphlet, *His Majesties Declaration Defended*. In the following month, July 1681, Shaftesbury was arrested on a charge of high treason.

Absalom and Achitophel was published on or about 17 November 1681, a week before Shaftesbury was to appear before a grand jury at the Old Bailey to answer the treason charge. We are told on good authority that Dryden's commission to write the poem came from the king himself, and it has often been supposed that the specific intention of both king and poet was to sway the jury against Shaftesbury and thus secure the verdict which the king wanted. But this assumption has recently been questioned: Dryden's intention, it has been suggested, was not so much to influence the outcome of the Old Bailey hearing as to contribute more generally to the propaganda war which was being waged on the Exclusion question, by reminding moderate-minded men of the resoluteness, justice and clemency of Charles's actions throughout the crisis, and by emphasising the dangerously seditious and disruptive nature of the campaign being fought by Shaftesbury and his supporters, and the preciousness of the institutions which were threatened by their actions.[4]

The poem is cast in the form of an extended biblical allegory, in which the struggles between King Charles and the Whigs are likened to the story (told in the Second Book of Samuel) of the rebellion led against David, King of Israel by his son Absalom and his wicked counsellor, Ahithophel the Gilonite. Each character in the modern story is given the name of an Old Testament equivalent. Charles is 'King David', Monmouth is 'Absalom', Shaftesbury is 'Achitophel', the Duke of Buckingham (one of Shaftesbury's chief allies) is 'Zimri', Titus Oates is 'Corah'. The English people are 'the Jews', and the institution of monarchy 'the Ark of the Covenant' – the special, and sacred, sign of God's favour to his chosen people. Achitophel first persuades Absalom to lead the rebellion against 'David', recruiting various subversives and malcontents to the cause. The Jews are tempted by Absalom's appeals to their self-interest, and the king's supporters are weak and few. But David brings the rebellion to an instant close by making a long speech which asserts his monarchical rights, and dispenses royal clemency to his enemies.

In treating contemporary events by means of this biblical parallel Dryden sought to 'place' the happenings of his own day within a larger perspective of moral and religious values. The biblical analogy which runs through the poem is intended to remind the reader that a king is the Lord's Anointed, and that rebellion against one's monarch is therefore not merely criminal but sacrilegious. Dryden is attempting to give new imaginative embodiment to the old idea of the divinity which hedges kings.[5]

The foregoing account serves to indicate Dryden's broad design when composing *Mac Flecknoe* and *Absalom and Achitophel*. And scholarship this century has done much to illuminate the complexity and ingenuity of Dryden's schemes of allusion in both poems, and to document the poems' rhetorical intentions and dense topicality.[6]

But the fullness and intricacy of an allusive scheme and the purposefulness of a rhetorical design do not, by themselves, guarantee the consistent imaginative success of the poet's end product. And many modern scholarly commentaries on both *Absalom and Achitophel* and *Mac Flecknoe* seem to fall short of accounting for two related reactions which intelligent general readers commonly have to the poems. First, some parts of *Absalom and Achitophel* are often felt to be conspicuously livelier and better written than others. From this the suspicion arises that, whatever his professional and political commitment to his task, Dryden's poetic imagination may not have been consistently fired throughout. Second (to take up a point made in the Introduction), some parts of both poems are often felt to remain tethered to their scholarly footnotes, with only limited interest and implications for readers not involved (or only involved in a partisan way) in the topical situation being referred to.

In what follows, I shall attempt to take account of both these common reactions to Dryden's two most famous satires, and to suggest why I believe they are, at least in some important respects, just.

Ridicule and allusion in *Mac Flecknoe*

Mac Flecknoe, it could be said, has had a greatness thrust upon it of late to which it never itself aspired. For the evidence suggests that Dryden designed the poem as little more than a witty, lightweight squib, intended to raise a laugh at Shadwell's expense among the members of a circle already well acquainted with the dramatist's work, and with Dryden's opinion of it.

The humour of *Mac Flecknoe* is, for much of the time, quite miscellaneous and opportunistic, with jokes of many different kinds and of many different levels of seriousness being heterogeneously jumbled together in an exuberant farrago. Dryden alights now on Shadwell's Jonsonian aspirations, now on his fatness, now on his consumption of opium, now on his plagiarism, now on his drinking, building in all the while sly allusions to Shadwell's plays and published critical opinions.[7]

The poem's mock-heroic diction can sometimes carry with it the main drift of a particular joke, so that its *essential* point is apparent even to readers who do not appreciate every topical nuance:

> My warbling Lute, the Lute I whilom strung
> When to King *John* of *Portugal* I sung,
> Was but the prelude to that glorious day,
> When thou on silver *Thames* did'st cut thy way,

With well tim'd Oars before the Royal Barge,
Swell'd with the Pride of thy Celestial charge;
And big with Hymn, Commander of an Host,
The like was ne'er in *Epsom* Blankets tost.

(35–42; K1 266)

Here we do not really need to know that Flecknoe used to boast of
having once had an audience with the King of Portugal, or that he
prided himself on his lute-playing, or that there was an incident at
Epsom in June 1676, involving Rochester and Etherege, in which
some fiddlers had been tossed in a blanket, and which is alluded to in
Shadwell's comedy, *The Virtuoso*. The essential ingredients of the
joke are conveyed by the Spenserian diction of the opening ('the
Lute I whilom strung') and the epic register of the Thames voyage
(the central five lines of the quotation could have been lifted from a
bona fide epic), combined with the deflation provided by the banality
of the last line. The passage illustrates something of what Dryden
meant when, praising the French poet Boileau's use of the mock-
heroic style in *Le Lutrin*, he remarked: 'Here is the Majesty of the
Heroique, finely mix'd with the Venom of [Satire]; and raising the
Delight which otherwise wou'd be flat and vulgar, by the Sublimity
of the Expression' (K2 665; W2 149).

But elsewhere a fine dividing line is crossed and the jokes then
seem to depend almost exclusively for their effect on the poet's and
reader's shared knowledge and shared opinion of particular events
or persons being referred to:

St. *André*'s feet ne'er kept more equal time,
Not ev'n the feet of thy own *Psyche*'s rhime:
Though they in number as in sense excell;
So just, so like tautology they fell,
That, pale with envy, *Singleton* forswore
The Lute and Sword which he in Triumph bore,
And vow'd he ne'er would act *Villerius* more.

(53–9; K1 266)

Here we are lost without the notes. On looking them up, we find that
St André was a French choreographer who was brought over to
stage the dances in *Psyche*. John Singleton was a musician who had
performed the part of Villerius, Grand Master of Rhodes, in Sir
William Davenant's opera *The Siege of Rhodes* (1656). *The Rehearsal*
had contained a parody of the opening scene of *The Siege of Rhodes*, in
which two characters had performed, under the direction of 'Mr
Bayes' (Dryden), a whole operatic battle-scene in recitative, armed
with a sword in one hand and a lute in the other! The joke is depen-

66

dent on the reader's knowledge of, and predictable response to, certain pieces of topical literary information.

Modern admirers of *Mac Flecknoe* have praised the power of Dryden's allusions and running mock-heroic analogy to raise the poem above the level of a mere lampoon. They are the means, it is suggested, whereby Dryden rises above simple ridicule of a minor literary rival to make deeper points about the nature of literary civilisation and the threat which is posed to such civilisation by Dullness.

But the relative limitations of *Mac Flecknoe* in these areas can be seen if the poem is set beside the later work for which it was often said it had provided the hint: Pope's *Dunciad*. Pope's canvas is altogether larger and more comprehensive than his master's. His imagination ranges beyond bad poets to consider all the areas of human activity in which Truth and Intelligence are peculiarly vulnerable to the encroachments of Pedantry, Modishness, Venality, and the thousand other forms which Dullness can take.

The liveliest parts of *The Dunciad* bring home vividly and delightfully to the imagination both the ludicrousness of Dullness and its potency. Near the beginning of *The Dunciad*, for example, the Goddess Dullness surveys her Empire of Chaos. She sees

> How hints, like spawn, scarce quick in embryo lie,
> How new-born nonsense first is taught to cry,
> Maggots half-form'd in rhyme exactly meet,
> And learn to crawl upon poetic feet.
> Here one poor word an hundred clenches makes,
> And ductile dulness new meanders takes;
> There motley Images her fancy strike,
> Figures ill pair'd, and Similies unlike.
> She sees a Mob of Metaphors advance,
> Pleas'd with the madness of the mazy dance.[8]

Pope's trick of metamorphosing the basic verbal ingredients of literary Dullness into little creatures with a life of their own tellingly suggests the extraordinary fecundity of the Goddess's power. We recall, noting both the similarity and the discrepancy, the spontaneous burgeoning of paradisal Nature at the Son's command in Book VII of *Paradise Lost*. In his suggestions of fly-blown filth ('Maggots half-form'd'), malleable aimlessness ('ductile dulness new meanders takes'), gaudiness ('motley Images'), lunacy ('madness of the mazy dance'), Pope alerts us to the aberrant and perverted nature of Dullness's realm. In appreciating the exasperation of the 'poor word' forced to make 'a hundred clenches' (where 'clenches' = 'puns'), the 'ill pair'd' nature of the similes, the disorder of the 'Mob of Metaphors', we are forced to recall the propriety of and the satisfaction offered by apt metaphors, well-judged similes and genuinely deft word-play. Pope's sense of literary excellence is here, as elsewhere, suggested by his witty presentation of its mirror image, so that by the time we reach Book IV, he has amply prepared the reader for the apocalyptic close, in which Dullness's empire is seen as engulfing and destroying the whole of civilisation. Pope's build-up allows us to appreciate exactly what is at stake:

> Then rose the Seed of Chaos, and of Night,
> To blot out Order, and extinguish Light,
> Of dull and venal a new World to mould,
> And bring Saturnian days of Lead and Gold.[9]

In contrast with Pope's comprehensive portrayal of the potent forces which always exist to destroy wit and confound merit, there is only one passage in *Mac Flecknoe* where Dryden makes any sustained attempt to suggest the poetic criteria against which the dullard Shadwell is offending. In the following lines, Flecknoe is congratulating Shadwell on being free of any real resemblance to Ben Jonson:

> Thou art my blood, where *Johnson* has no part;
> What share have we in Nature or in Art?
> Where did his wit on learning fix a brand,
> And rail at Arts he did not understand?
> Where made he love in Prince *Nicander*'s vein,
> Or swept the dust in *Psyche*'s humble strain?
> Where sold he Bargains, Whip-stitch, kiss my Arse,
> Promis'd a Play and dwindled to a Farce?
> When did his Muse from *Fletcher* scenes purloin,
> As thou whole *Eth'ridg* dost transfuse to thine?
> But so transfus'd as Oyl on Waters flow,
> His always floats above, thine sinks below.
> This is thy Province, this thy wondrous way,
> New Humours to invent for each new Play:
> This is that boasted Byas of thy mind,
> By which one way, to dullness, 'tis inclin'd.
> Which makes thy writings lean on one side still,
> And in all changes that way bends thy will.
> Nor let thy mountain belly make pretence
> Of likeness; thine's a tympany of sense.
> A Tun of Man in thy Large bulk is writ,
> But sure thou'rt but a Kilderkin of wit.

(175–96; K1 269–70)

Here the reference to Shadwell's 'mountain belly' is more than mere abuse. We are reminded, among other things, of the attractively self-mocking use made by Jonson of his own gargantuan appearance: the particular allusion is to Jonson's poem 'My Picture Left in Scotland', where Jonson refers to the 'mountain belly' and 'rocky face' which have prevented his mistress from giving due attention to the excellence of his poems. This makes a piquant contrast to the absurdly self-congratulatory nature of Shadwell's claim, in the Preface to *The Virtuoso*: 'Four of the Humors [in this play] are entirely new; and (without vanity) I may say, I ne'er produc'd a Comedy that had not some natural Humour in it not represented before, nor I hope ever shall.'[10] In recollecting the extravagant unreality of the love-scenes in Shadwell's opera *Psyche*, the reader is invited to let his mind play back over the decorousness and intelligence of the analysis of human behaviour in Jonson's comedies. In contemplating the way in which Shadwell had cobbled together half-digested ingredients from the works of others, the reader is invited to remember the skill with which Jonson had been able (as he himself put it in *Timber*) 'to convert the substance, or riches of another poet, to his own use . . . Not, as a creature, that swallows, what it takes in, crude, raw, or indigested; but, that feeds with an appetite, and hath a stomach to concoct, divide, and turn all into nourishment.'[11]

This passage on Shadwell and Jonson was certainly one of those which helped Pope in his more ambitious undertaking. It is echoed in Cibber's invocation to Dullness in Book I of *The Dunciad*. But in *Mac Flecknoe* it remains a sketch since elsewhere in the poem Dryden displays little of Pope's passion and poetic resource in bringing home the preciousness of the excellence which is threatened by the encroaching power of Dullness.

For similar reasons, Dryden's specific literary allusions in *Mac Flecknoe* often lack the depth and suggestiveness of the best of their counterparts in *The Dunciad*. At the beginning of the coronation scene there occur the following lines:

> The hoary Prince in Majesty appear'd,
> High on a Throne of his own Labours rear'd.
> At his right hand our young *Ascanius* sate
> *Rome*'s other hope, and pillar of the State.

(106–9; K1 267–8)

Flecknoe is here described in terms which recall Milton's Satan at the beginning of Book II of *Paradise Lost*:

> High on a Throne of Royal State, which far
> Outshone the wealth of *Ormus* and of *Ind*,
> Or where the gorgeous East with richest hand
> Showrs on her kings *Barbaric* Pearl and Gold,
> Satan exalted sat, by merit rais'd
> To that bad eminence.   (lines 1–6)

Flecknoe mounts a throne created by his own efforts and suited to his nature. Shadwell has already been depicted as the Christ to Flecknoe's John the Baptist ('Even I, a dunce of more renown than they, / Was sent before but to prepare thy way'). Here he is the dupe of his master's diabolic temptation.[12] The same passage in *Paradise Lost* was used by Pope in his depiction of Cibber's coronation in Book II of *The Dunciad*, and Pope, clearly, was aware of the Drydenian precedent:

> High on a gorgeous seat, that far out-shone
> Henley's gilt tub, or Fleckno's Irish throne,
> Or that where on her Curls the Public pours,
> All-bounteous, fragrant Grains and Golden show'rs,
> Great Cibber sate.[13]

But Pope has transformed the merest hint in *Mac Flecknoe*, and given it a far greater depth. Whereas in *The Dunciad* Pope feels and creates the threat of Chaos posed by Dullness with a religious intensity which gives a disturbing resonance and point to his alignment of Cibber-the-Dunce and Satan-the-destroyer, Dryden's Miltonic allusion seems, by comparison, superficial. Little is done elsewhere in *Mac Flecknoe* to follow up the Flecknoe-as-Satan parallel. Dryden seems more interested in drawing, opportunistically, on a moment of evil grandeur in a well-known contemporary epic than on exploiting (in Pope's manner) the precise resonance and associations of Milton's scene as part of a larger, and coherent, pattern of significant allusion.

Some of Dryden's other literary echoes in *Mac Flecknoe* show him to have used his predecessors in less creative and responsive ways than his great disciple. Here is the description of the training school for young actors which is situated (appropriately, Dryden suggests) near the brothels of the Barbican:

> Near these a Nursery erects its head,
> Where Queens are form'd, and future Hero's bred;
> Where unfledg'd Actors learn to laugh and cry,
> Where infant Punks their tender Voices try,
> And little *Maximins* the Gods defy.
>
>   (74–8; K1 267)

As well as incorporating a little joke at his own expense (Maximin is the absurd ranting tyrant in the heroic play *Tyrannick Love*), Dryden is drawing in his final triplet on two lines from Abraham Cowley's epic *The Davideis*, where Cowley had described the caverns beneath the earth in which (it was believed) the winds live until they have grown wings and can fly into the upper air:

> Beneath the dens where *unfletcht Tempests* lye,
> And infant *Winds* their tender *Voices* try.[14]

Cowley's wit half transforms the winds into little wingless birds learning to sing for the first time. In the passage quoted earlier, depicting embryonic nonsense in Chaos, Pope drew on the same passage in Cowley, to depict

> How hints, like spawn, scarce quick in embryo lie,
> How new-born nonsense first it taught to cry.

Pope, we note, has preserved Cowley's witty attribution to the winds of the helpless weakness of babyhood. And just as Cowley's baby winds have gradually to acquire the ability to fly, so Pope's Nonsense, at first raw and untutored, has to learn the skills that it will exercise for the rest of its life. Pope's allusion to Cowley preserves the older poet's playful wit, adapting it so that it contributes to his own depiction of Dullness's ability to spawn and cultivate a myriad forms of perverted life.

Dryden's use of the Cowley is more straightforwardly deflationary. A famous couplet is taken over and deployed for the purposes of simple mockery. Cowley's 'unfletcht' is deprived of its witty metaphorical force; these actors don't seem like tender little fledgelings, in the manner of Cowley's winds. The 'infant Punks' are simply juvenile versions of the whores they will turn into after drama school.

The comic geniality of *Mac Flecknoe*

But if *Mac Flecknoe* lacks the ambitiousness of critical purpose and allusive coherence and depth which have sometimes been attributed to it, it nevertheless contains some delightful, and characteristically Drydenian, comic strokes. Many of the most memorable turn on Dryden's depiction of the Absoluteness of Shadwell's dullness. At the opening of the poem, the folly of dull poets is seen as something not a million miles from that of poets' royal masters:

> All humane things are subject to decay,
> And, when Fate summons, Monarchs must obey:

71

This *Fleckno* found, who, like *Augustus*, young
Was call'd to Empire, and had govern'd long:
In Prose and Verse, was own'd, without dispute
Through all the Realms of *Non-sense*, absolute.
This aged Prince now flourishing in Peace,
And blest with issue of a large increase,
Worn out with business, did at length debate
To settle the succession of the State:
And pond'ring which of all his Sons was fit
To Reign, and wage immortal War with Wit;
Cry'd, 'tis resolv'd; for Nature pleads that He
Should onely rule, who most resembles me:
Sh— alone my perfect image bears,
Mature in dullness from his tender years.

(1–16; K1 265)

Dryden's wit here is playing subversively over matters which in his official 'public' writing he so often treated with straightforward solemnity. In this passage the weighty issues of monarchical succession, absolute rule and the divine right of kings are given a slyly double-edged treatment. Flecknoe has achieved the 'absolute rule' over his domain of *Non-sense* which Charles II was so frequently suspected of plotting to wield over his kingdom. Like Charles, Flecknoe is 'blest with issue of a large increase'. Charles had fathered twelve illegitimate children by 1676. (The Duke of Buckingham once remarked that a king is supposed to be the Father of his People, and Charles II was certainly a father of a good many of them.) As with Charles and other monarchs, Flecknoe's offspring bear a striking physical resemblance to their sire. Like Charles, Flecknoe is 'worn out with business' – we remember the contemporary accounts of Charles's notorious idleness, as well as noting the sexual *double entendre* in 'business'.

The mock-heroic effect here works in multiple directions. It is not, now, simply a case of the absurdity of Flecknoe being revealed in contrast to the majesty of royalty. The majesty of royalty is simultaneously being mocked. But the mockery is not merely sardonic or destructive. Every reader, I think, feels that there is something genuinely magnificent about both Flecknoe and his supremely foolish successor, and Dryden seems in the passage just quoted to have contemplated the two dullards and their kingly attributes not in a fit of spleen or animus or crypto-republicanism, but, rather, in a spirit of genial delight. *Mac Flecknoe*, wrote the eighteenth-century critic Joseph Warton, 'is full of *mirth*', and 'a vein of pleasantry is uniformly preserved through the whole'.[15]

The comic magnificence of the figure of Shadwell seems to derive particularly from the suggestion that whereas nature has endowed all human beings (including monarchs) with their fair share of folly, it is only in Shadwell that Folly's rule is pure and unalloyed, with no tincture of sense whatsoever. So, possessing a common human attribute to a supreme degree, Shadwell becomes a kind of heroic figure. He alone is 'fit / To Reign, and wage immortal War with Wit'. Just as, for example, Hercules showed in babyhood the strength that was to make him legendary, by strangling serpents in his cradle, so Shadwell seemed 'Mature in dullness from his tender years'. The completeness with which the promise of the child is realised in the mature man must, in this comic vision of things, be celebrated as one might celebrate any unparalleled human achievement. In the meritocracy of Folly, Shadwell has risen right to the top:

> Some Beams of Wit on other souls may fall,
> Strike through and make a lucid intervall;
> But *Sh*—'s genuine night admits no ray,
> His rising Fogs prevail upon the Day:
> Besides his goodly Fabrick fills the eye,
> And seems design'd for thoughtless Majesty:
> Thoughtless as Monarch Oakes, that shade the plain,
> And, spread in solemn state, supinely reign.
>
> (21–8; K1 265)

Here 'the sublimity of the expression' certainly does 'raise the delight which otherwise would be flat and vulgar'. Dryden's enjoyment of the careless lolling monarchs (we catch in 'Monarch Oakes' a sly hint of the celebrated Boscobel Oak which sheltered Charles II after his defeat at the battle of Worcester)[16] perhaps derives from the thought that only kings and fools (or both) are privileged to enjoy this degree of utterly unwavering confidence. In these circumstances, ignorance really is bliss. Here, in one of the best of the literary echoes in the poem, Dryden has drawn for inspiration on the scene in Boileau's *Lutrin* where the poet shares the nostalgia of La Mollesse (Sloth) for the good old days, when under her rule the kings of France lounged at idle ease:

> Helas! qu'est devenu ce temps, cet heureux temps,
> Où les Rois s'honnoroient du nom de Faineans,
> S'endormoient sur le Trône, et me servant sans honte,
> Laissoient leur sceptre aux mains ou d'un Maire ou d'un Comte?
> Aucun soin n'approchoit de leur paisible Cour.
> On reposoit la nuit, on dormoit tout le jour.
> Seulement au Printemps, quand Flore dans les plaines

Faisoit taire des Vents les bruyantes haleines,
Quatre boeufs attelez, d'un pas tranquille et lent,
Promenoient dans Paris le Monarque indolent.
Ce doux siecle n'est plus.

[Ah! whither fled those happy Times of Peace,
When idle Kings, dissolv'd in thoughtless Ease,
Resign'd their Scepters, and the Toils of State
To *Counts*, or some inferior *Magistrate*:
Loll'd on their Thrones, devoid of Thought or Pain;
And, nodding, slumber'd out a lazy Reign?
No anxious Cares did nigh the *Palace* creep,
But Day and Night was one continu'd Sleep,
Except the *Vernal* Month, when *Flora* gilds
The chearful Valleys, and the smiling Hills,
When the loud *North* his Airy Rule resigns
To gentle *Zephyrs*, and more peaceful Winds,
Four *Oxen* drew with *slow* and *silent* Feet
Th'unactive Monarch to some Country Seat.
But 'tis no more: That Golden Age is gone.[17]]

All Shadwell needs to do to maintain his power is simply to have confidence in his natural endowments:

let no alien S—*dl*—y interpose
To lard with wit thy hungry *Epsom* prose.
And when false flowers of *Rhetorick* thou would'st cull,
Trust Nature, do not labour to be dull.

(163–6; K1 129)

It is sometimes said that, had Shadwell not been selected as the subject of *Mac Flecknoe*, he would still enjoy a respectable reputation as a minor writer of comedies. The argument could I think be reversed: Dryden has taken a paltry contemporary and, in the liveliest parts of his poem, immortalised him as a comic colossus.

Party satire in *Absalom and Achitophel*

In his *Life of Dryden*, Dr Johnson commented on the enthusiasm with which *Absalom and Achitophel* was received on its first appearance:

Of this poem, in which personal satire was applied to the support of public principles, and in which therefore every mind was interested, the reception was eager, and the sale so large, that my father, an old bookseller, told me, he had not known .it equalled but by Sacheverell's trial [a famous eighteenth- century political trial].

The reason of this general perusal Addison [in no. 512 of *The Spectator*]

74

has attempted to derive from the delight which the mind feels in the investigation of secrets; and thinks that curiosity to decypher the names procured readers to the poem. There is no need to enquire why those verses were read, which to all the attractions of wit, elegance, and harmony added the co-operation of all the factious passions, and filled every mind with triumph or resentment.

(H1 373–4)

Later in the *Life*, Johnson added these further observations on the poem:

If it be considered as a poem political and controversial it will be found to comprise all the excellences of which the subject is susceptible: acrimony of censure, elegance of praise, artful delineation of characters, variety and vigour of sentiment, happy turns of language, and pleasing harmony of numbers; and all these raised to such a height as can scarcely be found in any other English composition.

(H1 436)

Johnson's remarks remind us of the particular kinds of pleasure and fascination which a contemporary audience must have found when they first read a work in which the leading poet of the day was treating matters of such urgent and widespread topical concern.

And it is easy to illustrate from Dryden's text each of the qualities singled out by Johnson for special mention – acrimony of censure:

> The *Jews*, a Headstrong, Moody, Murmuring race,
> As ever try'd th' extent and stretch of grace;
> God's pamper'd people whom, debauch'd with ease,
> No King would govern, nor no God could please;

(45–8; K1 218)

elegance of praise:

> What e'r he did was done with so much ease,
> In him alone, 'twas Natural to please.
> His motions all accompanied with grace;
> And *Paradise* was open'd in his face

(27–30; K1 217)

artful delineation of characters:

> His joy conceal'd, he sets himself to show;
> On each side bowing popularly low:
> His looks, his gestures, and his words he frames,
> And with familiar ease repeats their Names.
> Thus, form'd by Nature, furnish'd out with Arts,
> He glides unfelt into their secret hearts:

> Then with a kind compassionating look,
> And sighs, bespeaking pity ere he spoak,
> Few words he said; but easy those and fit:
> More slow than Hybla drops, and far more sweet.
>
> (688–97; K1 234–5)

The 'variety of sentiment' referred to by Johnson can be seen by all readers, as they move through the poem from oratorical *tour de force* to character-sketch to passage of general reflection. The 'vigour of sentiment' is especially noticeable in those 'penetrating remarks on human nature' for which Johnson thought Dryden 'to have been peculiarly formed':

> Youth, Beauty, Graceful Action, seldom fail:
> But Common Interest always will prevail:
> And pity never Ceases to be shown
> To him, who makes the peoples wrongs his own.
>
> (723–6; K1 235)

Johnson's 'happy turns of language' and 'pleasing harmony of numbers' are to be seen in all these quotations, and abound throughout the poem.

But recent commentators on *Absalom and Achitophel* have grounded their praise not on its numerous local felicities but on the aspect of the poem with which Johnson was least happy: its overall structure and design. They have described Dryden as the creator of a coherent and unified 'conservative myth', and have praised him for integrating and balancing in an architecturally designed whole, elements of forensic oratory, panegyric, satiric portraiture, and the final, *deus-ex-machina*-like, appearance of Charles, to convince the reader of the rightness of the royal cause. This has, I believe, involved some unwarranted exercise of charity towards unsatisfactory passages, and some taking of ingenious party strategy for artistic persuasiveness.[18]

As Johnson observed, the allegorical scheme on which the poem's design was grounded had to be forced to bring the contemporary events into line with the biblical narrative. 'The original structure of the poem', he wrote, 'was defective: allegories drawn to great length will always break; Charles could not run continually parallel with David' (H1 436–7).[19] Many of the historical figures in the poem are only related by the most tenuous connections to their biblical 'equivalents'. Some prominent persons in the biblical narrative could not be made to fit any of the actors in the political drama. And some of the biblical figures adduced in the poem play no part in the

76

story of Absalom's rebellion, but had to be found elsewhere in Scripture. The reader, therefore, might justifiably consider Dryden's alignment of modern and biblical events to be more ingenious than inevitable.

As an example of unsatisfactory writing in the poem we may consider the portraits of the 'short File' of King Charles's loyal supporters which precede the king's final speech. This section of the poem begins with the portrait of 'Barzillai', James Butler, Duke of Ormonde, Charles I's Lord Lieutenant of Ireland, who had followed Charles II (then Prince Charles) into exile during the Interregnum:

> In this short file *Barzillai* first appears;
> *Barzillai* crown'd with Honour and with Years:
> Long since, the rising Rebells he withstood
> In Regions Waste, beyond the *Jordans* Flood:
> Unfortunately Brave to buoy the State;
> But sinking underneath his Masters Fate:
> In Exile with his Godlike Prince he Mourn'd;
> For him he Suffer'd, and with him Return'd.
> The Court he practis'd, not the Courtier's art:
> Large was his Wealth, but larger was his Heart:
> Which, well the Noblest Objects knew to choose,
> The fighting Warriour, and Recording Muse.
>
> (817–28; K1 238)

Here the monotony of movement, awkward use of zeugma ('crown'd with Honour and with Years'), antitheses where no real contrast is being drawn ('For him he Suffer'd, and with him Return'd; 'Large was his Wealth, but larger was his Heart') and inertness of metaphor ('buoy the State . . . sinking') combine to produce an effect which seems both clumsy and weak.

The portrait of Ormonde is followed by a lament for Ormonde's son, Thomas, Earl of Ossory, who, after brave service in the Dutch and French wars, had died of a fever in 1680. The passage begins awkwardly:

> His Eldest Hope, with every Grace adorn'd.
> By me (so Heav'n will have it) always Mourn'd,
> And always honour'd, snatcht in Manhoods prime
> By' unequal Fates, and Providences crime:
>
> (831–4; K1 238)

Rather than evoking the qualities which made Ossory's life so valuable, thus giving his readers the means to appreciate more fully the pathos of his early death, Dryden continues in a declamatory mode, attempting to supply dignity with Virgilian allusion,[20] and then, when his treatment becomes too fanciful for his overall design, manoeuvring it back to the main subject by a somewhat stagey address to the Muse:

> Oh Narrow Circle, but of Pow'r Divine,
> Scanted in Space, but perfect in thy Line!
> By Sea, by Land, thy Matchless Worth was known;
> Arms thy Delight, and War was all thy Own:
> Thy force, Infus'd, the fainting *Tyrians* prop'd:
> And Haughty *Pharaoh* found his Fortune stop'd.
> Oh Ancient Honour, Oh Unconquer'd Hand,
> Whom Foes unpunish'd never coud withstand!
> But *Israel* was unworthy of thy Name:
> Short is the date of all Immoderate Fame.
> It looks as Heaven our Ruine had design'd,
> And durst not trust thy Fortune and thy Mind.
> Now, free from Earth, thy disencumbred Soul
> Mounts up, and leaves behind the Clouds and Starry Pole.
> From thence thy kindred legions mayst thou bring
> To aid the guardian Angel of thy King.
> Here stop my Muse, here cease thy painfull flight;
> No Pinions can pursue Immortal height:
> Tell good *Barzillai* thou canst sing no more,
> And tell thy Soul she should have fled before;
> Or fled she with his life, and left this Verse
> To hang on her departed Patron's Herse?

> (838–59; K1 238–9)

Here, it may be felt, Dryden relies on his classical allusion to carry a charge of significance which is not given sufficient imaginative life in the verse. While one appreciates the intent, one may not be convinced by the effect. And this tendency is one which is perhaps more pervasive in *Absalom and Achitophel* than is often admitted. A sceptical reader might feel that some of the allegorical parallelism which is so central to the poem's main design only has the desired effect if the allegory is being decoded by someone who already fundamentally shares the poet's assumptions.

It is, indeed, an awkward fact that Dryden was attempting to rest his polemical case and ground the significance of his allegory on principles and assumptions which were by no means regarded in all quarters as the exclusive preserve of the party for which he was propagandising. The same basic allegorical scheme and political arguments as Dryden's were deployed in one of the Whig replies to

Absalom and Achitophel, Elkanah Settle's *Absalom Senior*. But there it is the Tories who are seen as acting from self-interest, James ('Absalom') and his wicked adviser Halifax ('Achitophel') whose conduct is likely to bring disaster on the state, and the balanced constitution, where parliament acts as a divinely appointed check to potentially tyrannical absolutist monarchs, is the sacred status quo which must at all costs be preserved.[21]

In a series of echoes of Milton's *Paradise Lost*, Dryden has attempted to align the figure of Shaftesbury with that of Milton's Satan, thus displaying how his rôle in the affairs of the Exclusion crisis was that of diabolic tempter. This is most obvious at the point where he first tries to seduce Monmouth to his cause:

> Him he attempts, with studied Arts to please,
> And sheds his Venome, in such words as these
>
> (228–9; K1 223)

Here we are intended to remember Satan in Book IV of *Paradise Lost* 'Squat like a Toad, close at the eare of *Eve*', 'inspiring venom', and again, in Book IX, launching his 'fraudulent temptation'. A similar allusion occurs in the piece of overt Miltonic pastiche which comes at the moment when Monmouth has expressed some doubts as to whether he will fall in with Shaftesbury's plan:

> Him Staggering so when Hells dire Agent found,
> While fainting Vertue scarce maintain'd her Ground,
> He pours fresh Forces in . . .
>
> (373–5; K1 226)

The lines no doubt seemed a brilliant satirical stroke at the time and their strategic point is still, of course, appreciable. But for such echoes to seem to later readers more than a clever device to impute diabolic intent to 'the enemy', we need to have been convinced that Shaftesbury is not just a crafty and skilful politician but a potent force of evil, and a committer of *sacrilege*.

The fact that some non-partisan readers are not thus persuaded is perhaps partly attributable to the nature of Dryden's portrayal of Shaftesbury elsewhere (to be discussed below), partly to the weakness of Dryden's eulogy of Charles's followers, and partly to the enormous burden placed upon his scheme of allusions and metaphors to convince the reader of the *sanctity* of the persons and institutions which Shaftesbury's actions are threatening. This last subject is touched on most directly in the passage of general reflection which immediately precedes the character-sketches of the king's supporters:

If ancient Fabricks nod, and threat to fall,
To Patch the Flaws, and Buttress up the Wall,
Thus far 'tis Duty; but here fix the Mark:
For all beyond it is to touch our Ark.
To change Foundations, cast the Frame anew,
Is work for Rebels who base Ends pursue:
At once Divine and Humane Laws controul;
And mend the Parts by ruine of the Whole.
The Tampering World is subject to this Curse,
To Physick their Disease into a worse.

(801–10; K1 237–8)

Dryden is here attempting to express far more than the feeling, common to many political conservatives, that, though minor adjustments may be necessary, long-established institutions must be preserved, since there is little chance of them being replaced by anything better. It is his clear intention to show that the monarchy is the product of 'Divine', not merely 'Humane' laws. The 'ancient Fabricks' are *holy* buildings.

But readers not of Dryden's party may feel that little has been done in the poem, either here or elsewhere, to transform the notion of a divinely sanctioned monarchy into something more than a *donnée* of the biblical analogy which is continually *asserted* – not least in the lengthy unsolicited testimonial which Monmouth gives Charles in his first speech. Dryden, such readers may feel, has not managed to invest the kingship with that aura of sanctity with which Shakespeare surrounded the figure of Duncan in *Macbeth*, and which he brought alive imaginatively in a way that can impress readers and audiences with no independent investment in the idea of royal divinity.

In his final speech, many have felt Charles sounds more as if he is rehearsing political theory than speaking with an ungainsayable God-like authority. For such readers Joseph Spence's anecdote that 'King Charles obliged Dryden to put his Oxford speech into verse, and to insert it toward the close of *Absalom and Achitophel*' has poetic, if not literal truth.[22] Even some critics generally sympathetic to Dryden's design have found the speech disappointingly flat and dull.[23] And, at the one point in the poem where we are offered some imaginatively compelling thoughts about the divinity of kings, they touch, as we shall see, on a notion of divinity which is not easily compatible with the cautious conservatism of the 'ancient Fabricks' passage.

The portraits in Absalom and Achitophel

If the poem is, as I have suggested, dependent at times on the willingness of readers to relax critical judgement in the interests of affirming partisan solidarity, why did it retain a constant readership down the centuries? For though *Absalom and Achitophel* did not occupy the position of central prominence in Dryden's *oeuvre* for general readers in the eighteenth and nineteenth centuries as it does for academic students today, it nevertheless formed part of the repertoire of Dryden poems which were constantly read and enjoyed.

The evidence indicates that, once its immediately topical interest had worn off, *Absalom and Achitophel* was usually remembered not so much as a whole design, but for the excellence of some of its parts. The most frequently remembered moments were, of course, the celebrated portraits, particularly those of 'David', 'Achitophel' and 'Zimri'. And the tradition of singling them out for special mention starts with Dryden himself, who in 1693 wrote that 'the Character of *Zimri* in my *Absalom*, is, in my Opinion, worth the whole Poem' (K2 655; W2 137). Here is the 'Zimri' portrait:

> In the first Rank of these did *Zimri* stand:
> A man so various, that he seem'd to be
> Not one, but all Mankinds Epitome.
> Stiff in Opinions, always in the wrong;
> Was every thing by starts, and nothing long:
> But, in the course of one revolving Moon,
> Was Chymist, Fidler, States-Man, and Buffoon:
> Then all for Women, Painting, Rhiming, Drinking;
> Besides ten thousand freaks that dy'd in thinking.
> Blest Madman, who coud every hour employ
> With something New to wish, or to enjoy!
> Rayling and praising were his usual Theams;
> And both (to shew his Judgment) in Extreams:
> So over Violent, or over Civil,
> That every man, with him, was God or Devil.
> In squandring Wealth was his peculiar Art:
> Nothing went unrewarded, but Desert.
> Begger'd by Fools, whom still he found too late:
> He had his Jest, and they had his Estate.
> He laught himself from Court, then sought Relief
> By forming Parties, but coud ne'er be Chief:
> For, spight of him, the weight of Business fell
> On *Absalom* and wise *Achitophel*:

81

Thus, wicked but in will, of means bereft,
He left not Faction, but of that was left.

(544–68; K1 231)

The function of this portrait in the satirical design is to bring home to the reader the reckless irresponsibility of those who support the Whig cause. Dryden could afford to treat the Duke of Buckingham quite lightly, we are told, because in political terms Buckingham was far less of a threat than others in the Shaftesbury camp. And for the classically learned there is an extra dimension to be enjoyed, since Dryden had incorporated an allusion to another famous satirical portrayal of a versatile shyster – the time-serving Greek in the Third Satire of the Roman poet Juvenal. Dryden's own version of Juvenal's passage makes the similarity quite clear:

Quick Witted, Brazen-fac'd, with fluent Tongues,
Patient of Labours, and dissembling Wrongs.
Riddle me this, and guess him if you can,
Who bears a Nation in a single Man?
A Cook, a Conjurer, a Rhetorician,
A Painter, a Pedant, a Geometrician,
A Dancer on the Ropes, and a Physician.
All things the hungry *Greek* exactly knows:
And bid him go to Heav'n, to Heav'n he goes.

(133–41; K2 683)

Dryden reminds the reader that in Zimri we have an example of an anarchic type of human personality who, in all civilisations, presents a threat to order and probity.

All this is clearly very useful in revealing some of Dryden's polemical intentions (and some parts of the passage do reveal the poet's contempt for Buckingham's irresponsibility). But it falls short of explaining the most immediately striking feature of the liveliest parts of the 'Zimri' portrait, namely their tone. For some lines in the portrait seem to be written in a spirit closer to wonder and delight than to censorious hostility. Rather than regarding the chaotic contradictions of Zimri's behaviour simply as anathema, a threat to all he holds dear, Dryden sometimes suggests by his tone that he is fascinated and bemused by the spectacle. There is only a narrow dividing-line, we may reflect, between saying of Zimri that he is

A man so various, that he seem'd to be
Not one, but all Mankinds Epitome

and of Shakespeare that 'he was the Man who of all Modern and perhaps Ancient Poets, had the largest and most comprehensive Soul'.

Dryden's wonder at the chameleon-like transformations of this 'Blest Madman' who can become all men in rapid succession is captured in the verse by the jerky antitheses:

> Stiff in Opinions, always in the wrong;
> Was every thing by starts, and nothing long

and the tumbling, blurted-out lists:

> Was Chymist, Fidler, States-Man, and Buffoon:
> Then all for Women, Painting, Rhiming, Drinking.

These parts of the portrait read more like a miniature essay on the delightful absurdity of human perverseness than a polemical denunciation of a political enemy. They have an imaginative freedom which transcends their strategic purpose.

In no. 162 of *The Spectator*, Joseph Addison turned naturally to the Zimri portrait to conclude a series of general reflections (in the manner of Montaigne) on the changeability of Man:

There is scarce a State of Life, or Stage in it, which does not produce Changes and Revolutions in the Mind of Man. Our Schemes of Thought in Infancy are lost in those of Youth: these too take a different Turn in Manhood, till old Age often leads us back into our former Infancy. A new Title or an unexpected Success throws us out of ourselves, and in a Manner destroys our Identity. A cloudy Day or a little Sun-shine have as great an Influence on many Constitutions, as the most real Blessings or Misfortunes. A Dream varies our Being, and changes our Condition while it lasts; and every Passion, not to mention Health and Sickness, and the greater Alterations in Body and Mind, makes us appear almost different Creatures. If a Man is so distinguished among other Beings by this Infirmity, what can we think of such as make themselves remarkable for it even among their own Species? It is a very trifling Character to be one of the most variable Beings of the most variable Kind, especially if we consider that he who is the great Standard of Perfection has in him no Shadow of Change, but is the same Yesterday, to Day, and for ever.

As this Mutability of Temper and Inconsistency with our selves is the greatest Weakness of humane Nature, so it makes the Person who is remarkable for it in a very particular Manner more ridiculous than any other Infirmity whatsoever, as it sets him in a greater Variety of foolish Lights, and distinguishes him from himself by an Opposition of party-coloured Characters.

Addison then quotes a passage from the Third Satire of Horace's First Book which depicts a character ('the most humourous . . . in

Horace') which is 'founded upon this unevenness of Temper and Irregularity of Conduct'. In conclusion Addison remarks:

Instead of translating this Passage in *Horace*, I shall entertain my *English Reader* with the Description of a Parallel Character, that is wonderfully well finished by Mr. *Dryden*, and raised upon the same Foundation.[24]

And he ends the paper by quoting 'Zimri'.

In the Zimri portrait Dryden has transcended *parti-pris* to float large general thoughts about an important aspect of human nature. Something broadly similar might be said of the (very different) portrait of 'Achitophel':

> Of these the false *Achitophel* was first:
> A Name to all succeeding Ages Curst.
> For close Designs, and crooked Counsels fit;
> Sagacious, Bold, and Turbulent of wit:
> Restless, unfixt in Principles and Place;
> In Power unpleas'd, impatient of Disgrace.
> A fiery Soul, which working out its way, ⎫
> Fretted the Pigmy Body to decay: ⎬
> And o'r inform'd the Tenement of Clay. ⎭
> A daring Pilot in extremity;
> Pleas'd with the Danger, when the Waves went high
> He sought the Storms; but for a Calm unfit,
> Would Steer too nigh the Sands, to boast his Wit.
> Great Wits are sure to Madness near ally'd;
> And thin Partitions do their Bounds divide:
> Else, why should he, with Wealth and Honour blest,
> Refuse his Age the needful hours of Rest?
> Punish a Body which he coud not please;
> Bankrupt of Life, yet Prodigal of Ease?
> And all to leave, what with his Toyl he won,
> To that unfeather'd, two Leg'd thing, a Son:
> Got, while his Soul did hudled Notions try;
> And born a shapeless Lump, like Anarchy.
> In Friendship False, Implacable in Hate:
> Resolv'd to Ruine or to Rule the State.

(150–74; K1 220–1)

Dryden sometimes succumbs in *Absalom and Achitophel* to the temptation to treat his political opponents merely as contemptible blackguards, the motive for whose conduct is all too obvious, and therefore easily summarised and easily dismissed. But in the best strokes in this passage he seems genuinely disturbed and perplexed by the phenomenon he is describing. The questions ('Else, why should he . . .') seem more than a bullying rhetorical ploy: the 'restlessness' of an Achitophel is not attributable to some easily labelled motive (such as 'malice', 'Zeal', 'self-interest' or 'envy') but operates in mysterious and less predictable psycho-somatic regions which 'fret' and 'punish', and 'refuse rest' to the body. Shaftesbury had a suppurating wound in the side, the result of an operation on a cyst of the liver, and Dryden turns the fact to disturbingly potent poetical effect. Shaftesbury seems, in Dryden's portrayal, almost a vehicle for the working-out of powerful natural processes which he is apparently impotent to control. He is a man of great talent yet his 'wit' and 'daring' cannot be harnessed to work for 'calm', either of himself or others. The stress falls on the harm Achitophel is doing himself in destroying his 'Rest'. A recent commentator has justly observed that

when Dryden used the pigmy image in *Absalom and Achitophel* it was not merely an easy jibe at Shaftesbury's smallness, but, allied with the generalizing phrase 'Tenement of Clay' a comment on all mankind, on the propensity of the human mind to drive the body mercilessly, on the restless ambition of man, on the hunger of the imagination: . . . For all the dislike of Shaftesbury in *Absalom and Achitophel* – and the dislike and destructiveness in the portrait must not be minimized – there was an understanding of the psychological type of person to which he belonged.[25]

In the 'Achitophel' portrait, Dryden had written the first of what were to be a series of memorable portrayals of the restlessness and anguish which are the product of human strivings and ambitiousness. The best of these treatments, as we shall see in the next chapter, was his depiction of the mythical figure of Sisiphus in his translation of Lucretius's episode *Against the Fear of Death*. But he was also to touch on the subject in some striking prose sentences which he included in his Dedication to *Don Sebastian*, and which describe the character of ambitious men:

they have no sphere of their own, but like the Moon in the *Copernican* Systeme of the World, are whirl'd about by the motion of a greater Planet. This it is to be ever busie; neither to give rest to their Fellow creatures, nor, which is more wretchedly ridiculous, to themselves: Tho truly, the latter is a kind of justice, and giving Mankind a due revenge, that they will not permit their own hearts to be at quiet, who disturb the repose of all beside them.
(C15 60)

But, fine as 'Zimri' and 'Achitophel' are, the most imaginatively lively and suggestive of all the portraits in *Absalom and Achitophel* is the shortest, the opening depiction of 'King David':

In pious times, e'r Priest-craft did begin,
Before *Polygamy* was made a sin;
When man, on many, multiply'd his kind,
E'r one to one was, cursedly, confind:
When Nature prompted, and no law deny'd
Promiscuous use of Concubine and Bride;
Then, *Israel*'s Monarch, after Heaven's own heart,
His vigorous warmth did, variously, impart
To Wives and Slaves: And, wide as his Command,
Scatter'd his Maker's Image through the Land.

(1–10; K1 217)

We saw in Chapter 1 something of the diverse play of mind which is
at work in these lines, and how the very act of reading the passage out
loud prompts the reader to entertain a number of potentially subversive speculations: *Is* polygamy sinful? Or is it only made so by laws,
or priests? And, if the latter, what are the priests' motives? What is
the difference between polygamy and promiscuous fornication?

But the passage provokes further questions still in the mind of an
attentive reader. When, for example, we come to the phrase 'after
Heaven's own heart', we might be prompted to reflect: Is Dryden
seriously suggesting that in his notoriously promiscuous behaviour
Charles II was acting out God's will? And if the suggestion *isn't*
serious, then on whom does the joke rebound – Charles or God? Is
Dryden indulging in straightforward blasphemy?

That was certainly the view of Jeremy Collier, writing in 1698:

[In *Absalom and Achitophel*] we have Blasphemy on the top of the Letter,
without any trouble of Inference, or Construction. This poem runs all upon
Scripture Names, Upon Supposition of the true Religion, and the right Object of Worship. Here Profaneness is shut out from Defence, and lies open
without Colour or Evasion. Here are no Pagan Divinities in the Scheme, so
that all the Atheistick Raillery must point upon the true God. In the beginning we are told that *Absalom* was *David*'s Natural Son: So then there's a blot
in his *Scutcheon*, and a blemish upon his Birth. The *Poet* will make admirable
use of this Remark presently! This *Absalom* it seems was very extraordinary
in his Person and Performances. Mr. *Dryden* does not certainly know how
this came about, and therefore enquires of himself in the first place

> *Whether inspired with a diviner Lust,*
> *His Father got him* –

This is down right Defiance of the Living God. Here you have the very
Essence and Spirit of Blasphemy, and the Holy Ghost, brought in upon the
most hideous Occasion.[26]

Collier, we might concede, may have a point. But is Dryden one
step ahead, and taking more seriously than usual the two biblical

thoughts – that Man is made in God's image, and that his first duty was to 'go forth and multiply'? Some distinguished writers had, after all, expressed respect for the polygamy practised by some of the patriarchs of the Old Testament.

The suggestion takes us into further speculative regions: If Charles is the Lord's Anointed, God's representative on Earth, then his activities must be a performance of God's work. This is perhaps the proper exercise of the divine right of kings? So, rather than the seedy royal lecher of the court lampoons, we are dealing with a grand force of divine generosity:

> Then *Israel*'s Monarch, after Heaven's own heart,
> His vigorous warmth did, variously, impart
> To Wives and Slaves: And, wide as his Command,
> Scatter'd his Maker's Image through the Land.

The last clause, running across the line-ending, certainly has an irresistible vigour, but the notion of divinity being invoked seems closer to the Jupiter of Ovid's *Metamorphoses* than to the God of Christian scripture.

The jokes and speculations reverberate in these opening lines without settling on any one fixed point of view. Within the passage lurk several suggestions (some of them mutually incompatible): (i) In promiscuous copulation, King Charles is doing God's work; God approves lechery; the divine right which the king enjoys is the right to commit lecherous acts, (ii) fornication is 'natural', (iii) priests' activities are incompatible with piety, (iv) monogamous marriage is a curse, (v) (if the lines are read in a straightforwardly ironic spirit) King Charles's activity is a travesty of the proper conduct of a Christian king ('how does he character the King', asked an outraged anonymous pamphleteer on the poem's first appearance, 'but as a broad figure of scandalous inclinations').[27]

But to set the suggestions out like this as bald propositions is to ignore or destroy the wit which holds them in superfine equipoise. The suggestions remain teasing hints. The poet stands back, uncommitted to any of the suggestions as they stand (or perhaps committed to them all), inviting us to entertain speculations rather than to take up a 'point of view'.

Commentators sometimes explain the opening passage of *Absalom and Achitophel* as a piece of clever tactics (Dryden getting the embarrassing business of Charles's promiscuity and Monmouth's illegitimacy out of the way as soon as possible), or as a way of incorporating an acknowledgement of Charles's 'body natural' as well as his 'body politic'. But a close examination of the lines shows that their imaginative life is far less restricted than such descriptions might imply. The 'David' portrait, I believe, provides a commentator wishing to account for the common reactions to *Absalom and Achitophel* mentioned earlier in this chapter with his strongest clue.

It is clear that Dryden believed sincerely and honourably in the need for Englishmen to support the Stuart monarchy as the only bulwark against chaos and anarchy in the land. In that sense, his commitment to his polemical task in *Absalom and Achitophel* was deep and genuine. But, it may be suggested, when his poetic imagination was fired on the subject of the divinity of kings, its speculations were freer and more diverse than was easily compatible with the partisan presentation of a royalist-conservative political position. Dryden's strategic purpose necessitated his aligning Charles II and his cause with the absolute moral authority of the One True God of the Bible. But his deeper imaginative inclinations were prompting him to see Charles/David as a figure closer to the glorious lecher-gods of classical myth. The aspects of Charles which kindled Dryden's poetic imagination most vividly could not be made to feature too prominently in a piece of royalist propaganda. The polemical task of Dryden the Laureate, though undertaken with genuine commitment, can, in this respect, be thought of as having exercised a constraint upon the imaginative flights of Dryden the Poet. Whatever Dryden's political allegiances, the witty imaginings of the 'David' portrait (one may speculate from the end-product) were much closer to his *poetic* heart than the royalist doctrine which finds expression in David's final speech. Dr Johnson commented memorably on the stagey impression made by the ending of the poem:

As an approach to historical truth was necessary the action and catastrophe were not in the poet's power; there is therefore an unpleasing disproportion between the beginning and the end. We are alarmed by a faction formed out of many sects various in their principles, but agreeing in their purpose of mischief, formidable for their numbers, and strong by their supports, while the king's friends are few and weak. The chiefs on either part are set forth to view; but when expectation is at the height, the king makes a speech, and

'Henceforth a series of new times began'.

Who can forbear to think of an enchanted castle, with a wide moat and lofty battlements, walls of marble and gates of brass, which vanishes at once into air when the destined knight blows his horn before it?

(H1 437)

But the wide-ranging imaginings and speculations which had given

88

life to the 'David' portrait, and the acute psychological insight which had informed 'Zimri' and 'Achitophel' stayed with Dryden and were to give rise to more fine poetry later in his career, where, in the words of an early nineteenth-century critic, Dryden's 'genius sports at ease, freed from the shackles of a political or polemical task'.[28]

4

New directions: religion and translation in the 1680s

Dryden and the court: for and against

In 1681, the year in which *Absalom and Achitophel* was published and in which Dryden reached the age of fifty, his greatest period as a writer was, according to his earlier admirers, only just beginning. This chapter investigates the extraordinary burst of new energy which can be seen in Dryden's poetry in the early and middle 1680s, and the events and thinking which lay behind that burst of energy.

The 1680s, I shall suggest, were years in which Dryden underwent what might be called a 'spiritual metamorphosis', in which, as in the metamorphoses of Ovid's poem, or those observed by biologists, he was both utterly altered and yet simultaneously preserved in his new shape recognisable elements of his former self. The poetic by-products of this period of metamorphosis were of an extraordinarily varied kind – so varied that they seem at times mutually contradictory.

But within these apparent contradictions and contrarieties, there is an essential unity. In an attempt to locate and define this unity, it will first be necessary to chart in some detail the movements in Dryden's career and thinking which have a direct bearing on his period of spiritual metamorphosis.

The 1680s were, from any point of view, a period of prodigious and diverse activity for Dryden. On one level, his career continued in the pattern set by *His Majesties Declaration Defended* and *Absalom and Achitophel*. Dryden continued to propagandise for the royal cause, to attack the Whigs, and to celebrate and advise the Stuart monarchy in verse.

Absalom and Achitophel was followed the next year by two further contributions to the pamphlet war against the king's enemies: *The Medall: A Satire against Sedition* and *The Second Part of Absalom and Achitophel*. The first of these was occasioned by the striking of a medal by Shaftesbury's supporters to celebrate the verdict of *ignoramus* ('no charge to answer') passed by the Whig-packed Grand Jury before whom Shaftesbury appeared in November 1681. The second was substantially written by Nahum Tate, but contains some very lively interpolated lines by Dryden. The most famous of these are the satirical portraits of the two Whig poets 'Og' (Shadwell) and 'Doeg' (Elkanah Settle). Also in 1682 came the first performance of *The Duke of Guise*, a play written by Dryden in collaboration with Nathaniel Lee. *The Duke of Guise* suggests parallels between the Whigs' opposition to Charles and the struggles in the sixteenth century between the French king, Henry III, and the so-called 'Holy League'.

Dryden's activity as a court writer continued further into the 1680s. In 1684 he translated at the king's request a long prose work, again on the subject of the French religious wars, and again with parallels in the events of recent English history: Louis Maimbourg's *History of the League*. In 1685, on Charles's death, Dryden celebrated the king's achievement and heralded in the reign of James II with *Threnodia Augustalis: A Funeral-Panegyric Poem Sacred to the Happy Memory of King Charles II* and *Albion and Albanius*. The latter was an opera depicting the troubles and triumphs of Charles's reign and welcoming the new king in a series of quasi-allegorical tableaux. In the new reign, Dryden celebrated the birth of the king's son (the future 'Old Pretender') in *Britannia Rediviva: A Poem on the Birth of the Prince* (1688) and lent his support to James's propaganda-campaign for the Roman Catholic faith by translating (also in 1688) a second French prose work: Dominique Bouhours' *Life of St Francis Xavier*, an account of the expeditions of a pious sixteenth-century Jesuit missionary to China.

Though none of the works mentioned so far has ever been thought to rank as a whole among Dryden's finest achievements, this body of public work represents a considerable expenditure of personal commitment and professional skill. But during the very same years in which Dryden was so fully occupied with political controversy and with his official work as Poet Laureate and Historiographer Royal, other thoughts were preoccupying his mind and soul, and at a different and deeper level. These thoughts were not entirely new ones. From various pieces of evidence it is clear that for some years before the 1680s Dryden had been beginning to entertain serious misgivings about some aspects of the course which his earlier life and literary career had taken. In particular, he seems to have come to regret having squandered so much of his talent trying to please the tastes of a public whom he increasingly despised as shallow and fickle, and on having spent so much of his time flattering members of a court which he was coming to see as a breeding-ground for malice, hypocrisy, ambition and envy. At first these thoughts only surfaced occasionally and were either forgotten or suppressed. Dryden certainly underwent no sudden or immediate transformation as a result of his slowly-forming convictions. He continued for some time to flatter his courtier-patrons, and, long after first expressing doubts about the worth of his career as a dramatist, went on writing weak plays – though it is true that some of the plays of the later 1670s contain more serious matter and are less tainted with modishness than any he had written previously. Nevertheless, though Dryden's critical reflections produced no sudden *volte-face*, they were to increase in intensity, and eventually came to affect his work in crucial ways.

There are many passages in the prologues and epilogues where Dryden jeers at his theatre audiences or expresses dissatisfaction with his plays. Taken individually these remarks might perhaps not seem significant. The dual gambit of insulting one's audience and proclaiming one's own incompetence was, in the Restoration theatre (as now) a standard comic ploy. But the cumulative effect of such passages is telling, and they receive confirmation from remarks in several of Dryden's prefaces where the poet admits the extravagance and absurdity of some of his heroic plays, and expresses his annoyance and weariness at having for so long been forced to please an undiscerning audience.

In one prologue Dryden writes that a playwright is 'bound to please, not to Write well; and knows / There is a mode in Plays as well as Cloaths' (K1 34). In the prologue to her play *Sir Patient Fancy*, Mrs Aphra Behn has 'an elevated Poet' (clearly Dryden) remark of his own plays that 'these unwitty things will do, / When your fine fustian useless Eloquence / Serves but to chime asleep a drousy Audience'. 'Who', the poet cynically asks, 'at the vast expense of Wit would treat, / That might so cheaply please the Appetite?'[1] In another of his own prologues Dryden laments that the playwright

> Lives not to please himself but other men:
> Is always drudging, wasts his Life and Blood,
> Yet only eats and drinks what you think good.
>
> (Prologue to *Caesar Borgia*, 2–4; K1 204)

No less striking are the sharp and frequent pen-portraits of 'fawning' and 'servile' courtiers to be found in the plays. We get what is almost certainly a glimpse of autobiography in one of the later plays, when a character addressing a king comments on the court

> Where, like a Statue, thou hast stood besieg'd,
> By Sycophants and Fools, the growth of Courts;

> Where thy gull'd eyes, in all the gawdy round,
> Met nothing but a lye in every face,
> And the gross flattery of a gaping Crowd,
> Envious who first should catch, and first applaud
> The Stuff of Royall Nonsence . . .

The courtiers' sycophancy to the king contrasts sharply with their treatment of the latest arrival at court:

> when I spoke,
> My honest homely words were carp'd, and censur'd,
> For want of Courtly Stile: related Actions,
> Though modestly reported, pass'd for boasts:
> Secure of Merit if I ask'd reward,
> Thy hungry Minions thought their rights invaded,
> And the bread snatch'd from Pimps and Parasits.
>
> (*Don Sebastian*, IV. iii. 438–50; C15 184–5)

Dryden had used similarly strong language over ten years before in the dedication to *Aureng-Zebe* to describe the 'courtiers without wit' who behave with envious and cowardly viciousness towards those truly witty men whom they find vulnerable to their attack:

> They fawn and crouch to men of parts, whom they cannot ruine: quote their Wit when they are present, and when they are absent, steal their Jests: But in those who are under 'em, and whom they can crush with ease, they show themselves in their natural Antipathy; there they treat Wit like the common Enemy, and give it no more quarter, than a Dutch-man would to an English Vessel in the *Indies*; they strike Sail where they know they shall be master'd, and murder where they can with safety.
>
> (1676 text)

By 1686 it is clear that Dryden had come to regard some areas of his earlier work not merely as regrettable but as a *desecration* of his sacred calling as a poet. For Dryden cast the following lines which he included in an elegy written in that year on the death of a young poetess, Mrs Anne Killigrew, in the language of vehement religious repentance:

> O Gracious God! How far have we
> Prophan'd thy Heav'nly Gift of Poesy?
> Made prostitute and profligate the Muse,
> Debas'd to each obscene and impious use,
> Whose Harmony was first ordain'd Above
> For Tongues of Angels, and for Hymns of Love?
> O Wretched We! why were we hurry'd down
> This lubrique and adult'rate age,

(Nay added fat Pollutions of our own)
T' increase the steaming Ordures of the Stage?

(55–65; K1 461)

What had led Dryden to such a pitch of feeling? Why was he prompted to use language with such a specifically religious charge to reflect on earlier activity which might at first seem a purely literary matter? And what was the upshot of such feelings for his subsequent literary development?

Contexts of Dryden's spiritual metamorphosis

The dynamics of Dryden's writing life were as often shaped by his reading as they were by historical or public events. From the mid 1670s onwards, Dryden received a number of challenges and shocks and was subjected to various influences and pressures which caused him to come by slow degrees to the realisations expressed in the Killigrew Ode: that the poetic ideals which he had been following were a prostitution of his art; if he was to produce work of permanent worth he would have to learn to distinguish more clearly between fashionable novelty (and the conceit which is always involved in the production of such novelty) and lasting excellence.

The challenges and shocks seem to have begun in the mid 1670s. Thoughout his life Dryden was abused and derided by minor literary rivals. But in 1675 there had appeared the most balanced and discerning of all the attacks on him, the poem 'An Allusion to Horace' by John Wilmot, Earl of Rochester. Rochester had hailed Dryden as unquestionably the greatest living poetic genius, but had also accurately pin-pointed the ways in which he had played to the gallery by filling his dramatic writing with a blend of modish intellectuality and would-be-rakish salaciousness. Dryden's plays, Rochester had noted, have 'justly pleased the town', being 'embroidered up and down / With wit and learning', but (Rochester had advised Dryden):

> 'Tis . . . not enough, when your false sense
> Hits the false judgment of an audience
> Of clapping fools, assembling a vast crowd,
> Till the thronged playhouse crack with the dull load;
> Though ev'n that talent merits in some sort,
> That can direct the rabble, and the court.[2]

Later in his poem, Rochester had noted the patronising complacency of some of Dryden's published critical judgements (and the

Sin of Pride which had prompted them), and ended by advising the poet to

> Scorn all applause the vile rout can bestow,
> And be content to please those few who know.[3]

In 1674, the year before Rochester's poem, Thomas Rymer had published his translation of the *Reflections on Aristotle's Treatise of Poesie* by the French critic René Rapin. In his Preface, Rymer had paid Dryden a generous tribute by making a favourable comparison of the description of Night from *The Indian Emperour* with treatments of the same subject by distinguished poets of the ancient and modern world. But in the best parts of the *Reflections* themselves, Rapin had presented a grander and more dignified conception of poetry and the poet's function than any which Dryden had served hitherto, or which he could have found described in such a sustained form in the existing body of English literary criticism.

Dryden was deeply impressed both by the work of Rapin and of his translator. In 'The Author's Apology for Heroick Poetry, and Poetic Licence' of 1677 he declared the French writer to be 'alone sufficient, were all the other critics lost, to teach anew the rules of writing'. And in a letter of the same year he called Rymer's *Tragedies of the Last Age* 'the best piece of Criticism in the English tongue', and added: 'I thinke myself happy that he has not fallen upon me, as severely and wittily as he has upon Shakespeare and Fletcher, for he is the only man I know capable of finding out a poets blind sides' (L 13–4). Many years later, after the appearance of the *Short View of Tragedy*, in which Rymer had severely criticised *Othello* as 'a Bloody farce, without salt or savour', Dryden remarked that, while Shakespeare's work was not touched by Rymer's strictures, 'I . . . and such as I, have reason to be afraid of him' (L 72).

Dryden had every reason to be worried by critics whose work had been inspired by the recent literary achievements in France. For, in the very same decades when his output consisted largely of the plays discussed in Chapter 2, French audiences and readers were being offered almost yearly the major literary masterpieces of the century: the plays of Molière and Racine, the poems of La Fontaine, the poetry and critical work of Boileau, the maxims of La Rochefoucauld, the philosophical and devotional writings of Pascal and the novels of Mme de Lafayette.

If Dryden had been impressed by the criticism of Rapin, he was equally or even more enthusiastic about the work of Boileau. In his own work he was indebted both to Boileau's precept and to his example. *Mac Flecknoe*, we have seen, owed something to the precedent of Boileau's mock-heroic poem, *Le Lutrin*. Dryden was equally attentive to the implications of Boileau's critical work. In 1683 he made alterations and improvements to Sir William Soame's translation of *L'Art Poétique*, replacing Boileau's French examples with names from English literary history. In particular, Dryden came to value the way in which Boileau both advocated and engaged in a kind of spiritual commerce with the poets of former ages. 'What [Boileau] borrows from the Ancients', he wrote, 'he repays with Usury of his own: in Coin as good, and almost as Universally valuable' (K2 608; W2 81).

In the same year as the Rymer/Rapin *Reflections* and Boileau's *Le Lutrin* and *L'Art Poétique* there also appeared the final version of the most ambitious English literary masterpiece of the age. It is said that after his first reading of *Paradise Lost*, Dryden was moved to exclaim, 'This Man Cuts us All Out, and the Ancients too'.[4] But the full magnitude of what Milton had achieved and the comprehensiveness and dignity of the Miltonic vision of Man were in fact slow to impress themselves upon him. In later life he was to confess to the critic John Dennis that at the time when he had asked Milton's permission to write *The State of Innocence* he 'knew not half the extent of his greatness'.[5] As he grew older, Dryden drew increasingly on the phrasing and thought of *Paradise Lost* in a way that clearly reveals the depth of his preoccupation with Milton's masterpiece.[6]

As well as these literary stimuli, there were circumstances in Dryden's personal life which helped to dislodge him from his former complacency and infatuation with worldly success. Official favour had not brought the security which he had hoped for, and his salary from the Royal Exchequer was frequently in arrears. So strongly did Dryden feel about this aspect of his career that he even included in his funeral panegyric on Charles II some splendidly double-edged lines on the poets of his former master's court:

> Tho little was their Hire, and light their Gain,
> Yet somewhat to their share he threw;
> Fled from his Hand, they sung and flew,
> Like Birds of Paradise, that liv'd on Morning dew.
> Oh never let their Lays his Name forget!
> The Pension of a Prince's praise is great.
>
> (*Threnodia Augustalis*, 377–82; K1 452)

Dryden's first-hand experience of court life cannot have encouraged any simple-minded admiration of the institution or of the values which prevailed there. Neither can the severe beating-up which he received in December 1679 at the hands of an aristocrat's thugs for his supposed hand in some satirical verses about court personalities.

Dryden was also beginning to reflect more generally on the uncertainties of human life. It has been convincingly argued that the death in 1683 of the promising young poet John Oldham (on whom Dryden wrote a serenely dignified elegy, and whose achievements in verse-translation in some respects anticipate Dryden's own) caused him to reflect deeply and seriously on mortality in general, and on the mortality of poets in particular.[7]

Tonson and translation

In 1679, with the publication of his adaptation of *Troilus and Cressida*, Dryden had entered into a partnership with an enterprising young publisher, Jacob Tonson, which was to last, with only minor interruptions, for the rest of the poet's life. It was to prove most fruitful, in both artistic and financial terms, for poet and publisher alike.[8] Since going into business in the late 1670s, Tonson had concentrated largely on the publication of plays. But in 1680, prompted partly by the precarious state of the theatre at that time and partly by the success some years earlier of a composite English translation of the poems of Horace, Tonson mounted a publishing venture which was to be prophetic of things to come. In that year he assembled a translation 'by several hands' of Ovid's *Heroides*, a set of imaginary love-letters in verse from the heroines of classical mythology. Dryden was asked to submit a Preface and versions of two of Ovid's poems, and to revise a third by his patron the Earl of Mulgrave. Dryden's Preface contains some interesting and often-quoted remarks about the principles of translation, but the versions themselves are often coarse and monotonous. However, Tonson's venture was a great success, and marked the beginning of what would become the main activity of the last fifteen years of Dryden's writing career – the production and editing of verse translations from the classical poets.

Dryden, it seems, was actively engaged in the early 1680s in discussions with various literary friends (particularly Wentworth Dillon, Earl of Roscommon, to whose *Essay on Translated Verse*, 1684, he contributed an enthusiastic prefatory poem) about the potential of translation as a poetic medium, and the ways in which the genre might contribute to the general literary life of the nation. In this, they were seeking to consolidate and extend the work of earlier

English poets – most notably Ben Jonson and Cowley – who had already attempted in a piecemeal way to enrich modern literature by creative renderings of older authors. The details of the Dryden/Tonson/Roscommon circle remain to be documented, but it is clear that over the next few years Dryden became established at the centre of a collaborative translating venture in which Tonson acted as publisher, and to which Dryden not only contributed many hundred lines of his own verse, but also acted as a recruiter of translators,[9] an adviser to other poets,[10] and a radiant source of ideas and inspiration.

In the years after 1680, the literary publications of the Tonson house were prodigious, both in quantity and quality.[11] Tonson provided English readers with new English versions of the classical writers Plutarch, Horace, Virgil, Juvenal, Persius and Lucan, as well as substantial portions of Ovid, Seneca, Cicero, Chaucer, Boccaccio, Homer, Pascal and Cervantes. Nor did Tonson restrict his operations to translation. He produced new editions of the English poets – Cowley, Milton, Spenser, Shakespeare, Denham, Waller, Suckling and Fletcher – and a series of Miscellanies containing many important new poems, original and translated. Not all these publications involved Dryden directly, but many were his own work (or composite ventures to which he contributed both poetry and editorial advice) and all were the products of a literary circle in which he was chief mentor and source of inspiration. Dryden's financial involvement with Tonson increased after 1688, when the loss of his Laureate salaries made it necessary for him to support himself by his pen. But by that date his career as a translator was already well established. By the later 1680s he had been transported from an environment where his work had been largely to provide ephemeral entertainment, into a *milieu* whose gradually developing enterprise was nothing short of an attempt to provide for cultivated readers of both sexes reading editions of the best English and foreign literature, past and present. The contributors to Tonson's first volume of translations, the 1680 *Ovid*, had mostly been members of the old circle of court wits and minor dramatists. But increasingly during the 1680s and 90s Dryden found himself at the centre of a circle of young writers who were better read, more serious about literature, and more versatile, accomplished and poetically ambitious than most of his friends and rivals of the 1660s and 70s.

The Christian poetry of the 1680s

By the early 1680s, then, various factors were encouraging Dryden to reconsider the earlier course of his literary career. The Killigrew Ode shows that Dryden felt this reconsideration to have profound implications for his spiritual life as well. These were the years when, Sir Walter Scott noted, 'reiterated disappointment, and satiety of pleasure, prompted [Dryden's] mind to retire within itself and think upon hereafter'.[12]

In 1682, when he published *Religio Laici: or A Laymans Faith*, Dryden was a member of the Church of England. The impulse for this poem (unlike much of his other work of the period) seems to have come from Dryden himself. The poem's immediate occasion was the controversial translation into English of a French work, the *Histoire Critique du Vieux Testament* by the French Catholic theologian, Richard Simon. Simon had demonstrated the unreliability of the texts of the Bible and had argued for the consequent need for Christians to accept the arbitration of the Church and the authority of Church traditions on all controversial questions of scriptural interpretation.

Dryden's poem consists of a series of reflections, couched for the most part in a verse which is plain, spare, and often pointed and pithy, on the nature of authority in religious matters. He questions, in turn, the teachings of the Deists (who believed that adequate knowledge of God could be attained by the exercise of Reason alone), of the Roman Catholics (whose reliance on the authority of tradition and priestly say-so Dryden judges to be excessive), and of the Protestant sectaries (whose claims to be able to interpret Scripture by the unaided exercise of the 'inner light' he regards as deluded and dangerous). Dryden then goes on to argue for the necessity of a religious stance in which the reading of Scripture, respect for Church tradition and the exercise of Reason are all allowed to play no more or less than their proper part. Only by restraining his innate tendencies towards fruitless theological speculation (and the discord and wrangling which are their inevitable consequence), Dryden suggests, will Man attain that 'common quiet' which it is the peculiar prerogative of religion to provide. The ideal stance, Dryden suggests in *Religio Laici*, can be best achieved within the Church of England.

By 1685 Dryden had been prompted to modify his position, and in that year he was received into the Roman Catholic Church. The precise circumstances of his conversion remain, and will perhaps always remain, obscure. We know, however, that Dryden became aligned with the body of moderate opinion within the small English Catholic community. He strongly dissociated himself from the extreme positions of the Jesuits (who argued that English Catholics could legitimately work for the overthrow of any heretic on the English throne – thus showing themselves, in Dryden's eyes, to be as subversive as the Protestant sectaries) and the 'Blackloists' (an English Catholic splinter group who had tried to exalt Tradition to the status of sole guide in questions of scriptural interpretation and who claimed that Faith had the status of quasi-'scientific' truth).[13]

In 1687, in the midst of political troubles and tensions which were mounting towards the end of James II's reign, Dryden published his first and only major declaration and defence of his Catholic faith, *The Hind and the Panther*. Dryden's second Christian poem is an altogether larger and more ambitious piece than *Religio Laici*. It is cast as an extended beast-fable. Dryden found partial precedent for this form in some of the more recondite traditions of Renaissance writing.[14] But his reasons for writing his Catholic poem as a beast-fable were not merely antiquarian or whimsical. *The Hind and the Panther* is, like *Religio Laici*, a poem directed against religious bigotry by a writer who is avowedly not claiming for his doctrinal discussions any privileged authority or divine inspiration. By setting his poem in the world of beasts and birds, Dryden gives it a lightness of touch which is not an evasive frivolity but a kind of tact – a built-in guarantee against the very kind of portentous dogmatism which the poem seeks to expose. For in Dryden's hands the depiction of the animal world was almost always touched with a humour which, among other things, directs the mind inevitably toward human foibles and pretensions.

The Hind and the Panther attempts a defence of the moderate Catholic position on questions of reason, faith and Church authority (voiced in the speeches of the 'milk white hind') against the criticisms of its Anglican detractors (represented by the 'spotted panther'), and addresses itself to the particular problems and dangers facing the English Catholics and the nation as a whole in 1687. The bird fables of the poem's Third Part treat the damage being done to the Catholic cause by the extreme policies of James II's advisers, and offer dark forebodings of the fate which might await the English Catholics under any future Protestant monarch. The delicately sympathetic yet wry wit of these fables (in which the contemporary parties and personalities are imagined as swallows, pigeons, buzzards, martins and domestic poultry) both brings home the danger and political violence of the current conflicts, and simultaneously charms the reader into a sense of the inhumane absurdity of doctrinal discord. By exploiting the humorous incongruities (and similarities) between the fables' ornithological settings and the human events to which they refer, Dryden is able to tease his readers out of complacent or fixed attitudes to the current controversies, and to tap areas of their sensibilities which would normally lie dormant when contemplating such matters.

The Hind and the Panther reveals some of the ways in which Dryden's religious thinking had shifted in emphasis during the 1680s. Most noticeably, it puts more stress than had *Religio Laici* on the vital need for a Church with sufficient authority to stifle the dangerous and potentially anarchic excesses of Protestant individualism, and insists that the Catholic Church alone has such authority.

But the two Christian poems of the 1680s also have a great deal in common. It is difficult to believe that only strategic considerations caused Dryden to stress, in *The Hind and the Panther*, the common theological ground shared by the Anglican and Catholic churches, and to avoid dwelling on what (to Anglicans) were the more offputting aspects of Catholic worship and doctrine – miracles, saints, the rôle of the Virgin Mary. A main concern of Dryden's is to stress the common core of Christian belief which men of good will from different denominations can share.

Both *Religio Laici* and *The Hind and the Panther* put a significant stress on the 'quiet' and 'rest' from 'endless anguish' which religious faith and the resistance of vain theological speculation bring to the believer. Both poems emphasise the unknowableness of ultimate truths. In *Religio Laici* the prime folly of the Deists is that they fancy themselves capable of comprehending through their own Reason truths which are by definition outside its scope:

> How can the *less* the *Greater* comprehend?
> Or *finite Reason* reach *Infinity*?
> For what cou'd *Fathom GOD* were *more* than *He*.
>
> (39–41; K1 312)

The same thought finds expression in Part I of *The Hind and the Panther*:

> Let reason then at Her own quarry fly,
> But how can finite grasp infinity?
>
> (I. 104–5; K2 472)

In *Religio Laici* Dryden had likened religion to the light of the sun which eclipses lesser lights. In *The Hind and the Panther* Dryden returns to the image, now emphasising the dazzling mystery of God's presence:

> Thy throne is darkness in th' abyss of light,
> A blaze of glory that forbids the sight;
> O teach me to believe Thee thus conceal'd,
> And search no farther than thy self reveal'd;
>
> (I. 66–9; K2 471)

In both poems, Dryden's desire for a religious certainty which involves accepting the mystery of ultimate truths (rather than trying to attain knowledge of God's secrets) does not involve the abdication of Reason, but rather a just recognition of the scope (and therefore the limitations) of that 'noble' human faculty. Reason, faith, private reflection upon Scripture and due reverence for the traditions of the Church all have their contributions to make in both the Anglican and Catholic phases of Dryden's religion.

Profoundly abhorrent to both the Anglican and Catholic Dryden are those groups (in both Protestant and Catholic camps) who claim doctrinal certainty from their own resources. Such men, Dryden suggests, think themselves entitled to stir up dissent and disorder in both Church and State on the basis of little more than an egotistical delusion. In *The Medall* Dryden had written of the sects' wilful imposition on Scripture of the meanings that they wanted to see in it:

> Happy who can this talking Trumpet seize;
> They make it speak whatever Sense they please!
> 'Twas fram'd, at first, our Oracle t'enquire;
> But, since our Sects in prophecy grow higher,
> The Text inspires not them; but they the Text inspire.
>
> (162–6; K1 257)

In his 'Postscript' to the translation of the *History of the League* Dryden had specifically equated the religious bigotry and violence (the two are seen as inseparable) of the Protestant sects and of the Jesuits: 'Their Tenets in Politicks are the same; both of them hate Monarchy, and love Democracy: both of them are superlatively violent; they are inveterate haters of each other in Religion, yet agree in the Principles of Government' (C18 403).

Fallen Man in *Religio Laici* and *The Hind and the Panther*

But Dryden's point about the sects and the Jesuits is not a narrowly partisan one. Much of the enduring power of his writing about the religious extremists, and about the form which religious conduct should properly take, seems to stem not so much from narrow party antagonisms as from an acute and thorough awareness of the inherently fallible and self-deluding nature of Man. In *The Medall*, Dryden had included some large general reflections in his evocation of the anarchic impulses in the crowd to which he shows Shaftesbury appealing:

> Ah, what is man, when his own wish prevails!
> How rash, how swift to plunge himself in ill;
> Proud of his Pow'r, and boundless in his Will!
>
> (132–4; K1 257)

Dryden perceives Man's doubts and uncertainties with equal acuteness. The much-admired opening of *Religio Laici* offers us a carefully pondered evocation of the benighted course of human life:

> Dim, as the borrow'd beams of Moon and Stars
> To *lonely, weary, wandring* Travellers
> Is *Reason* to the *Soul*: And as on high,
> Those rowling fires *discover* but the Sky
> Not light us *here*; So Reason's glimmering Ray ⎫
> Was lent, not to *assure* our *doubtfull* way, ⎬
> But *guide* us upward to a *better Day*. ⎭
> And as those nightly Tapers disappear
> When Day's bright Lord ascends our Hemisphere;
> So pale grows *Reason* at *Religions* sight;
> So *dyes*, and so *dissolves* in *Supernatual Light*.
>
> (1–11; K1 311)

This passage alone would be enough to prevent us from taking Dryden's own description of the verse of *Religio Laici* ('unpolish'd, rugged Verse . . . / As fittest for Discourse, and nearest Prose') too literally. For while these lines might seem superficially to have the rhetorical structure of a piece of discursive prose, it is also clear that Dryden conveys his 'point' to the reader's imagination in a strikingly suggestive series of related metaphors and images, and by the steady, dignified movement of the verse rather than simply by a process of reasoning. The 'Majestick' manner described in the poem's preface is sufficiently flexible to evoke the sadly resigned course of a man's life ('To *lonely, weary, wandering* Travellers') as well as the stately grandeur of the Sun in the heavens ('When Day's bright Lord ascends our Hemisphere': where the verse moves with a vital spring in its step).

So dense is the passage with poetic thought that it is worth dwelling on a little further. Dryden's images are precise and telling. The moon and planets reflect the light of the (unseen) sun. Their light is thus 'borrow'd, 'lent' them by the sun, just as human life and the reasoning powers which accompany it are 'lent' to Man by God for a short space of time. The reflected light, like human reason, is entirely dependent for its very existence as well as for such power as it possesses on an unseen source of energy. Reason's light, like that of the planets, is 'glimmering' – genuine, but sporadic and uncertain. Its existence reveals the existence of God (as the planets reveal the existence of the sun) but does not illuminate that existence. Man's path through life will remain 'doubtful' (a word which seems to encompass the meanings 'unclear' and 'hesitating'). His reason has been given him not so that life will be any less of a trial or a mystery, but as a means whereby he might recognise the existence of the source whence it was derived in the first place. He does this by looking 'upward' to the sky, raising his sights beyond the tribulations of this world to the glories of the heavens. The images force the imagination to make complex and fruitful connections between the imagined traveller benighted on the highway and the human soul contemplating the mysteries of religion.

The train of imagery is continued into the following lines, which depict the vain attempts of the pagan philosophers Epicurus and Aristotle to discover the Summum Bonum, the happiness which it is the peculiar prerogative of religion to provide:

> Some few, whose Lamp shone brighter, have been led
> From Cause to Cause, to *Natures* secret head;
> And found that *one first principle* must be:
> But *what*, or *who*, that *UNIVERSAL HE*;
> Whether some *Soul* incompassing this Ball
> *Unmade, unmov'd*; yet *making, moving All*;
> Or various *Atoms* interfering Dance
> Leapt into *Form*, (the Noble work of *Chance*;)
> Or this great *All* was from *Eternity*;
> Not ev'n the *Stagirite* himself could see;⎫
> And *Epicurus Guess'd* as well as He:⎭
> As *blindly grop'd* they for a *future State*;
> As *rashly Judg'd* of *Providence* and *Fate*:
> But least of all could their Endeavours find
> What most concern'd the good of Humane kind:
> For *Happiness* was never to be found;
> But vanish'd from 'em, like Enchanted ground.
> One thought *Content* the Good to be enjoy'd:

This, every little *Accident* destroy'd:
The *wiser Madmen* did for *Vertue* toyl:
A Thorny, or at best a barren Soil:
In Pleasure some their glutton Souls would steep; ⎫
But found their Line too short, the Well too deep; ⎬
And leaky Vessels which no *Bliss* cou'd keep. ⎭

(12–35; K1 311–12)

Dryden does not simply view these benighted and groping pagan travellers from the confident vantage-point of one who knows. These men's lamp genuinely did shine 'brighter'. Epicurus's vision of a universe consisting of atoms colliding at random in a void was a vision of a *'Noble* work of Chance'. But the images of happiness vanishing before the philosophers like a conjurer's illusion, and of the men who, wishing to soak their bodies in the cooling depths of a well, find that they haven't enough cord to let themselves down to water level are almost comic. They serve to remind us that the world will inevitably seem cruel and frustrating to anyone, however distinguished (and the revered Aristotle is in this respect no more favoured than the reviled Epicurus), who seeks to explain its workings and ends merely by recourse to his own reasoning.

The passage ends with another telling image: the pagans' activities have resulted in a kind of crazy dance ('wilde Maze') resembling a planetary orbit with no sun at the centre, or the line drawn by a compass without a fixed foot:

Thus, *anxious Thoughts* in *endless Circles* roul,
Without a *Centre* where to fix the *Soul*:
In this wilde Maze their vain Endeavours end.
How can the *less* the *Greater* comprehend?
Or *finite Reason* reach *Infinity*?
For what cou'd *Fathom GOD* were *more* than *He*.

(36–41; K1 312)

In context, the rhetorical questions might seem to denote sympathetic fellow-feeling as much as admonitory exasperation. We are therefore not surprised when, later in the poem, we find Dryden siding charitably with those theologians who could not bring themselves to conceive of a God who would refuse a wise pagan like Socrates a place in heaven.[15]

Dryden makes frequent returns in both *Religio Laici* and *The Hind and the Panther* to Man's propensity to disrupt or frustrate his own happiness by wilfully placing excessive reliance on his own judgement or on his deluded self-image. The depiction of the Protestant sectaries near the end of *Religio Laici* allows us to view their activity not as a freak aberration peculiar to 'the enemy' but as a natural process which, once started, develops under its own momentum. In characteristically Drydenian fashion the chain of events is depicted in the form of a miniature drama-cum-narrative. We are shown how, first, the Catholic priests jealously guarded their monopoly on interpretation of the Scriptures. Then, after the Bible had been translated at the Reformation, each Protestant extremist took it upon himself to expound the Scriptures as he wished. The fragile vulnerability of the Bible to such coarse exponents is captured in the very way they handle the book:

> The tender Page with horney fists was gaul'd;
> And he was gifted most that loudest baul'd
>
> (404–5; K1 321)

The sectaries seem driven to their activity by a mysterious and irresistible physical urge:

> Plain *Truths* enough for needfull *use* they found;
> But men wou'd still be itching to *expound*
>
> (409–10; K1 321)

Their worship is rendered as a bizarre metamorphosis which grotesquely travesties the sacrament of Holy Communion:

> While Crouds unlearn'd, with rude Devotion warm,
> About the Sacred Viands buz and swarm,
> The *Fly-blown Text* creates a *crawling Brood*;
> And turns to *Maggots* what was meant for *Food*.
>
> (417–20; K1 321–2)

In our mind's eye the bustling Enthusiasts seem instantly transformed into a mass of crawling grubs. The 'warmth' (that is, 'Zeal') of their devotion is, at the same time, the warmth of a day when the flies are buzzing around a joint destined for the meal table. Our minds are directed towards the apparently inevitable process whereby Man generates the means to rob himself of his most precious possession:

> A *Thousand daily Sects rise up and dye*;
> A *Thousand more the perish'd Race supply*.
> So all we make of Heavens discover'd Will
> Is, not to have it, or to use it ill.

> The Danger's much the same; on several Shelves
> If *others* wreck *us*, or *we* wreck our *selves*.
>
> (421–6; K1 322)

Dryden employs the same technique – of charting a general human trait by means of a miniature narrative – in Part I of *The Hind and the Panther*, when writing of the evils of religious persecution. The passage moves from a specific historical situation (the persecution of the Huguenots in France) to a set of large reflections about the characteristics inherent in the nature of Man which cause persecution in the first place. Since the passage works as a single unit, it will be useful to follow it through, step by step.

Dryden begins with a specific reference to the Huguenot persecutions (couched within the terms of his beast-fable):

> From *Celtique* woods is chas'd the *wolfish* crew:
>
> (235; K2 476)

But he immediately checks himself and moves to a general reflection:

> But ah! some pity e'en to brutes is due:
> Their native walks, methinks, they might enjoy
> Curb'd of their native malice to destroy.
> Of all the tyrannies on humane kind
> The worst is that which persecutes the mind.
>
> (236–40; K2 476)

Persecution, Dryden continues, goes against the inherent nature of Man, against the very ingredients in humanity which differentiate Man from the animals and which reveal Man's divine origins:

> Let us but weigh at what offence we strike,
> 'Tis but because we cannot think alike.
> In punishing of this, we overthrow
> The laws of nations and of nature too.
> Beasts are the subjects of tyrannick sway,
> Where still the stronger on the weaker prey.
> Man onely of a softer mold is made;
> Not for his fellows ruine, but their aid.
> Created kind, beneficent and free,
> The noble image of the Deity.
>
> (241–50; K2 476)

These preliminary thoughts lead into a miniature replay of the biblical (or Miltonic) account of Creation. First the beasts are made by God in a single stroke of effortless ease (captured in the rapid run of the last line):

>One portion of informing fire was giv'n
>To Brutes, th' inferiour family of heav'n:
>The Smith divine, as with a careless beat,
>Struck out the mute creation at a heat:

(251–4; K2 476)

The creation of Man is an altogether more carefully pondered affair:

>But, when arriv'd at last to humane race,
>The god-head took a deep consid'ring space:
>And, to distinguish man from all the rest,
>Unlock'd the sacred treasures of his breast:
>And mercy mix'd with reason did impart;
>One to his head, the other to his heart:
>Reason to rule, but mercy to forgive:
>The first is law, the last prerogative.

(255–62; K2 476)

Dryden's first man, like Milton's, combines magisterial authority with a physical delicacy and vulnerability. His rule is that of the most clement and beneficent of monarchs, and rests on a mutual love of great beauty between lord and subjects. He is, in Dryden's account, quite literally full of the milk of human kindness:

>And like his mind his outward form appear'd;
>When issuing naked, to the wondring herd,
>He charm'd their eyes, and for they lov'd, they fear'd.
>Not arm'd with horns of arbitrary might,
>Or claws to seize their furry spoils in fight,
>Or with increase of feet t' o'ertake 'em in their flight.
>Of easie shape, and pliant ev'ry way;
>Confessing still the softness of his clay,
>And kind as kings upon their coronation day:
>With open hands, and with extended space
>Of arms, to satisfie a large embrace.
>Thus kneaded up with milk, the new made man
>His kingdom o'er his kindred world began:

(263–75; K2 476–7)

But then in just a few lines the picture is alarmingly reversed:

>Till knowledge misapply'd, misunderstood,
>And pride of Empire sour'd his balmy bloud.
>Then, first rebelling, his own stamp he coins;
>The murth'rer *Cain* was latent in his loins,
>And bloud began its first and loudest cry
>For diff'ring worship of the Deity.

108

> Thus persecution rose, and father space
> Produc'd the mighty hunter of his race.
>
> (276–83; K2 477)

The milk of human kindness has, in a disconcertingly physical image, mysteriously and suddenly curdled. Adam's begetting of his son is seen as an act of stubborn and proud defiance, transmitting genetically the wilfulness which will become the murderousness of Cain and consequently the intolerance and blood-lust of the whole human race. The momentary beauty of Man in God's original creation, has been almost immediately transformed into something more fearful. The effect is to make one wonder whether the 'cannot' in the earlier lines –

> Let us but weigh at what offence we strike,
> 'Tis but because we cannot think alike.
>
> (241–2; K2 476)

should not have been italicised, to bring home the fact that what is being referred to is more a harsh law to be bitterly lamented than a trivial blindness out of which Man could be easily reasoned. The overall effect is to remind us of Man's godlike potential and then, in rapid succession, to impress upon us how totally and irremediably fallen is the present state of humanity, the only state which we will ever know.

We may surmise that a significant part of Dryden's ability to write so tellingly in both *Religio Laici* and *The Hind and the Panther* of Man's pride, vanity and capacity for self-delusion must be attributed to the acuteness of his diagnosis of these propensities in himself. 'To find in our selves the Weaknesses and Imperfections of our wretched kind', he wrote in the Epistle Dedicatory to *Don Sebastian*, 'is surely the most reasonable step we can make towards the Compassion of our Fellow-Creatures' (C15 62). In Parts I and III of *The Hind and the Panther* there occur passages which have often been taken as confessions by Dryden of what he had come to think of as grievous personal sins.

The term 'confessions' must here be understood with tact. Both the passages referred to express with considerable passion and emphasis the need for humans to repent and reject certain vices. But the second passage is cast dramatically as part of a speech by the Hind. And there is no question in either case of an embarrassing *cri de cœur* from the poet disturbing the poem's overall decorum. Any personal pressure which lies behind the passages is firmly under artistic control.

But it is interesting that in both the 'confessional' passages in *The Hind and the Panther* Dryden puts a strong emphasis on the need to conquer the sin of pride. The first passage presents some striking images of the delusions which, Dryden says, had misled him from youth well into middle age:

> My thoughtless youth was wing'd with vain desires,
> My manhood, long misled by wandring fires,
> Follow'd false lights; and when their glimps was gone,
> My pride struck out new sparkles of her own.
> Such was I, such by nature still I am,
> Be thine the glory, and be mine the shame.
> Good life be now my task: my doubts are done.
>
> (I. 72–8; K2 472)

Long after the buoyant flights of (misplaced) youthful confidence, Dryden suggests, a man can remain deluded by the will-o'-the-wisps ('wandering fires') and (?) wreckers' beacons ('false lights') which circumstances seem to contrive to deceive him. But even when these have passed, the mind can (on its own anvil, as it were) 'strike out' equally delusive glimmerings of its own. And he knows that the attractions of self-generated delusions are never easy to shrug off: indeed, it is only by fixing the mind on something beyond or above the narrow perspective of an individual view that they can even be recognised for what they are.

The same emphasis on the need to conquer Pride is prominent in the passage in Part III on worldly fame (the Hind is speaking):

> If joyes hereafter must be purchas'd here
> With loss of all that mortals hold so dear,
> Then welcome infamy and publick shame,
> And, last, a long farwell to worldly fame.
> 'Tis said with ease, but oh, how hardly try'd
> By haughty souls to humane honour ty'd!
> O sharp convulsive pangs of agonizing pride!
> Down then thou rebell, never more to rise,
> And what thou didst, and do'st so dearly prize,
> That fame, that darling fame, make that thy sacrifice.
>
> (III. 281–90; K2 511)

The nature of the 'pride' and 'worldly fame' being referred to here is deliberately kept general. Yet the acute pain which the pursuit of such fame causes and the difficulty (or impossibility) of any human being able to extricate himself from that pursuit are tellingly captured in several phrases ('*sharp convulsive pangs*', '*agonizing* pride', '*darling* fame', 'to humane honour *ty'd*').

In the light of the other evidence it is difficult to resist the speculation that at least part of the impulse behind both these 'confessional' passages in *The Hind and the Panther* came from the reflections which Dryden had been entertaining about the course of his earlier career. There are perhaps more than accidental resemblances between the wording of the rejection of 'worldly fame' in the passage quoted above, the vehement repentance for his 'prostitution' of his Muse in his theatrical writings (voiced in the Killigrew Ode) and the thoughts uttered years before, in the *Aureng-Zebe* Dedication about 'the wretched affectation of Popularity'. This was the same piece in which Dryden had declared his weariness of writing for the stage and his hatred of certain kinds of Courtier:

A popular man is, in truth, no better than a Prostitute to common Fame, and to the People. He lies down to every one he meets for the hire of praise; and his Humility is onely a disguis'd Ambition.

(1676 text)

Sylvae

If *Religio Laici* and *The Hind and the Panther* contain many passages of substantial general interest, it must be admitted that both poems, and particularly the latter, remain for long stretches closely tied to the immediate circumstances in which they were written, and densely and specifically allusive to contemporary events, debates, and political and religious dilemmas.

In poetic terms, the most sustainedly free-standing and vivid manifestation of the period of rethinking and self-scrutiny in which Dryden had been engaged during the 1680s is to be found in the verse translations which he contributed to the second of Jacob Tonson's collections of Miscellany Poems, the remarkable little volume entitled *Sylvae*.

Sylvae appeared in 1685, the same year in which Dryden was received into the Catholic Church. The composition of the poems which he contributed to the volume had clearly excited Dryden: in his preface he speaks of the 'hot fits' of activity which had brought them into being – in contrast to the 'cold prose fits' in which he had at the same time composed his version of Maimbourg's *History of the League*. Having started in a desultory fashion to translate a few poems by Theocritus and Horace, he tells us, he was surprised to find 'something that was more pleasing in them, than my ordinary productions' (K1 390; W2 18). So he went on to do more.

The Preface to *Sylvae* reveals the spirit of delighted discovery with which Dryden surveyed his achievement on completing the volume. His comments on the authors he had been translating and on the art of translation have a freshness, directness and confidence which tends to make the elegance of much of his earlier criticism seem rather formal, and its interest rather academic. In the 1680 preface to *Ovid's Epistles*, for example, Dryden had made a famous tripartite division of translation into Metaphrase, 'or turning an Authour word by word, and Line by Line, from one Language into another', Paraphrase, 'where the Authour is kept in view by the Translator, so as never to be lost, but his words are not so strictly follow'd as his sense, and that too is admitted to be amplyfied, but not alter'd', and Imitation, 'where the Translator (if now he has not lost the Name) assumed the liberty not only to vary from the words and sence, but to forsake them both as he sees occasion: and taking only some general hints from the Original, to run division on the ground-work, as he pleases' (K1 182; W1 268). But by 1685 he has, in the light of practical experience, adopted a more flexible approach. Whereas in 1680 he had been doubtful about the translator's right to add anything which cannot be directly traced to the text of his original, and had specifically disapproved of those translators who were content to depart from both the words and sense of their original in order to write 'as . . . that Authour would have done, had he liv'd in our Age, and in our Country' (K1 184; W1 270), in the *Sylvae* preface he has moved closer to seeing translation as a kind of vigorous artistic collaboration across the ages. Wherever he has enlarged on the literal sense of his originals, Dryden says,

I desire the false Criticks wou'd not always think that those thoughts are wholly mine, but that either they are secretly in the Poet, or may be fairly deduc'd from him: or at least, if both these considerations should fail, that my own is of a piece with his, and that if he were living, and an *Englishman*, they are such, as he wou'd probably have written.

(K1 390–1; W2 19)

Dryden's new-found confidence is amply justified by the quality of the poems to which his remarks refer. The translations of episodes from each of the five books of Lucretius's *De Rerum Natura* and of certain Odes of Horace contained in *Sylvae* have had many distinguished admirers. Not surprisingly, since these poems speak with a directness, urgency and compelling rhythmic assurance, and have a generality and range of imaginative implication which Dryden had never managed so sustainedly in any of his previous publications.

It is one of the most extraordinary facts about Dryden's literary career that in the very same year that he was engaged in the last stages of the religious reflections which were to lead to his assumption of Catholicism he was also composing a series of poems which are unashamedly pagan in inspiration. These poems assert, with an imaginative vibrancy and conviction which it is impossible to believe was merely assumed on Dryden's part, the belief that, since the soul is mortal and man's life is beset by a host of delusions and vain desires, the ultimate wisdom is to 'live in the present'. Man should, the poems suggest, enjoy the present hour to the full, taking no thought for the morrow, since the future is unknowable and man is subject to inexorable forces and processes over which he can have no control.

It is also an extraordinary fact that, the year before Dryden expressed vehement repentance of the impious obscenities with which he felt he had defiled some of his earlier works, he had published, in two of his Lucretian translations, poems which treat the power of sexual love with an uninhibited frankness and freedom which he had never remotely matched before.

Lucretius: Against the Fear of Death

By general consensus, one of the finest of the *Sylvae* poems is that which Dryden entitled *Translation of the Latter Part of the Third Book of Lucretius: Against the Fear of Death*. In his preface Dryden had given an excellent description of the 'noble pride and positive assertion', the 'sublime and daring Genius', the 'fiery temper' and 'perpetual torrent of Verse' (K1 395; W2 25) which characterise the Latin poet's writing and which he had tried to emulate in his version. But he had proceeded immediately to disclaim any complicity with Lucretius's argument that, since the soul dies along with the body, it is absurd to fear the grave. Without the prospect of an afterlife of the kind offered by Christianity, Dryden had protested, there is nothing to prevent anyone from indulging in bestial excesses in this life, and nothing to reconcile one to the palpable injustices which abound in the world.

But no such inhibitions or reservations restrain the translation itself. In his version Dryden has achieved a passionate imaginative identity with the vehement mortalism on which Lucretius insists in his turbulently sweeping verse-paragraphs. The fallacy which clouds most men's thinking about death, the poem asserts, is that consciousness survives when the body dies. But, Lucretius insists, a human body is a knot intrinsicate of soul and body:

> we are only we
> While Souls and bodies in one frame agree.
>
> (17–18; K1 405)

When the body dies, so, inevitably, does the consciousness:

> So, when our mortal frame shall be disjoyn'd,
> The lifeless Lump, uncoupled from the mind,
> From sense of grief and pain we shall be free;
> We shall not feel, because we shall not *Be*.
>
> (9–12; K1 405)

To reinforce the point, we are shown the tumult of atomic activity which, in the Lucretian understanding of things, constitutes the ultimate reality in the world we inhabit. Even, the poet insists, if the atoms have combined at some time in the past to produce persons identical to us, we can have no memory of the fact, since the faculties of perception will, by definition, have perished along with the dissolution of the physical frame. Dryden's enjambment conveys a powerful sense of the hectic movement of the atoms across a void, and some striking phrases ('pause of Life', 'gaping space') capture the absoluteness of the chasm between life and nothingness:

> For backward if you look, on that long space
> Of Ages past, and view the changing face
> Of Matter, tost and variously combin'd
> In sundry shapes, 'tis easie for the mind
> From thence t' infer, that Seeds of things have been
> In the same order as they now are seen:
> Which yet our dark remembrance cannot trace,
> Because a pause of Life, a gaping space
> Has come betwixt, where memory lies dead,
> And all the wandring motions from the sence are fled.
>
> (31–40; K1 406)

Lucretius acknowledged a great debt to the Greek philosopher Epicurus. But it will already be apparent that the exhortation to live life in the present to be found in *Against the Fear of Death* is something far removed from the facile hedonism which is nowadays (as it was in Dryden's day) often popularly associated with the term 'epicurean'.[16] Indeed, certain verbal details in his version make it quite clear that Dryden saw in Lucretius's poem an indictment of those self-styled libertines of his own day who affected to live by the motto 'Eat, drink and be merry, for tomorrow we die'. Such revellers receive a stern blast of the poet's scorn:

> Yet thus the fools, that would be thought the Wits,
> Disturb their mirth with melancholy fits,
> When healths go round, and kindly brimmers flow,
> Till the fresh Garlands on their foreheads glow,
> They whine, and cry, let us make haste to live,
> Short are the joys that humane Life can give.
> Eternal Preachers, that corrupt the draught,
> And pall the God that never thinks, with thought;
> Ideots with all that thought, to whom the worst
> Of death, is want of drink, and endless thirst,
> Or any fond desire as vain as these.
>
> (97–107; K1 407)

The 'Wits'' merrymaking (and, in using the word, Dryden's mind is clearly on the Restoration libertines whom he had observed at close quarters) is shallow and anxiety-ridden. The 'kindly' brimmers and 'glowing' garlands bring them no joy because their hold on the life which they are professedly making such haste to live is so precarious. Their crime is not their revelling as such but their failure to have any real understanding of the human happiness at whose shrine they purport to worship. The criticism is reinforced and extended in Nature's great speech which stands at the centre of Dryden's translation.

Nature's tirade, like the poem as a whole, impresses us as much by its tone and spirit as by its paraphrasable argument. Her scornful contempt for the ingratitude of humans in complaining that they are about to die, is captured in the disdainful half-mimicry of human protest which forms part of her first insistent rhetorical question:

> What dost thou mean, ungrateful wretch, thou vain,
> Thou mortal thing, thus idly to complain,
> And sigh and sob, that thou shalt be no more?
>
> (123–5; K1 408)

Man complains that he is about to die, Nature continues, and yet he has derived no more benefit from the life which has been given him than a body which has excreted its food without having first derived from it any of the nutriment or pleasure which that food offers. Nature's images are precise and earthy. Life is envisaged as something which must properly be felt and relished in every fibre of the body:

For if thy life were pleasant heretofore,
If all the bounteous blessings I cou'd give
Thou hast enjoy'd, if thou hast known to live,

(where the emphasis on 'live' brings out what a paltry parody of 'living' it is that most men engage in)

And pleasure not leak'd thro' thee like a Seive,
Why dost thou not give thanks as at a plenteous feast
Cram'd to the throat with life, and rise and take thy rest?
But if my blessings thou hast thrown away,
If indigested joys pass'd thro' and wou'd not stay,
Why dost thou wish for more to squander still?

(126–34; K1 408)

Nature, she says, is not responsible if man fails to make use of her gifts. She makes her point in a triplet which, in the circular movement of its last line, seems to contain both a humorous admission of exasperated defeat and a miniature enactment of the cyclical process which it describes:

To please thee I have empti'd all my store,
I can invent, and can supply no more;
But run the round again, the round I ran before.

(138–40; K1 408)

The poet's scorn for the young 'Wits' is matched by Nature's contempt for the aged who will not resign life with equanimity when their appointed time has arrived, even though their capacity to enjoy life has long since passed. The old man's perverseness in being unwilling to die is seen as the final stage of a perverseness which has been his in different guises throughout life:

But if an old decrepit Sot lament;
What thou (She cryes) who hast outliv'd content!
Dost thou complain, who has enjoy'd my store?
But this is still th'effect of wishing more!
Unsatisfy'd with all that Nature brings;
Loathing the present, liking absent things;
From hence it comes thy vain desires at strife
Within themselves, have tantaliz'd thy Life,
And ghastly death appear'd before thy sight
E're thou hadst gorg'd thy Soul, and sences with delight.
Now leave those joys unsuiting to thy age,
To a fresh Comer, and resign the Stage.

(151–62; K1 409)

Why are these tirades not merely shrugged off by the reader as callous, and the poem as a whole (for all its energy) rejected as a remorseless and merely dispiriting jeremiad? Why is the effect, in fact, quite the opposite of depressing – one, rather, of exhilaration and release? Partly because Nature's criticisms do not merely depend on her say-so. There is an irresistible tang of truth to be found in many of the poem's direct portrayals of the Vanity of Human Wishes.

In this poem, for example, Sisiphus is not a figure to be found among the mythological inhabitants of Hades, but on the hustings and in the courts of this world. In his portrait of this figure, Dryden's verse evokes in its surging, restless rhythms, the heady elation which the demagogue feels and the mysterious inner necessity which prompts his activity. Here we have an unforgettable image of the kind of subversive politician whom he had earlier characterised in the 'Achitophel' portrait:

> The *Sisiphus* is he, whom noise and strife
> Seduce from all the soft retreats of life,
> To vex the Government, disturb the Laws;
> Drunk with the Fumes of popular applause,
> He courts the giddy Crowd to make him great,
> And sweats and toils in vain, to mount the sovreign Seat.
>
> (200–5; K1 410)

The self-defeating agony which accompanies such activity is equally memorably given in the laboured trudge of the lines which follow:

> For still to aim at pow'r, and still to fail,
> Ever to strive and never to prevail,
> What is it, but in reasons true account
> To heave the Stone against the rising Mount
>
> (206–9; K1 410)

And the nemesis which awaits this Sisiphus is captured in the vivid rush of the final fourteener:

> Which urg'd, and labour'd, and forc'd up with pain,
> Recoils and rowls impetuous down, and smoaks along the plain.
>
> (210–1; K1 410)

Later, when the poet is summing up his catalogue of the vain desires which torment men's lives, the whole of mankind is seen as suffering from a mysterious unrest which constantly stimulates it to action which can never satisfy or fulfil. It is no accident, therefore, that Dryden's thoughts here turned to the scene in Shakespeare's *Macbeth* where Banquo's ghost appears to remind the hero of the horrors he has committed to attain what he thought were his own most deeply cherished wishes:

> Thus every màn o're works his weary will,
> To shun himself , and to shake off his ill; }
> The shaking fit returns and hangs upon him still. }
> No prospect of repose, nor hope of ease;
> The Wretch is ignorant of his disease.
>
> (287–92; K1 412)

But it is clear that Dryden, like Lucretius, saw this poem not merely as chastising deluded humanity but as offering him consolation, and consolation, moreover, which could be effective this side of the grave. There are, Dryden wrote in the Preface to *Sylvae*, arguments in the poem 'which are strong enough to a reasonable Man, to make him less in love with Life, and consequently in less apprehensions of Death' (K1 396; W2 26). In the lines which immediately follow those quoted above, Dryden writes that, were 'The Wretch' to understand the disease from which he is suffering

> he wou'd know the World not worth his care:
> Then wou'd he search more deeply for the cause;
> And study Nature well, and Natures Laws
>
> (294–6; K1 412)

And in the fragment from the Second Book of Lucretius which precedes *Against the Fear of Death* in *Sylvae* and forms a preface to the longer poem, Dryden had imagined the pleasure of ascending

> To Vertues heights, with wisdom well supply'd,
> And all the *Magazins* of Learning fortifi'd;
> From thence to look below on humane kind,
> Bewilder'd in the Maze of Life, and blind:
> To see vain fools ambitiously contend
> For Wit and Pow'r; their lost endeavours bend
> T'outshine each other, waste their time and health,
> In search of honour, and pursuit of wealth.
>
> (8–15; K1 403)

The same fragment ends:

> For life is all in wandring errours led;
> And just as Children are surpriz'd with dread,
> And tremble in the dark, so riper years
> Ev'n in broad day light are possest with fears:
> And shake at shadows fanciful and vain,
> As those which in the breasts of Children reign.
> These bugbears of the mind, this inward Hell,

No rayes of outward sunshine can dispel;
But nature and right reason, must display
Their beames abroad, and bring the darksome soul to day.

(58–67; K1 404)

Read hastily, and out of context, these passages might suggest that the Lucretian consolation resides either in the advocacy of a quietistic retirement (where the wise man withdraws from life to regard his fellow humans with untouched detachment or *Schadenfreude*) or in the cultivation of a rational, logical, understanding of human weakness, terror, and delusion which will by itself make the human lot more tolerable.

Dryden himself seems to have interpreted the Lucretian consolation in something like the first of these two senses ten years before composing the *Sylvae translations*. *In the Dedication to Aureng-Zebe* he had, significantly, likened his own playwriting career to a Sisiphus-like torture. In the same piece, he had turned to Lucretius for thoughts about the nature of 'true greatness'. 'True greatness', Dryden had there remarked (drawing for support on the Lucretian description of the gods living undisturbed by danger and fear, oblivious of the striving and warrings of mankind), 'if it be any where on Earth, is in a private Virtue; remov'd from the notion of Pomp and Vanity, confin'd to a contemplation of it self, and centring on it self'. The Lucretian desire to 'look below on humane kind' from 'Vertues heights', however, did not much appeal to Dryden at this date, since 'The truth is, the consideration of so vain a Creature as man, is not worth our pains.'

By 1684 Dryden had come to see the Lucretian consolation as something more active and vital. For by then he had come to see Lucretius's exhortation to study nature and nature's laws not as an invitation to withdraw from life or to indulge in abstract speculation, but rather as a command to turn aside from an obsession with superficial preoccupations, anxieties and pleasures and to contemplate the magnitude and grandeur of the natural processes of which human life is merely a small part. And he had come to see that the serenity to be had from contemplating mankind 'with wisdom well supply'd / And all the *Magazins* of Learning fortifi'd' was not the kind of peace that comes from a cold detachment from man and his doings, but rather the tranquillity and content which derives from the ability to enjoy to the full the true goods of life, and to separate them from the desires which, for all their apparent attractiveness, imprison man in a hell of frustration and unfulfilment. Such a tranquillity can only be achieved, Lucretius suggests, by

119

seeing humanity from a sufficiently large and inclusive perspective. Behind this crucial extension of Dryden's interest in Lucretius can be seen the influence of a literary figure whose importance for Dryden's period of self-scrutiny and inner reflection in the 1680s was as great as that of any of the writers mentioned earlier in this chapter. For some years now Dryden had been reading and reflecting on the work of the great French essayist Michel de Montaigne. It is perhaps not surprising that Dryden had come to find much congenial matter in the work of a writer who had insisted so fully on the changeability and inconsistency of the human mind and on man's infinite capacity for self-delusion and unwarranted self-aggrandisement.

Dryden did not fail to notice that, in his essay *That to Philosophise is to Learn to Die*, Montaigne had quoted and commented extensively on the closing pages of Lucretius's Third Book to support his own arguments against the fear of death. In particular, Montaigne had insisted that to fancy that one can avoid death is to suffer from a monstrous delusion, to think egotistically that the Doom of Man can be reversed for an individual. He who fears death pathetically seeks exemption from the processes which govern all nature:

Your death is a part of the order of the universe, 'tis a part of the life of the world . . . 'Tis the condition of your creation; death is a part of you, and whilst you endeavour to evade it, you avoid your selves . . . Equality is the soul of equity. Who can complain of being comprehended in the same destiny wherein all things are involved?[17]

Montaigne's last question can perhaps be usefully seen as a master-idea behind Dryden's translation, the thought which above all justifies the scornful harangues and denunciations and which gives them a positive purpose and effect. For man's delusions are seen in the poem not merely as a folly but a kind of blasphemy against the nature of things. The study of nature's laws which Lucretius advocates is a study of the vast natural cycles in which any individual human life is only a small ingredient:

Is Nature to be blam'd if thus she chide?
No sure; for 'tis her business to provide,
Against this ever changing Frames decay,
New things to come, and old to pass away.
One Being worn, another Being makes;
Chang'd but not lost; for Nature gives and takes:
New Matter must be found for things to come,
And these must waste like those, and follow Natures doom.

All things, like thee, have time to rise and rot;
And from each others ruin are begot;
For life is not confin'd to him or thee;
'Tis giv'n to all for use; to none for Property.

(163–74; K1 409)

The stately march and gravity of the verse here, with its obvious biblical echoes, gives a sense of the grandeur and dignity of the inexorable processes being described. From this perspective, the poet suggests, each individual life is to be seen not as a piece of private property which its owner has the right to squander as he pleases but as a sacred trust which, during the short time in which it is given to man, must be properly *used*.

It is therefore perhaps not surprising that, despite all the scorn at the false ideals and aspirations of man, the poet is able at one point to show a warm appreciation of some of the true goods of life. Lucretius is scornful of those who lament that when they die, they will miss the domestic pleasures of wife, children and friends: to lament thus is vain, since when one is dead one's desire for such things (as well as one's pleasure in them) will be no more. It is the survivors whose lamentation has some point.

But in the course of his tirade, Lucretius gives a telling miniature evocation of the domestic pleasures in question:

But to be snatch'd from all thy houshold joys,
From thy Chast Wife, and thy dear prattling boys,
Whose little arms about thy Legs are cast
And climbing for a Kiss prevent their Mothers hast,
Inspiring secret pleasure thro' thy Breast,
All these shall be no more.

(76–81; K1 407)

Perhaps the most striking feature of these lines is the conspicuous unsentimentality of the details selected. The poet does not evoke a fireside idyll, but recalls the children's (from one point of view) tiresome pestering of their parents. Dryden's mind here perhaps turned again to *Macbeth*, this time to the tender rebuke which Lady Macduff offers her little son, just before they are both murdered: 'Poor prattler, how thou talk'st.' He also stresses the 'secret' pleasure which the father feels – his open expression of joy perhaps being prevented by surface annoyance, or suppressed in deference to his wife's attempts to get on with her work.

Horace: Odes III. 29

This is a touching and telling passage, but the main emphasis in *Against the Fear of Death* is, it must be admitted, on those forces which prevent man from laying a secure hold on the good things of life, rather than on those good things themselves. Elsewhere in *Sylvae*, in his translations from Horace, Dryden offered images of that very happiness which the conditions of life so often preclude.

Horace's Second Epode had long been one of the most celebrated classical treatments of the longing of urban man for peace of mind and human satisfactions in a humble rural environment. In his version, Dryden improved on Ben Jonson's and Abraham Cowley's fine renderings of the same poem by achieving an apparently effortless mellifluousness of verse-music and harmoniousness of compositional arrangement which mirrors the content of soul which is the poem's subject. In his translation of Horace's *Odes I.9*, he conveyed a vivid sense of the joyful release to be found in convivial mirth.

In the best of his Horatian renderings, Dryden tried to capture what it might be like to speak from the stance towards life commended by Lucretius's Nature. Dryden judged that in his translation of the twenty-ninth Ode of Horace's Third Book ('Paraphras'd in Pindarique Verse; and Inscrib'd to the Right Honourable Lawrence Earl of Rochester') he had captured the 'Briskness', 'Jollity' and 'good Humour' which are especially characteristic of this Roman poet even more satisfactorily than in his other Horatian versions.[18] The Ode is cast in the form of an invitation. Horace calls upon his patron Maecenas to leave for a while 'The smoke, and wealth, and noise of *Rome*' and to partake of the poet's hospitality in the country. As it proceeds, the poem develops into a celebration and demonstration of precisely what Horace means when, in stanza III, he exhorts his patron:

> Come, give thy Soul a loose, and taste the pleasures of the poor.
>
> (21; K1 435)

The Ode begins with a series of images which prepare us for the final affirmation – the heat of the day, the bustle of Rome, the nervous anxiety of Maecenas's busy public life. Dryden renders the last in terms which have obvious application to the city life of his own day:

> Thou, what befits the new Lord May'r,
> And what the City Faction dare,

> And what the *Gallique* Arms will do,
> And what the Quiver bearing Foe,
> Art anxiously inquisitive to know:
>
> (40–4; K1 435)

The poet then turns to the comforts offered by the realisation that the future is unknowable. In his rendering, Dryden has made a daring blend of the wise Christian God ordering things beneficently for his chosen creatures, and an epicurean deity utterly unconcerned with the human lot:

> But God has, wisely, hid from humane sight
> The dark decrees of future fate;
> And sown their seeds in depth of night;
> He laughs at all the giddy turns of State;
> When Mortals search too soon, and fear too late.
>
> (45–9; K1 435)

The next stanza shows the nature of the comfort offered by such a realisation. The poet reveals his full cognizance of the destructive power of Fortune. It is likened to a river in full spate destroying the habitations and terrain of a valley. But at the same time Dryden displays in the rapid *élan* of his verse that he is in a state of mind where he is able to contemplate with equanimity, even pleasure, natural phenomena which would ordinarily seem overwhelmingly awesome:

> Enjoy the present smiling hour;
> And put it out of Fortunes pow'r:
> The tide of bus'ness, like the running stream,
> Is sometimes high, and sometimes low,
> A quiet ebb, or a tempestuous flow,
> And alwayes in extream.
> Now with a noiseless gentle course
> It keeps within the middle Bed;
> Anon it lifts aloft the head,
> And bears down all before it, with impetuous force:
> And trunks of Trees come rowling down,
> Sheep and their Folds together drown:
> Both House and Homested into Seas are borne,
> And Rocks are from their old foundations torn,
> And woods made thin with winds, their scatter'd honours mourn.
>
> (50–64; K1 436)

The confidence to enjoy such destruction comes from an inner conviction, the knowledge that, unlike those rebuked by Lucretius's Nature, the poet has not let pleasure leak through him like a sieve. A similar emphasis is put on the word 'liv'd' as in the Lucretius version. The poet's defiant delight is conveyed in his vibrant rhythms:

> Happy the Man, and happy he alone,
> He, who can call to day his own:
> He, who secure within, can say
> To morrow do thy worst, for I have liv'd to day.
> Be fair, or foul, or rain, or shine,
> The joys I have possest, in spight of fate are mine.
> Not Heav'n it self upon the past has pow'r;
> But what has been, has been, and I have had my hour.

(65–72; K1 436)

When Dryden makes the well-established comparison between Fortune and a fickle woman, he enjoys the freedom to evoke her amorality with a lightness of touch which shows him to be more delighted than disgusted by her perverse waywardness:

> Fortune, that with malicious joy,
> Does Man her slave oppress,
> Proud of her Office to destroy,
> Is seldome pleas'd to bless.
> Still various and unconstant still;
> But with an inclination to be ill;
> Promotes, degrades, delights in strife,
> And makes a Lottery of life.
> I can enjoy her while she's kind;
> But when she dances in the wind,
> And shakes her wings, and will not stay,
> I puff the Prostitute away:
> The little or the much she gave, is quietly resign'd:
> Content with poverty, my Soul, I arm;
> And Vertue, tho' in rags, will keep me warm.

(73–87; K1 436–7)

The version of Horace's twenty-ninth Ode makes it particularly clear that to speak of the Horatian and Lucretian translations in *Sylvae* as offering 'philosophical consolation' is misleading if it suggests that the poems offer a series of wise precepts which the reader can be expected to put easily into practice in his subsequent daily life. It would be naive to assume that, after writing *Against the Fear of Death*, Dryden would have found it much easier in his ordinary dealings to put aside the worldly desires so tellingly anatomised by Lucretius, or that, after composing the version of Horace's twenty-ninth Ode, he could have lived his subsequent life in the state of exultant insouciance embodied in the poem – or that he would have expected his readers to be able to do so.

The release and wisdom which the study of Lucretius and Horace had given Dryden was one which found expression primarily *in the exercise of his art*, in the act of finding *those particular words and rhythms*. While writing the poems, we may deduce, Dryden must have momentarily achieved something of the freedom of spirit which the poems commend. The poems embody their own precepts. They thus allow the reader to feel something of the same liberation of spirit, and the resultant release of pleasure which we imagine must have possessed the author in the act of writing.

'The mind', wrote Dr Johnson in the Preface to his edition of Shakespeare, 'can only repose on the stability of truth.' Johnson's remark accounts more than anything else for one's feeling that in reading *Against the Fear of Death* one is being exposed not to a misanthropic tirade or a moral lesson, but to something deeply exhilarating and pleasurable. The 'repose', the deep satisfaction, offered by the poem (and, in its different way, by the version of Horace's twenty-ninth Ode) derives from our consciousness of being released from our ordinary anxieties and preoccupations by being confronted with a view of human life which we recognise is truer and larger than any we could manage in the ordinary heat of living. Thus, while we are reading a work of *literature* we recognise that we are, in important senses, more fully and truly alive than is usually possible in 'real life'. And that feeling is profoundly pleasurable.

Lucretius and Venus

Similar thoughts account for the success of another of the *Sylvae* poems, the episode from the Fourth Book of Lucretius entitled *Concerning the Nature of Love*. On one level, this episode can be seen as a series of warnings against the torments and delusions of sexual passion. Its depiction of love, and lovers' behaviour, can be seen as another instance of the Lucretian denunciation of the Vanity of Human Wishes. In the Preface to *Sylvae*, Dryden remarked wryly of the passage:

I am not yet so secure from that passion, but that I want my Authors Antidotes against it. He has given the truest and most Philosophical account both of the Disease and Remedy, which I ever found in any Author: For which reasons I Translated him.

(K1 396–7; W2 27)

But Dryden's translation of the episode shows that in one sense he needed no such 'Antidotes'. For the descriptions of sexual passion in

125

the poem are written in a manner that, though they may momentarily take our breath away by their fullness of detail and sharp explicitness, show their author to be entirely lacking in that embarrassment and coyness which comes from fear or insecurity. They are thus utterly unembarrassing to read. So intent is Dryden's focus on the facts of the case, so devoted a student of 'Nature's Laws' does he show himself to be, so thoroughgoing is his fascination with this force to which man and woman must, of necessity, submit, and which is capable of giving such pleasure and such pain, that the poem quite avoids two of the pitfalls into which it might so easily have fallen: on the one hand, a self-protective cynicism about sexuality, born of fear, disillusionment, or loathing, and, on the other, the desire to titillate or snigger.

As it is, the consolation and pleasure which the poem offers lie in its ability to allow us to concentrate, with unsalacious and un-prurient (but not humourless) attentiveness, on aspects of human lovemaking which are so often evaded by the diversionary tactics of euphemism, pornography or quasi-religiosity. Dryden's descriptions of sexual intercourse combine a surging rhythmic drive with a diction which is biologically precise, but which also incorporates strokes of distancing wit. The result is that we are allowed to view the hectic activity of lovers *in flagrante* in a way that is simultaneously engaged and detached. We are imaginatively participating in the scene to a degree that prevents any danger of our interest being merely voyeuristic. But at the same time we are allowed to stand back sufficiently to enable us to take a clear look at phenomena in which we are normally too closely involved to see so steadily:

> So Love with fantomes cheats our longing eyes,
> Which hourly seeing never satisfies;
> Our hands pull nothing from the parts they strain,
> But wander o're the lovely limbs in vain:
> Nor when the Youthful pair more clossely joyn,
> When hands in hands they lock, and thighs in thighs they twine;
> Just in the raging foam of full desire,
> When both press on, both murmur, both expire,
> They gripe, they squeeze, their humid tongues they dart,
> As each wou'd force their way to t'others heart:
> In vain; they only cruze about the coast,
> For bodies cannot pierce, nor be in bodies lost:
> As sure they strive to be, when both engage,
> In that tumultuous momentary rage,
> So 'tangled in the Nets of Love they lie,
> Till Man dissolves in that excess of joy.

Then, when the gather'd bag has burst its way,
And ebbing tydes the slacken'd nerves betray,
A pause ensues; and Nature nods a while,
Till with recruited rage new Spirits boil;
And then the same vain violence returns,
With flames renew'd th' erected furnace burns.
Agen they in each other wou'd be lost,
But still by adamantine bars are crost;
All wayes they try, successeless all they prove,
To cure the secret sore of lingring love.

(67–92; K1 415)

Of all the subjects which Dryden tackled, love is often thought to be the area where he had least success. Critics this century can be roughly divided into those who see his handling of the subject as jolly and robust but superficial, and those who condemn it more roundly as coarse, sniggering, salacious and even depraved. The objections are long-standing. Wordsworth, in one of his letters, referred to Dryden as having had no other notion of love except as 'absolute sensuality and appetite'. And in his *History of England*, Lord Macaulay remarked that 'What was innocent contracted a taint from passing through his mind. He made the grossest satires of Juvenal more gross, interpolated loose descriptions in the tales of Boccaccio, and polluted the sweet and limpid poetry of the Georgics with filth which would have moved the loathing of Virgil.'[19]

There is evidence in Dryden's work to support some of these strictures. As we have seen, and as he himself noted in the Killigrew Ode, he had in some of his earlier plays succumbed to the bad habits of his age. The 'fires', 'torments', 'pantings' and 'pains' of the lovers in the plays and songs are often little more than the last gasps of Petrarchan cliché. And the mixture of prurience and sentimentality in some of Dryden's earlier treatments of love and lovers reveals that love is not being taken seriously as a great *power*.

But the version from Lucretius's Fourth Book might suggest that Dr Johnson was not censuring Dryden in his famous remarks on his love poetry:

Dryden's was not one of the 'gentle bosoms': Love, as it subsists in itself, with no tendency but to the person loved and wishing only for correspondent kindness, such love as shuts out all other interest, the Love of the Golden Age, was too soft and subtle to put his faculties in motion. He hardly conceived it but in its turbulent effervescence with some other desires: when it was inflamed by rivalry or obstructed by difficulties; when it invigorated ambition or exasperated revenge.

(H1 458)

From *Concerning the Nature of Love* we might conclude that, so intense was Dryden's awareness, at his best, of the power of sexual passion, and of the universality of sexual love, and so fully did he respond in his imagination to both its torments and delights, that he could rarely summon up much interest in idyllic or romantic portrayals of lovers. He was all-too-conscious that, the facts of the case being as they are, such portrayals can easily lapse into cliché, sentimentality, or self-parodic solemnity.

But Dryden is also able to render with equal intensity and conviction Lucretius's passionate and delighted celebration of the creative fecundity of sexual love. In the invocation to Venus which opens the first Book of *De Rerum Natura*, the Roman goddess is seen as an embodiment and concentration of the procreative power whose influence pervades not only the human realm but also that of the animals. It is also felt in the great regenerative and cyclical processes of so-called 'inanimate' nature. In his rendering of this passage, Dryden achieves a hymn-like note which both conveys, in the large roll of its sentences and the urgency of its repeated phrases, the grandeur of the processes being described, and also (by putting the emphasis at key moments on sharp, active verbs) their vitality:

> Delight of Humane kind, and Gods above;
> Parent of *Rome*; Propitious Queen of Love;
> Whose vital pow'r, Air, Earth, and Sea supplies;
> And breeds what e'r is born beneath the rowling Skies:
> For every kind, by thy prolifique might,
> Springs, and beholds the Regions of the light:
> Thee, Goddess thee, the clouds and tempests fear,
> And at thy pleasing presence disappear:
> For thee the Land in fragrant Flow'rs is drest,
> For thee the Ocean smiles, and smooths her wavy breast; }
> And Heav'n it self with more serene, and purer light is blest. }
>
> (1–11; K1 401)

The hymn modulates into a wide survey of Venus's sphere of influence. Venus's power, the poet shows, is manifested in bright colour, sharp sensation, energetic muscular action. Again the emphasis falls, at the crucial points, on active verbs and participles ('teeming', 'bound', 'Strook', 'Stung', 'scatter'st'):

> For when the rising Spring adorns the Mead,
> And a new Scene of Nature stands display'd,
> When teeming Budds, and chearful greens appear,
> And Western gales unlock the lazy year,
> The joyous Birds thy welcome first express,

> Whose native Songs thy genial fire confess:
> Then salvage Beasts bound o're their slighted food,
> Strook with thy darts, and tempt the raging floud:
> All Nature is thy Gift; Earth, Air, and Sea:
> Of all that breaths, the various progeny,
> Stung with delight, is goaded on by thee.
> O're barren Mountains, o're the flow'ry Plain, ⎫
> The leavy Forest, and the liquid Main   ⎬
> Extends thy uncontroul'd and boundless reign. ⎭
> Through all the living Regions dost thou move,
> And scatter'st, where thou goest, the kindly seeds of Love.
>
> (12–27; K1 401–2)

Lucretius's invocation to Venus ends with a passage which, like Nature's speech in Book III of *De Rerum Natura*, was a favourite of Montaigne's. Venus is imagined as a bringer of peace, since, at those moments when her lover Mars falls prey to her charms, he has no spare energies for stirring up the warfare which agitates the world. In his essay *Upon Some Verses of Virgil* (which we know Dryden had been reading while composing the *Sylvae* poems) Montaigne paid eloquent tribute to the power and immediacy of Lucretius's description which, he says, 'does not so much please, as it fills and ravishes' the mind.

Dryden's version of the passage shows him revelling in the love-play of the two gods, his enjoyment resting in part on a humorous relish of the thought that, if, in succumbing to sexual passion, man *can* be submitting to a force which dooms him to agony and frustration, he can also (looked at from another point of view) be thought of as participating in one of the great creative and beneficent processes of nature, whose hallmarks are pleasure and delight:

> To thee, Mankind their soft repose must owe,
> For thou alone that blessing canst bestow;
> Because the brutal business of the War
> Is manag'd by thy dreadful Servant's care:
> Who oft retires from fighting fields, to prove
> The pleasing pains of thy eternal Love:
> And panting on thy breast, supinely lies,
> While with thy heavenly form he feeds his famish'd eyes:
> Sucks in with open lips, thy balmy breath,
> By turns restor'd to life, and plung'd in pleasing death.
> There while thy curling limbs about him move,
> Involv'd and fetter'd in the links of Love,
> When wishing all, he nothing can deny,
> Thy Charms in that auspicious moment try;

With winning eloquence our peace implore,
And quiet to the weary World restore.

(43–58; K1 402–3)

The warm humour with which the seduction of Mars is imagined is worlds away from the kind of prurient salaciousness which merely degrades its subject. Such a moment, coming where it does, has the power to make us feel momentarily that it is, indeed, love which makes the world go round.

Dryden's Christianity and paganism

What were the lasting effects on Dryden's life and career of the period of self-scrutiny and reflection which he went through during the early and mid 1680s? On the personal level, it led to a commitment to Roman Catholicism which was sustained till the poet's death. After the Revolution of 1688, Dryden tactfully but firmly resisted offers to receive him back into government favour.[20] One significant effect of his conversion was the decision of all three of his sons (two of whom were promising poets whose work had appeared beside their father's) to follow him into the Catholic Church and to make the journey to Rome.

But, poetically, I have suggested, the most sustainedly signficant product of Dryden's spiritual transformation was the burst of vivid creative energy evidenced in the best of the poems included in the miscellany *Sylvae* of 1685. To trace the connections between the (apparently quite different) Christian and pagan effects of Dryden's spiritual metamorphosis clearly requires some considerable tact. I shall end with a few tentative suggestions.

In the 1680s Dryden seems to have gone simultaneously through two spiritual metamorphoses, one in his capacity as man and the other in his capacity as poet. The two metamorphoses came into various states of complex interconnection with one another, but never achieved absolute identity.

Dryden the man sought as an Anglican and found as a Catholic that peace of mind and spiritual reassurance which comes from belonging to a Church with sound authority and established tradition. The precise nature of that peace of mind, and the struggles which Dryden felt he had put behind him when he achieved it, remain obscure. *The Hind and the Panther* has much to say on the doctrinal and political aspects of religion, but practically nothing about the more private, spiritual dimension. What we do learn of Dryden's spiritual struggles has to be inferred from the discreetest hints in the poetry itself, and from the general doctrinal positions which the poet eventually assumed as the result of his private meditations. It does however seem safe to suggest that the comfort which Dryden derived from his Catholicism was centred on a mystery, the ineffable and inscrutable mystery of a God whose mind and purpose mortal man can never fathom. And his Catholicism seems to have given him a heightened sense of the error of some of his own former actions, and the resolve to make 'good life' his object henceforth.

The burst of new poetic energy found in *Sylvae* seems also to have derived from something which we might call a new-found spiritual confidence. But the ultimate truths on which the spiritual confidence of Dryden the poet rested are much more clearly presented in his work than are those of Dryden the man. In both the Christian poems and the *Sylvae* translations, Dryden depicted the delusions, vanities, desires and egotisms which beguile and disturb man, in both his public and private rôles, and which cause him to subvert the state, the Church and his own peace of mind. In the classical translations these delusions are firmly and clearly attributed to a failure to apprehend the workings of those laws and processes of Nature which are observable by all and from which no man can be exempt.

To divide Dryden the man from Dryden the poet in this way is clearly to oversimplify. We are dealing here with the complex movements of a subtle and sophisticated mind, not with a bizarre case of schizophrenia. As well as the obvious differences, there are important points of resemblance (noted by Dryden and exploited in his translations) between the teaching of the Gospels and the vision of life's joys and evils presented in the poems of Lucretius and Horace.

But it remains true that Dryden's new-found contact with pagan antiquity was to prove far more fruitful for his subsequent work than his Catholic faith. For whereas he wrote only one short Catholic poem after *The Hind and the Panther*, the vast bulk of his work after 1687 (and almost all the best) was to be devoted to the results of his spiritual communings with a number of congenial master-spirits from pagan Greece and Rome.

In Tonson's fourth miscellany of 1694 there appeared a poem, 'On the Happyness of a Retir'd Life. By Mr. CHARLES DRYDEN. Sent to his Father from *ITALY*.' In the light of the evidence presented in this chapter, it is difficult not to see a special significance in the fact that Dryden's eldest son, a fellow Catholic (he was currently Chamberlain to Pope Innocent XII in Rome), and also a fellow poet, chose to address his father, now deprived of his public posts and working in retirement on his translation of Virgil, in a manner which seems deliberately to refer to the poems of consolation which, nine years before, John Dryden had contributed to *Sylvae*:

> As in a Shipwrack some poor Sailer tost,
> By the rude Ocean, on a Foreign Coast;
> Vows to the Gods, he never more for Gain
> Will tempt the Danger of the Faithless Main:
> But hugs himself upon the friendly Shoar,
> And loves to hear the raging Billows Roar,
> That spend their Malice, and can hurt no more.
> Just so the Wretch, who can no longer stand
> The Shocks of Fortune, and is wreck'd at Land;
> Lays down the Burthen of his Cares, to find
> A Solitary Place, and Quiet Mind:
> Chusing Content with Poverty to meet,
> Before a Fortune, infamously great.
> Thus, in respect of Gold and Silver, Poor,
> But Rich in Soul, and Virtues better Store:
> He Digs in Nature's Mines, and from her Soil
> He Reaps the noble Harvest of his Toil;
> His Thoughts mount upward to their Mother Sky,
> And, pur'd from Dross, exert th'Etherial Energy;
> The dusky prospect of his Life grows Clear,
> And Golden Scenes of Happiness appear.
>   Then from the Summet of Philosophy,
> Secure himself, Mankind he may descry,
> Industrious in the search of their own Misery.
> Like moiling Ants, in various paths they run,
> And strive in vain the Rubs of Life to shun.
> To different Ends their Actions they Address,
> Which meet, and center in Unhappiness.
> One Toils, and Struggles, in pursuit of Fame,
> And grasps, with greediness, an empty Name:
> Wing'd with Ambition, others soar so high,
> They fall, and cannot bear so thin a Sky:
> This Wretch, like *Croesus*, in the midst of Store
> Sits sadly Pyning, and believes he's Poor.
>   The Wise Man Laughs at all their Pains, secure
> From Lording Passions, which those Fools endure.
> Despair and Hope are banish'd from his Breast;
> Agues, and Feavers that allow no Rest:
> And Lust, and Pride, the Mother of Disdain,
> And Thirst of Honour, with her anxious Train,

No longer Warring, Peace of Soul deny,
But Exiles of the Mind their once lov'd Mansions fly.
Nor Love misplac'd, nor Malice now controul,
Right Reason's use, the Guardian of the Soul.
His Thoughts unbiass'd, and no longer tost,
Of Solid Judgment now securely Boast.
The fierce, unruly Race of Passions dye,
And the free'd Soul asserts her Liberty.

5

'Studying Nature's Laws':
the *Juvenal* and *Virgil*

Dryden in the 1690s

On the accession of the Protestant King William III in 1689, Dryden was deprived of his posts of Poet Laureate and Historiographer Royal, and the pensions which went with them, and was forced to support himself for the last twelve years of his life by his writing. He returned for a while to the theatre with two new tragedies, *Don Sebastian* (first performed, 1689) and *Cleomenes* (1692), a comedy, *Amphitryon* (1690), a tragi-comedy, *Love Triumphant* (1694), and an opera (with music by Henry Purcell) *King Arthur* (1691). But his writing in the 1690s was increasingly to take the form of verse-translation from the classics, the medium which he had so successfully employed in *Sylvae*.

The third Tonson Miscellany in 1693, *Examen Poeticum* ('A Swarm of Poems'), contained substantial translated extracts by Dryden from Ovid's *Metamorphoses* and Homer's *Iliad*. In the same year, Tonson published a complete composite translation of *The Satires of Decimus Junius Juvenalis . . . Together with The Satires of Aulus Persius Flaccus*. This collection was edited by Dryden, who personally contributed a lengthy introductory *Discourse Concerning the Original and Progress of Satire*, versions of Juvenal's First, Third, Sixth, Tenth and Sixteenth Satires, and the complete rendering of Persius.

In the mid 1690s most of Dryden's energies went into the preparation of the major English poetic project of the decade, a complete one-man translation of *The Works of Virgil* which was eventually published in a handsome folio volume in 1697. For this venture, Dryden and Tonson employed the method of subscription-publishing, whereby support for the book was guaranteed in advance by encouraging intending purchasers to lay out a deposit, the balance to be paid on the volume's appearance. One hundred and one choice subscribers – many of them members of the aristocracy – paid extra to have their names and coats of arms inscribed at the foot of the engraved plates which accompanied the text. The Dryden *Virgil* sold well, and Tonson's technique of subscription-publishing was to mark an important stage in the liberation of the writing profession from the constraints imposed by patronage.[1]

There are some signs that Dryden had felt resentment and bitterness at the change in his fortunes after 1688. In the Dedication to *Examen Poeticum*, he had grumbled about the habit of all governments to reward and protect 'Time servers and Blockheads' (K2 790; W2 157). In his poem addressed to William Congreve in 1694 he had remarked on the irony of the Laureateship now being in the hands of the Monarch of Non-sense himself, the loyal Whig Thomas Shadwell. In the Prologue to *Amphitryon*, he had likened his own position, as a poet no longer able to exercise his talent for political satire, to that of 'the lab'ring Bee, when his sharp Sting is gone', who 'Forgets his Golden Work, and turns a Drone' (1–2; K2 558). And in a transparently autobiographical insertion in *The Third Satyr of Juvenal*, he had described himself (in the person of Juvenal's Umbricius) as going into exile in the country

> conducted on my way by none:
> Like a dead Member from the Body rent;
> Maim'd and unuseful to the Government.
>
> (88–90; K2 682)

It is clear that one of the sources of Dryden's resentment at his fall from official favour was that it forced him to support himself once more by writing for the stage. When *Don Sebastian* was published in 1690, he used the occasion of that play's Preface to explain why:

Having been longer acquainted with the Stage, than any Poet now living, and having observ'd how difficult it was to please, that the humours of Comedy were almost spent, that Love and Honour (the mistaken Topicks of Tragedy) were quite worn out, that the Theaters cou'd not support their charges, that the Audience forsook them, that young men without Learning set up for Judges, and that they talk'd loudest, who understood the least: all these discouragements had not only wean'd me from the Stage, but had also given me a loathing of it. But enough of this: the difficulties continue; they increase, and I am still condemn'd to dig in those exhausted Mines.

(C15 65–6; W2 45)

Some of Dryden's plays of this period show notable advances over most of those from his earlier phase as a dramatist. Modern scholars have discovered a political interest in these plays (in the form of covert allusions to the régime of William III[2]), and have also praised them for their intrinsic artistic merits. *Don Sebastian*, in particular, has often been thought of as Dryden's best play, and it contains writing of undeniable passion and dignity, particularly in the famous reconciliation scene between the hero and his former enemy, the nobleman Dorax. But despite the play's strengths, much of the verse of *Don Sebastian* tends to seem disappointingly stiff and declamatory when set beside the supply flexible couplets of *Sylvae* and *The Hind and the Panther*. *Amphitryon* has also been enthusiastically praised by modern scholars, one writer going as far as to call it 'one of the greatest comedies in English'.[3] In it, Dryden tackled a subject, the comedy of divine sexuality, which he had handled with conspicuous success in the 'David' portrait in *Absalom and Achitophel*, and in the Lucretian and Virgilian translations of *Sylvae*, and to which he was to return in *Alexander's Feast*. In all those works, he was able to treat the immoral and irresponsible conduct of the gods and demi-gods as something both sublime and delightful. But readers moving from these poems to *Amphitryon* are likely to be conscious of the limitations which were imposed on Dryden's imagination when he was required to handle the same subject in the idiom of cuckoldry farce. For in the play, the divine characters have little of that more-than-human humanity which they take on in the poems, and the events of the story are often reduced to the all-too-human level of bedroom manoeuvring.

Despite the bitternesses, frustrations and disappointments of the post-Revolution years, the dominant note to be found in Dryden's writing in the 1690s is one of accomplishment, confidence and contentment. The confidence, it seems, came from the poet's conviction that his genius, when engaged by a worthy subject, was becoming steadily richer and more mature without losing anything of its former acuteness and penetration. In the Dedication to his translation of Virgil's *Georgics*, Dryden expressed the opinion that Virgil had written his poem 'in the full strength and vigour of his Age, when his Judgment was at the height, and before his Fancy was declining' (K2 913). Horace had declined in vigour and inspiration (if not in 'Judgment') in the works which he published in his old age. But in northern Europe, wrote the sixty-six-year-old English poet, circumstances favour a longer flowering:

[Man] seems at Forty to be fully in his Summer Tropick; somewhat before, and somewhat after, he finds in his Soul but small increases or decays. From Fifty to Threescore the Ballance generally holds even, in our colder Clymates: For he loses not much in Fancy; and Judgment, which is the effect of Observation, still increases: His succeeding years afford him little more than the stubble of his own Harvest: Yet if his Constitution be healthful, his Mind may still retain a decent vigour; and the Gleanings of that *Ephraim*, in Comparison with others, will surpass the Vintage of

Abiezer.[4] I have call'd this somewhere by a bold Metaphor, a green Old Age.

(K2 913–14)

Indications of Dryden's equanimity and contentment during this decade are provided by various passages in the prose. In the Dedication to *Don Sebastian* he remarked on the happiness of one, who

centring on himself, remains immovable, and smiles at the madness of the dance about him. He possesses the midst, which is the portion of safety and content: He will not be higher, because he needs it not; but by the prudence of that choice, he puts it out of Fortunes power to throw him down.

(C15 60)

Such a poise, Dryden insisted, should not come from any attempt (like that of the Stoics) to steel oneself into obliviousness of the painfulness and delusions of human life, but from an open-eyed acceptance of the conditions of life as they really are. In the Dedication to *Amphityron*, Dryden struck just such a note of equable *insouciance*:

I suffer no more, than I can easily undergo; and so long as I enjoy my Liberty, which is the Birth-right of an *English* Man, the rest shall never go near my Heart. The Merry Philosopher, is more to my Humour than the Melancholick; and I find no disposition in my self to Cry, while the mad World is daily supplying me with such Occasions of Laughter.

(C15 224)

Though 'naturally vindicative', Dryden wrote in the *Discourse Concerning . . . Satire*, he has not replied to any of the scurrilous attacks made against him, but has 'possess'd [his] Soul in quiet' (K2 646; W2 126). The few surviving letters of the last years give attractive glimpses of the poet, happily and busily preoccupied with his 'studies'.

Dryden's equanimity in the 1690s is closely connected with the fact that, in the best work of the decade, he was able to put into practice the principles which he both advocated and embodied in the best poems of the 1680s. For it is no accident (it will be the purpose of this chapter to suggest) that Dryden recalled a phrase from his own translation of Horace *Odes* III. 29 ('he puts it out of Fortunes power') in the passage, quoted above, from the *Don Sebastian* Dedication, in which he discussed the nature of philosophical contentment. Dryden's classical translations of the 1690s can be seen as a series of attempts to follow the advice of his own Lucretius, and to come to an imaginative accommodation with the sorrows and vicissitudes of the world, by devoting himself to 'study[ing] Nature well, and Natures Laws'.

Juvenal and the *Georgics*: philosophical poetry

In some of the remarks which he made after translating five of Juvenal's *Satires* and the *Georgics* of Virgil, Dryden displayed something of the fresh, personal engagement which had been so noticeable in his comments on Lucretius and Horace in the Preface to *Sylvae*. He had clearly found in both poets matter which spoke directly to his own passions and preoccupations.

After remarking, in the Dedication to his translation, that the *Georgics* are 'the best Poem of the best Poet', Dryden launched into a pointed attack (in some ways reminiscent of the *Aureng-Zebe* Dedication) on the malice and hypocrisy of courts. It is, however, he observed, a good thing to have experienced the evils of public life at first hand, if only because such an experience gives depth and substance to one's subsequent decision to withdraw from them into a better kind of life. 'A young Man', he noted, 'deserves no praise, who out of melancholy Zeal leaves the World before he has well try'd it, and runs headlong into Religion' (K2 916). The pleasures of a retired country life advocated and described in the *Georgics*, Dryden continued, are not a matter of passive withdrawal from the world, but rather of active contemplation, possession and enjoyment of the true goods of life, and an abandonment of all that might distract one from such a quest:

> *Virgil* seems to think that the Blessings of a Country Life are not compleat, without an improvement of Knowledge by Contemplation and Reading . . . 'Tis but half possession not to understand that happiness which we possess: A foundation of good Sense, and a cultivation of Learning, are requir'd to give a seasoning to Retirement, and make us taste the blessing . . . Such only can enjoy the Country, who are capable of thinking when they are there, and have left their Passions behind them in the Town.

> (K2 917)

The *Discourse* which Dryden prefixed to his *Juvenal* is a far more formal, full-dress, essay than the *Georgics* Dedication. For much of the piece, Dryden is concerned to take up debates about classical satire established long before his own day in the writings of such humanist commentators as Isaac Casaubon, Daniel Heinsius and Julius Caesar Scaliger.[5] What is the etymology of the word 'satire'? Where and how did the genre originate? What are its relations to Greek and Roman drama and epic? Are the satires of Horace or those of Juvenal the best representatives of the genre? How does satire perform the functions which are traditionally thought to be its particular concern: to instruct and to improve? What is the most appropriate style for satire?

In these parts of the *Discourse*, Dryden is, it might be felt, making elegant contributions to an academic debate rather than attempting to articulate his more intimate responses to the body of poetry which he has just been translating. And his contributions have, moreover, been found to be confusing and contradictory.[6] But at one point in the *Discourse*, Dryden begins to write about Juvenal in a way that gives us a more direct and vivid glimpse at the reasons which attracted him to the Roman poet. In this passage, Dryden sounds more like a passionate admirer of Juvenal than a cautious and formal Advocate for the Defence before a jury of continental pedants:

> *Juvenal* is of a more vigorous and Masculine Wit, he gives me as much Pleasure as I can bear: He fully satisfies my Expectation, he Treats his Subject home: His Spleen is rais'd, and he raises mine: I have the Pleasure of Concernment in all he says; He drives his Reader along with him; and when he is at the end of his way, I willingly stop with him: If he went another Stage, it wou'd be too far, it wou'd make a Journey of a Progress, and turn Delight into Fatigue. When he gives over, 'tis a sign the Subject is exhausted; and the Wit of Man can carry it no farther.
>
> (K2 649; W2 130)

To judge from this passage, what Dryden most enjoyed in Juvenal was not the improving morality and righteously indignant denunciatory passion for which the Roman satirist had been praised by such commentators as Scaliger, but rather Juvenal's mastery of a vigorously hyperbolic wit, which both takes the reader's breath away by its sheer energy and audacious brinkmanship, and involves him to the full in the vividness of its imaginings.

Such an impression is amply confirmed by the translations themselves. For there it is clear that Dryden conceived of Juvenal not as a Roman Jeremiah, or a bitterly frustrated soul crying out in anguish, but as a creator of witty personae, who revelled in the hyperbole, inconsistency, unfairness, opportunism and frequent scurrility of his portraits of Roman life, and who always stood in a sophisticated, rather than a simple-mindedly earnest, relation to his own tirades.[7] Juvenal, Dryden's translations suggest, was a poet whose celebrated 'indignation' and deployment of a stately epic register for the purposes of satirical denunciation can never be taken at face value.

And yet Dryden, it appears, did not think of Juvenal merely as an irresponsibly amoral opportunist, jeering at mankind from a position of facile cynicism. For the ending of his translation of *The Tenth*

Satyr shows that he saw Juvenal's witty and scurrilous railings against mankind (in which all human claims to dignity and self-respect and most of man's natural pieties are scoffed remorselessly into oblivion) as having been conducted not in a spirit of nihilistic disgust, misanthropy, or glib sarcasm, but in the interests of identifying the true goods of life. Dryden seems to have thought that to expose oneself to the lurid half-truths of Juvenalian satire was a valuable stage in that comprehensive exploration of nature's laws which leads to spiritual content.

It is only by some such argument, I believe, that one can account for the fact that, at the end of *The Tenth Satyr*, Dryden makes his English Juvenal sound remarkably like the Horace of *Odes* III. 29, in his defiantly daring assertion of the need to live in the present, neglecting the false attractions of worldly fame and the self-torturing desires which normally prevent man from truly living, accepting the buffets of fortune, and possessing the true goods of life, in full and confident recognition and relish of their present delight:

> Forgive the Gods the rest, and stand confin'd
> To Health of Body, and Content of Mind:
> A Soul, that can securely Death defie,
> And count it Nature's Priviledge to Dye;
> Serene and Manly, harden'd to sustain
> The load of Life, and Exercis'd in Pain;
> Guiltless of Hate, and Proof against Desire;
> That all things weighs, and nothing can admire:
> That dares prefer the Toils of *Hercules*
> To Dalliance, Banquets, and Ignoble ease.
>   The Path of Peace is Virtue: What I show,
> Thy Self may freely, on Thy Self bestow:
> Fortune was never Worshipp'd by the Wise;
> But, set aloft by Fools, Usurps the Skies.
>
>   (548–61; K2 734–5)

As well as revealing connections between Dryden's classical interests of the 1690s and those of the previous decade, this passage allows one to discern direct links between what might at first seem his two quite distinct interests in the *Satires* of Juvenal and Virgil's *Georgics*.

For Dryden's translation of the *Georgics* shows him to have believed that, in its descriptions of the work and life of the Italian countryside, Virgil's poem both discovered and celebrated the mysterious continuities running through the human and animal worlds and the world of what is usually called 'inanimate' nature, and sought to define the nature of true human contentment by its delighted contemplation of the principles and laws by which the whole system of life on earth is kept in motion. It is therefore perhaps not surprising that, in his rendering of the *Georgics*, Dryden was able to bring to perfection that poetry of fanciful animism which, as we saw in Chapter 2, had fascinated him since his very first years as a poet. It is his mastery of this particular mode which, above all, makes Dryden's *Georgics* at one and the same time a great philosophical poem and a great nature poem.

Nature's laws in *Virgil's Georgics*

Virgil's Georgics deals, in turn, with husbandry and the proper seasons for planting and harvesting (Book I), with vineculture and the planting of trees (Book II), with the rearing of animals (Book III), and with bee-keeping (Book IV). Midway through Book II, the poet pauses to describe the season of Spring, so propitious for the growing of young plants:

> The Spring adorns the Woods, renews the Leaves;
> The Womb of Earth the genial Seed receives.
> For then Almighty *Jove* descends, and pours
> Into his buxom Bride his fruitful Show'rs.
> And mixing his large Limbs with hers, he feeds
> Her Births with kindly Juice, and fosters teeming Seeds.
> Then joyous Birds frequent the lonely Grove,
> And Beasts, by Nature stung, renew their Love.
> Then Fields the Blades of bury'd Corn disclose, ⎫
> And while the balmy Western Spirit blows, ⎬
> Earth to the Breath her Bosom dares expose. ⎭
> With kindly Moisture then the Plants abound,
> The Grass securely springs above the Ground.
>
> (438–50; K2 948)

The renewal of nature in Spring is here imagined as an act of vigorous and delightful impregnation. The rain, moistening the rich earth and encouraging germination, is at the same time the generative juice poured by an amorous Jove into his joyously compliant wife the Earth, who is as 'buxom' as any newly married English girl following to the letter the demands of the pre-Reformation marriage service.[8] The vigour of the 'pouring' is emphasised by the way the positioning of the verb causes the voice to pause momentarily at the line-ending. The sexual act and the amorous twinings of the classical gods are thus linked in the reader's imagination with the grand and miraculously restorative processes of 'inanimate' nature. Human copulation (the poetic logic suggests – since these gods make love in a very human way) is a collaboration with one of the great beneficent processes of nature.

The beasts, prompted by the onset of the new season to procreate, are 'stung', goaded on by a sharply physical and irresistible force within their own beings. The fields in which the blades of corn are beginning to push their way through the earth are imagined as 'disclosing' a hitherto closely guarded secret. Earth, still imagined as a beautiful young woman, disrobes and reveals her naked beauty in the warm air, confident that she will not be chilled by winter blasts. The 'breath' of the Spring air is also the breath of life. The grass, still tender and soft, is imbued in the verse with confidence and elasticity. It *securely springs* above the Ground'. The whole description is coloured by a delightful comedy which has the effect of enhancing, rather than diminishing, the reader's sense of the miraculous plenitude of what is being evoked. The fanciful linking of the human, the divine and the inanimate are combined with a sensuous precision. The vigorous active verbs insist on the vitality of nature's rebirth. The opening line reminds us of nature's rôle as artist and restorer, adorner and renewer.

Both the comedy and the wonder are sustained in what follows:

> The tender Twig shoots upward to the Skies,
> And on the Faith of the new Sun relies.
> The swerving Vines on the tall Elms prevail,
> Unhurt by Southern Show'rs or Northern Hail.
> They spread their Gems the genial Warmth to share:
> And boldly trust their Buds in open Air.
> In this soft Season (Let me dare to sing,)
> The World was hatch'd by Heav'ns Imperial King: }
> In prime of all the Year, and Holydays of Spring.
> Then did the new Creation first appear;
> Nor other was the Tenour of the Year:
> When laughing Heav'n did the great Birth attend,
> And Eastern Winds their Wintry Breath suspend.
>
> (451–63; K2 948)

The young plants, momentarily imbued with human consciousness, are ardent and trusting. The vines exercise their power of persuasion, hugging the trunks of the elm trees. The warmth of the Spring sun is 'genial' – both 'kindly' and 'productive of growth'. The immense act of earth's creation is depicted (in a stroke of rich comedy) as the hatching of a chick from an egg. We are momentarily whisked up in our imaginations to a godlike height from which the vast cosmic miracle is assimilated to the miniature miracle of the new-born chick breaking its shell. Spring is a 'Holyday', a religious festival and, at the same time, a moment of relaxation and jollity. Heaven 'attends' the 'great Birth' of nature like a midwife, and laughs with amused sympathy when the child/chick/earth emerges.

The wit of the passage encourages a complex and many-faceted response to nature in the reader. We see the processes of the natural world in rapid succession (and sometimes simultaneously) from positions of amused distance and warm intimacy. And all the time the poetic fancy invites us to acknowledge the numerous resemblances and overlaps between human and non-human nature: the world, the poetry suggests, is moved by a single great spirit which rolls through all things, a spirit to be conceived of not in a mood of solemn reverence but one of delighted appreciation.

Similar thoughts arise in Book III of *Virgil's Georgics* when the poet describes a young horse:

> The Colt, that for a Stallion is design'd,
> By sure presages shows his Generous Kind,
> Of able Body, sound of Limb and Wind.
> Upright he walks, on Pasterns firm and straight;
> His motions easy; prancing in his Gate.
> The first to lead the way, to tempt the flood;
> To pass the Bridge unknown, nor fear the trembling wood.
> Dauntless at empty noises; lofty neck'd;
> Sharp headed, Barrel belly'd, broadly back'd . . .
> The fiery Courser, when he hears from far,
> The sprightly Trumpets, and the shouts of War,
> Pricks up his Ears; and trembling with delight,
> Shifts place, and paws; and hopes the promis'd Fight.
> On his right shoulder his thick Mane reclin'd,
> Ruffles at speed; and dances in the wind.
>
> (118–26; 130–5; K2 960–1)

By alighting on just the right details, the poet has conveyed with great economy the essence of the colt's nervous vitality and youthful pride. The young horse is high-stepping, in full control of its supple muscles. He is without surplus flesh. His hearing is keen, and picks up the brassily bright ('sprightly') but distant sound of the battle-trumpets. He is keyed up, and shows this in his sharp, nervous movements. He evidences the pride of life within him, flourishing his mane with delight. The flourish is not merely described, but conveyed directly in the runaway *élan* of the last line of the passage. The verse of this extract steps tautly and vigorously, and moves with something of the same combination of spring, dash, and emphatic precision as the animal which it portrays.

The descriptive language is partly the no-nonsense phrasing which might be appropriate on the lips of a professional horse-dealer ('Of able Body, sound Limb and Wind'), but the horse is also said to 'prance' (a word that can equally be used of the capering of young humans), and the animal's perception of the 'trembling' wood (the adjective conveying the forbidding mystery of a wind-tossed forest as it appears to an imaginative beholder) and his own 'trembles' of delight are reactions which he shares with more conscious beings. By such means, Dryden manages to encompass the powerful feelings of similarity and difference which are such a part of every human's observations of the non-human world. Dryden's imputing of human perceptions and emotions to the young horse is not sentimentalism, or a cutting of nature down to human size, but an acknowledgement (enacted in the rhythms of the verse itself) of the wonderful spirit of proud, joyful life which man shares with members of the animal world. The humour with which such descriptions are so often coloured is a means of incorporating a simultaneous recognition of the sense of unlikeness which we feel when observing the animals, a sense which must have its due if our wonder at the animal world is to avoid falling into sentimentality or self-parodically portentous solemnity.

It is in the area of love that the *Georgics* impresses on the reader most forcibly the interconnections between the human and animal worlds:

> Thus every Creature, and of every Kind,
> The secret Joys of sweet Coition find:
> Not only Man's Imperial Race; but they
> That wing the liquid Air, or swim the Sea,
> Or haunt the Desart, rush into the flame:
> For Love is Lord of all; and is in all the same.
>
> (*The Third Book of the Georgics*, 375–80; K2 967)

The helpless subservience to the power of love which man feels equally with the animals (the neutrally biological 'Coition' usefully covers the sexual activity of both realms)[9] might be thought to make the force of the phrase 'Man's Imperial Race' ironical, the effect being to deprive man of his claim to rule with dignity, since he is subject to base animal instincts. But the large majestic sweep of the passage's survey – from air, to sea, to desert (the reader's mind is invited to contemplate in one rapid kaleidoscopic movement the universal power of sexual feeling) – serves not to denigrate or debase human sexuality, but to aggrandise it by showing that, in submitting to his sexuality (with all the pains and pleasures it brings), man is obeying a general law which, like all general laws, must impress any beholder by its sheer grandeur and dignity.

But the poet's sense of universal sway exercised by love does not prevent him from touching his depiction of some of its effects with a pungent humour, which, as in the examples discussed above, often draws attention, simultaneously, to the differences and similarities between human and animal lovers. Here, for example, is a lioness, for whom the promptings of love even override the bonds of motherhood, and who pursues the promptings of her instincts with remorseless ferocity:

> 'Tis with this rage, the Mother Lion stung,
> Scours o're the Plain; regardless of her young:
> Demanding Rites of Love, she sternly stalks;
> And hunts her Lover in his lonely Walks.
>
> (381–4; K2 967)

The sense-organs of the young horse are given an extra acuteness by the power working within:

> The Stallion snuffs the well-known Scent afar;
> And snorts and trembles for the distant Mare:
> Nor Bitts nor Bridles, can his rage restrain;
> And rugged Rocks are interpos'd in vain.
>
> (391–4; K2 968)

The pains and joys of love are equally felt by less dignified members of the animal kingdom:

> The bristled Boar, who feels the pleasing wound,
> New grinds his arming Tusks, and digs the ground.
> The sleepy Leacher shuts his little Eyes;
> About his churning Chaps the frothy bubbles rise:
> He rubs his sides against a Tree; prepares
> And hardens both his Shoulders for the Wars.
>
> (397–402; K2 968)

The Petrarchan cliché 'pleasing wound' is here given a new lease of life by the vivid demonstration of the pain and agony which love costs both humans and animals. The most extreme example (brought home with sharp physical explicitness and the by now familiar Drydenian employment of vigorous active verbs) is found among the horses:

> But far above the rest, the furious Mare,
> Barr'd from the Male, is frantick with despair.
> For when her pouting Vent declares her pain,
> She tears the Harness, and she rends the Rein.
>
> (419–22; K2 968)

In his *Essay on Virgil's Georgics*, prefixed to Dryden's translation in the 1697 edition, Joseph Addison remarked that, in the sections of Book IV which describe the life of bees, Virgil 'Ennobles the Actions of so trivial a Creature, with Metaphors drawn from the most important Concerns of Mankind' (p. 101). But Dryden's translation of *The Fourth Book of the Georgics* shows that he was not convinced that Virgilian contemplation of these tiny creatures who 'share with Man one common Fate, / In Health and Sickness, and in Turns of State' (366–7; K2 989) was so straightforwardly committed to a sense of human superiority as Addison implies.[10] The location of human habits, personalities, laws and history in the miniature environment of the hive can, rather, serve to impress upon us the littleness of human affairs, allowing us to 'look below on human kind' with something of the philosophical detachment which Dryden's Lucretius had found so pleasurable. Yet at the same time the bees' behaviour, even their follies, are described with such unsentimentally affectionate precision that the overall effect is to cause us to think anew about both human and apian life, and to see a profound aptness in the poet's observation that

> some have taught
> That Bees have Portions of Etherial Thought:
> Endu'd with Particles of Heavenly Fires:
> For God the whole created Mass inspires;
> Thro' Heav'n, and Earth, and Oceans depth he throws
> His Influence round, and kindles as he goes.
>
> (321–6; K2 988)

Dryden imagines his Virgilian bees as engaging in activities remarkably like those which had produced such strife in the human affairs of his own century:

> if intestine Broils allarm the Hive,
> (For Two Pretenders oft for Empire strive)
> The Vulgar in divided Factions jar;
> And murm'ring Sounds proclaim the Civil War.
> Inflam'd with Ire, and trembling with Disdain,

Scarce can their Limbs, their mighty Souls contain.
With Shouts, the Cowards Courage they excite,
And martial Clangors call 'em out to fight:
With hoarse Allarms the hollow Camp rebounds,
That imitates the Trumpets angry Sounds:
Then to their common Standards they repair;
The nimble Horsemen scour the fields of Air.
In form of Battel drawn, they issue forth,
And ev'ry Knight is proud to prove his Worth.
Prest for their Country's Honour, and their King's,
On their sharp Beaks they whet their pointed Stings;
And exercise their Arms, and tremble with their Wings.

(92–108; K2 982)

The bees are at one and the same time fragile little insects with tiny sharp stings, gossamer-thin wings and minute legs, and companies of Roundheads and Cavaliers (or supporters of James and William) rallying to the standard. But the effect of the contemporary allusion (as so often in Dryden's later verse) is not that of a piece of topical satire having been surreptitiously and inappropriately smuggled into a version of a Latin poem. For Dryden is not concerned here to make specific political points, but to show, using examples from his own experience, the whole political and military activity of man in an interesting new light.[11] The bees' vigour and vitality is allowed its due in the description. But there is also something absurd about these little creatures with stings and probosci (albeit inspired by 'Ire' and 'Disdain', and possessing 'mighty Souls' which can hardly be sustained by their frail bodies) fighting for their king and his cause. And the treatment may prompt us to ponder whether it is any less absurd when humans do such things.

Dryden's apian monarchs have 'gorgeous Wings the Marks of Sov'raign Sway' (120; K2 983). The 'Regal Race' of bees are 'With ease distinguish'd' (137; K2 983). Their magnificence is genuinely impressive. The bee-king's 'Royal Body shines with specks of Gold' (140; K2 983). They are as striking in presence as any human *roi soleil*. And the contending apian monarchs fight with real heroism:

With mighty Souls in narrow Bodies prest,
They challenge, and encounter Breast to Breast;
So fix'd on Fame, unknowing how to fly,
And obstinately bent to win or dye.

(124–7; K2 983)

The rejected bees are as pathetic as any human (Stuart?) monarch and his supporters in defeat:

> That other looks like Nature in disgrace,
> Gaunt are his sides, and sullen is his face:
> And like their grizly Prince appears his gloomy Race:
> Grim, ghastly, rugged, like a thirsty train
> That long have travel'd through a desert plain,
> And spet from their dry Chaps the gather'd dust again.
>
> (143–8; K2 983)

Yet the mingling of human and apian attributes in these passages, as well as allowing genuine sympathy and admiration, simultaneously encourages in the reader a certain detachment from, even amusement at, the events portrayed. These 'narrow' bodies and 'Chaps' are, we remember, the minute mandibles and abdomens of insects, and there is something comically futile as well as touchingly grand about the fighting monarch's 'obstinacy'.

The bees' unquestioning loyalty to their king is, moreover, not regarded with the solemn approval which one might expect from a conservative, monarchist poet:

> The King presides, his Subjects Toil surveys;
> The servile Rout their careful *Caesar* praise:
> Him they extol, they worship him alone,
> They crowd his Levees, and support his Throne:
> They raise him on their shoulders with a Shout:
> And when their Sov'raigns Quarrel calls 'em out,
> His Foes to mortal Combat they defy,
> And think it honour at his feet to die.
>
> (314–20; K2 988)

In his recreation of Virgil's bees, Dryden had been able to do justice to his conservative impulses in encouraging our respect and affection for the little creatures whose task it is

> To fortify the Combs, to build the Wall,
> To prop the Ruin, lest the Fabrick fall.
>
> (262–3; K2 986)

Here, it might be felt, the fragile delicacy of apian engineering in wax serves to create a more potent symbol of the valuable but vulnerable structures in a society which need to be constantly maintained if that society is not to collapse into disorder and anarchy than had been present in the more famous lines from *Absalom and Achitophel* (see above, p. 80) on which they are based. But Dryden can also mock, in his depiction of the bees, the delusions of a society which places all its faith in the actions of its king and whose members are prepared to die unquestioningly in the royal cause. In *The Fourth*

Book of the Georgics Dryden has found a means of treating the painful concerns of his own life and times from a position which is both detached and sympathetic, both vividly involved and serenely and amusedly distanced. He has done this by contemplating the laws of nature whose operation is as potent among the smallest of insects as it is among members of the species which often considers itself the crown of God's creation.

Nature's laws in the *Juvenal*

If in *Virgil's Georgics*, Dryden was fascinated with the numerous and diverse overlaps, correspondences and connections between the human world and that of the animals, the insects and the plants, translating the *Satires* of Juvenal gave him the opportunity to explore the particular kinds of insights afforded into the delusions and absurdities of human affairs by the exercise of a hyperbolically extravagant wit.

In his sixteen *Satires*, published in the reigns of the emperors Trajan and Hadrian (c.100–127 A.D.), Juvenal had deployed his distinctive satirical imagination to create a Rome teeming with larger-than-life monsters of all kinds – sexual perverts, gluttons, legacy-hunters, haughty patrons, child-castrators, scholarly pedants, hack poets, unscrupulous immigrants, ambitious politicians. The satires translated by Dryden deal with the perils of life in Rome (Satire III), the vices and lusts of women (Satire VI), the Vanity of Human Wishes (Satire X) and the evils of standing armies (Satire XVI). Dryden also translated Juvenal's First Satire, which serves as an introduction to the whole collection, explaining what it was that, allegedly, prompted Juvenal to write (his famous 'indignation'), and why he chose satirical writing in preference to epic or mythological poetry.

Much of *The Tenth Satyr* consists of a series of portraits of figures – famous and obscure, ancient and near-contemporary – whose behaviour and fortunes illustrate the folly of all human aspirations and desires. Among these is Sejanus, a Roman politician whose career is succinctly summarised for the benefit of modern readers in one of Dryden's own *Explanatory Notes*:

Sejanus was *Tiberius*'s first Favourite; and while he continu'd so, had the highest Marks of Honour bestow'd on him; Statues and Triumphal Chariots were every where erected to him. But as soon as he fell into Disgrace with the Emperor, these were all immediately dismounted; and the Senate and Common People insulted over him as meanly, as they had fawn'd on him before.

(K2 735)

The rapidity and ignominy of Sejanus's fall is vividly captured in the description of the pulling-down of his statues:

> Down go the Titles; and the Statue Crown'd,
> Is by base Hands in the next River Drown'd.
> The Guiltless Horses, and the Chariot Wheel
> The same Effects of Vulgar Fury feel:
> The Smith prepares his Hammer for the Stroke.
> While the Lung'd Bellows hissing fire provoke;
> *Sejanus* almost first of *Roman* Names,
> The great *Sejanus* crackles in the Flames:
> Form'd in the Forge, the Pliant Brass is laid ⎫
> On Anvils; and of Head and Limbs are made, ⎬
> Pans, Cans and Pispots, a whole Kitchin Trade. ⎭

(87–97; K2 723)

The imaginative energy is in the details, the relish with which the smith meditates his hammer-blow, the almost human malice of the puffing bellows – and the emphasis falls, in the sustained run of the final triplet, on the contemptuous 'low term' 'Pispots'. The biblical lament 'How are the mighty fallen' is transformed so as to deprive the mighty of all traces of dignity. Insult is added to insult when the poet imagines the conversations among members of the mob who are observing the destruction. The lines precisely capture the smug tones of those who always back the winning side – after the event:

> Good Lord, they Cry, what Ethiop Lips he has,
> How foul a Snout, and what a hanging Face:
> By Heav'n I never cou'd endure his sight;
> But say, how came his Monstrous Crimes to Light?
> What is the Charge, and who the Evidence
> (The Saviour of the Nation and the Prince?)
> Nothing of this; but our old *Caesar* sent
> A Noisie Letter to his Parliament:
> Nay Sirs, if *Caesar* writ, I ask no more:
> He's Guilty; and the Question's out of Door.

(102–11; K2 723)

Yet, lest the reader imagine that Sejanus is a remote *exemplum*, safely insulated from his (the reader's) experience by barriers of time and station, the satirist makes the general conclusion of his portrait plain. Who, he asks, would be so foolish as to seek high office like

Sejanus, and have his 'Levees Crowded with resort, / Of a depending, gaping, servile Court' (146–7; K2 724)? The answer comes immediately: *all of us*, since the wish for high rank is at root the wish for life-and-death power over one's fellow men and women, and that is a wish more often entertained than acknowledged:

> I well believe, thou wou'd'st be Great as he;
> For every Man's a Fool to that Degree:
> All wish the dire Prerogative to kill;
> Ev'n they wou'd have the Pow'r, who want the Will:
>
> (156–9; K2 724)

And if one settles for a less spectacular form of eminence, that, too, comes in for a withering blast of the poet's scorn:

> Wou'dst thou not rather choose a small Renown,
> To be the May'r of some poor Paltry Town,
> Bigly to Look, and Barb'rously to speak;
> To pound false Weights, and scanty Measures break?
>
> (162–5; K2 724–5)

In *The Sixth Satyr* attention is turned on women. Dryden's headnote to his version of this poem is noticeably teasing and tricksy in tone. Such a work as Juvenal's Sixth Satire, he suggests, can't possibly be defended on the grounds that it contains an 'improving moral', since Juvenal's accusations are so self-evidently untrue ('amongst the Men, all the happy Lovers, by their own Experience, will disprove his Accusations', K2 694). The Sixth is, Dryden says, by general admission, the wittiest of Juvenal's satires, 'and truly he had need of all his parts, to maintain with so much violence, so unjust a Charge' (K2 694). Even if Roman women were, perhaps, as Juvenal describes, the same clearly can't be said of the English ladies! If this poem can't be justified by the conventional defences of satire, the case had better rest on Juvenal's wit. But then, a few sentences later, Dryden makes a remark that gives us a deeper glimpse into the nature of his interest in *The Sixth Satyr*. Juvenal, Dryden observes, 'makes [women's] Lust the most Heroick of their Vices: The rest are in a manner but digression' (K2 695). To see why the remark is illuminating, it is necessary to look in detail at the most heroically lustful of all Juvenal's women, Messalina, wife of the Emperor Claudius:

> The good old Sluggard but began to snore,
> When from his side up rose th'Imperial Whore:
> She who preferr'd the Pleasures of the Night
> To Pomps, that are but impotent delight,
> Strode from the Palace, with an eager pace,

To cope with a more Masculine Embrace:
Muffl'd she march'd, like *Juno* in a Clowd,
Of all her Train but one poor Wench allow'd,
One whom in Secret Service she cou'd trust;
The Rival and Companion of her Lust.
To the known Brothel-house she takes her way;
And for a nasty Room gives double pay;
That Room in which the rankest Harlot lay.
Prepar'd for fight, expectingly she lies,
With heaving Breasts, and with desiring Eyes:
Still as one drops, another takes his place,
And baffled still succeeds to like disgrace.
At length, when friendly darkness is expir'd,
And every Strumpet from her Cell retir'd,
She lags behind, and lingring at the Gate,
With a repining Sigh, submits to Fate:
All Filth without and all a Fire within,
Tir'd with the Toyl, unsated with the Sin.
Old *Caesar*'s Bed the modest Matron seeks;
The steam of Lamps still hanging on her Cheeks
In Ropy Smut; thus foul, and thus bedight,
She brings him back the Product of the Night.

(163–89; K2 700–1)

To dismiss, or defend, this passage as a piece of righteous misogynism is to overlook the freedom and gusto of its imaginings. From the start, the poet shows himself able to enjoy phenomena which might, in other handlings, seem merely pathetic, disgusting or frightening. The episode opens with a playful variation on a stock poetic gambit: the heroine's awakening. But where the *aubades* of romance or epic heroines occur in the morning, and are normally accompanied by the sunrise and birdsong, Messalina rises at night, accompanied by her husband's snores. Yet her rise is one which has its own kind of magnificence. Messalina is 'th'Imperial Whore', not only 'the Empress who acts the whore' but 'an Empress among whores'. We share something of her contempt for the impotent 'Pomps' which are all that her husband can offer her by way of 'delight' (the 'impotence' seems partly Claudius's as well as that of the Pomps). Muffled in her cloak, she takes on something of the mysterious majesty of the goddess to whom she is likened. We laugh at the lovers who, one after another, retire exhausted, awed ('baffled') at her resilience and ashamed of their own inability to satisfy her. There is a genuine sadness in the depiction of her wistful lingering for more:

> She lags behind, and lingring at the Gate,
> With a repining Sigh, submits to Fate.

The final line does not quite exclude the thought that, in returning to her husband's bed bearing the marks of her night's activities, she is not entirely unlike a huntsman bringing his beloved, or his king, the trophies of the chase. Her deeds are certainly not described in morally neutral terms: her feelings are 'Lust', the brothel-room is 'nasty', and her deeds are 'sin'. But moral disapproval is not the dominant note or *raison d'être* of the scene. The poet's treatment, with its distinctive blend of hyperbole, scurrilously vivid detail, comedy, sympathy and straightforward celebratory beauty, allows us to contemplate what might have seemed a particularly distasteful case of nymphomania with pleasure, the pleasure coming, in no small part, from our appreciation, and almost admiration, of an insatiable natural force which must have its way. If King Lear was driven mad by the thought that 'Downe from the waste they are Centaures, though Women all above', Dryden's version gives us grounds for thinking that Juvenal contemplated the same thought with wonder and even delight.

Content of mind in the *Juvenal* and *Georgics*

Not only do Dryden's *Juvenal* and *Georgics* display, in their very different ways, the equanimity and delight which comes from contemplating some of the laws whose operation is observable in the world of human and non-human nature. They also contain direct reflections on the character of philosophical contentment and serenity.

The note of defiant self-possession which, as we have seen, Dryden struck at the end of his version of *The Tenth Satyr* of Juvenal, is dependent in context on the conviction that one must enjoy the present, since the future is unfathomable, man's wishes and hopes are inevitably vain, and the gods' wishes are inscrutable. Thus, to set one's hopes on future gain or glory is to throw away the substance for the shadow. Sejanus, it was shown earlier in the poem,

> went astray,
> In ev'ry Wish, and knew not how to pray.
>   (166–7; K2 725)

Men's wishes and prayers, the poet suggests, are all too often an attempt to impose their wills where they can simply have no influence. The wise man, therefore, adopts a position of serene acceptance:

153

What then remains? Are we depriv'd of Will?
Must we not Wish, for fear of wishing Ill?
Receive my Counsel, and securely move;
Intrust thy Fortune to the Pow'rs above.
Leave them to manage for thee, and to grant
What their unerring Wisdom sees thee want:
In Goodness as in Greatness they excel;
Ah that we lov'd our selves but half so well!

(533–40; K2 734)

In the passage from the *Amphitryon* Dedication, quoted earlier, Dryden had remarked that 'The Merry Philosopher' was more 'to his Humour than the Melancholick' and had observed that he found no disposition in himself to cry 'while the mad World is daily supplying me with such Occasions of Laughter'. 'The Merry Philosopher' being alluded to is the Democritus of *The Tenth Satyr* of Juvenal:

In his own Age *Democritus* cou'd find
Sufficient cause to laugh at Humane kind:
Learn from so great a Wit; a Land of Bogs
With Ditches fenc'd, a Heav'n Fat with Fogs,
May form a Spirit fit to sway the State;
And make the Neighb'ring Monarchs fear their Fate.
He laughs at all the Vulgar Cares and Fears;
At their vain Triumphs, and their vainer Tears:
An equal Temper in his Mind he found,
When Fortune flatter'd him, and when she frown'd.
'Tis plain from hence that what our Vows request,
Are hurtful things, or Useless at the best.

(73–84; K2 722)

There are obvious connections between the Dryden of the 1690s finding in life and manifesting in his verse an 'equal Temper' when frowned upon by fortune, and Democritus's simultaneously heady and serene laughter at the follies of mankind – not a facile or inane laughter, but one based on a just appreciation of the laws which underlie the otherwise overwhelmingly disturbing and perplexing surface of life.

We saw earlier how, in *Virgil's Georgics*, Dryden was able to incorporate reflections on the painful events of his own times within a larger philosophical perspective on life. In the passage from the *Juvenal* quoted above, the reference to 'a Land of Bogs/With Ditches fenc'd' which 'May form a Spirit fit to sway the State; / And make the Neighb'ring Monarchs fear their Fate' has no direct counterpart in Juvenal's Latin. The momentous events of Dryden's

154

own century (the 'Land of Bogs' would seem equally appropriate for Cromwell's Huntingdonshire and William of Orange's Holland) are contemplated, in the context of Juvenalian translation, from a certain distance, and with a certain amused serenity. The allusion is, again, not a mere throwback to Dryden's earlier mode of topical comment, but, rather, an incorporation of his interest in contemporary events within the larger vision of human life suggested by his classical reading.

That Dryden sustained his amused Democritean view of the events of his own times to the end of his life can be seen from the lightness of touch with which, in his last work *The Secular Masque*, he was able to look back, through the fictional personae of various classical gods, on the century through which he had lived:

> *Momus.* All, all, of a piece throughout;
> Pointing ⎱
> to *Diana.* ⎰ Thy Chase had a Beast in View;
> to *Mars.* Thy Wars brought nothing about;
> to *Venus.* Thy Lovers were all untrue.
> *Janus.* 'Tis well an Old Age is out,
> *Chro* [*nos*]. And time to begin a New.
>
> (86–91; K4 1764–5)

'By the introduction', wrote Sir Walter Scott, 'of the Deities of the chace, of war, and of love, as governing the various changes of the seventeenth century, the poet alludes to the sylvan sports of James the First, the bloody wars of his son, and the licentious gallantry which reigned in the courts of Charles II. and James his successor.'[12] The lilting anapaestic ease with which the elderly poet is able to look back on the century which had caused him so much pain and bitterness indicates something of the depth of Dryden's equanimity and freedom of soul in his last years.

Like the *Juvenal*, *Virgil's Georgics* makes explicit connections between exposing oneself to the study of nature's laws and the cultivation of an inner content. In the closing sections of *The Second Book*, the poet expresses his desire to be a Lucretian investigator of the nature of things, to study the movements of the stars, the eclipses of the sun and moon, the motions of the tides, and the causes of earthquakes and the seasons (676–84; K2 954). But if such an enterprise is not possible, the next best thing, he says, would be to be allowed to enjoy and celebrate what Abraham Cowley (translating the same passage of Virgil) had called the 'substantial blessedness' of a country life. The two activities are, in any case, seen as closely related:

> Happy the Man, who, studying Nature's Laws,
> Thro' known Effects can trace the secret Cause.
> His Mind possessing, in a quiet state,
> Fearless of Fortune, and resign'd to Fate.
> And happy too is he, who decks the Bow'rs
> Of Sylvans, and adores the Rural Pow'rs:
> Whose Mind, unmov'd, the Bribes of Courts can see;
> Their glitt'ring Baits, and Purple Slavery.
> Nor hopes the People's Praise, nor fears their Frown, ⎫
> Nor, when contending Kindred tear the Crown, ⎬
> Will set up one, or pull another down. ⎭
> Without Concern he hears, but hears from far,
> Of Tumults and Descents, and distant War.
>
> (698–710; K2 955)

Dryden's rendering of this famous passage puts the main stress on the philosophical equanimity which results both from having one's 'free Soul, aspiring to the Height / Of Nature' (686–7) in Lucretian enquiry, and from being a 'Country King' who can enjoy his 'peaceful Realm' (660) without the strife, greed, ambition and servility to popular fame which (as Dryden knew all too well) mark the courts of ordinary monarchs. Countryman and philosopher-poet can look at the strife which rends nations 'when contending Kindred tear the Crown' with interest, but without anxiety. The countryman's relish of his surroundings, though, must be a *conscious* relish, unsentimentally grounded in the perceivable realities of country life:

> Thus ev'ry sev'ral Season is employ'd:
> Some spent in Toyl, and some in Ease enjoy'd.
> The yeaning Ewes prevent the springing Year;
> The laded Boughs their Fruits in Autumn bear.
> 'Tis then the Vine her liquid Harvest yields,
> Bak'd in the Sun-shine of ascending Fields.
> The Winter comes, and then the falling Mast,
> For greedy Swine, provides a full repast.
> Then Olives, ground in Mills, their fatness boast,
> And Winter Fruits are mellow'd by the Frost.
> His Cares are eas'd with Intervals of bliss,
> His little Children climbing for a Kiss,
> Welcome their Father's late return at Night;
> His faithful Bed is crown'd with chast delight.
> His Kine with swelling Udders ready stand,
> And, lowing for the Pail, invite the Milker's hand.
>
> (749–64; K2 956)

The countryman's life follows the pattern of the seasons with due times appointed for work and for relaxation. Each season affords its own plentiful supply of fruits. The succulent weight of the autumnal apples is suggested by the bending of the boughs which bear them (a touch which Keats was perhaps to remember when composing his *Ode to Autumn*).[13] The vigorous rooting of the swine, the oiliness of the olives, and the cows, lowing to have their distended udders relieved as much as to bestow their milk on the farmer, are all evoked with economy and affectionate precision. The countryman's life is not a mere idyll, but his anxieties are relieved and diverted by his appreciation of the blessed comforts of his home, the affection of his children (whose clambering is depicted with something of the unsentimental appreciation which had characterised the similar scene in *Lucretius: Against the Fear of Death*) and, above all, by the 'chaste delight' – the combination of frank sensual enjoyment and trusting fidelity – which marks his relationship with his wife. As in Milton's Eden, the pleasures of the marriage-bed form the 'crown' of the countryman's life. Beside such solid joys, the glamour and pretensions and ambitions of court are mere phantasms.

The challenge of the *Aeneid*

In undertaking to render the whole of Virgil's *Aeneid*, Dryden was taking on the most ambitious and daunting challenge of his translating career. ''Tis one thing', he wrote, 'to take pains on a Fragment, and Translate it perfectly; and another thing to have the weight of a whole Author on my shoulders' (K3 1051; W2 242). Hitherto it had been his practice to render only those passages from ancient authors which 'had most affected [him] in the reading' (K1 390; W2 19), episodes and poems in rendering which he was 'giving the original through himself, and finding himself through the original'.[14] Now he was for the first time committed to rendering a single author in his entirety.

In sharp contrast to the confident *Sylvae* Preface, Dryden's *Dedication to the Aeneis* is, for much of the time, a cautious and defensive document, in which its author keeps returning to the peculiar difficulties involved in producing a complete English *Aeneid*. In the *Postscript* to the translation, Dryden wrote, in a temporary mood of dejection, that he had composed his version 'in [his] Declining Years: struling with Wants, oppress'd with Sickness, curb'd in [his] Genius' (K3 1424; W2 258). He was evidently wearied by the enterprise, and felt that it had not been entirely successful.

There were, however, good reasons why the task should have fallen to him. Tonson saw the great commercial potential of a new English version of the greatest Latin poem, and a composite translation of Ovid's *Metamorphoses* being planned in the early 1690s was temporarily shelved so that Dryden could work full time on the more prestigious project.[15] The celebrated stylistic mastery and organisational coherence of the *Aeneid* would clearly necessitate the English translation being the work of a single hand, and that hand would, equally clearly, have to be that of the most distinguished living English poet, if the new *Aeneid* were to convey anything of the 'Propriety of Thought, Elegance of Words, and Harmony of Numbers' (K3 1045) which, everyone thought, so characterised Virgil's original.

But the difficulties facing Dryden were real. Not only was the *Aeneid* a work of vast length (nearly 10,000 lines), but it was also a peculiarly *Roman* poem. Its Romanness lay partly in Virgil's mastery of stylistic effects which were felt to be crucial ingredients of the poem's distinctive beauty, but which were dependent on particular features of the Latin language – such as the kinds of compression and patterning allowed by a heavily inflected language, and the 'sweetness' which is possible in languages which are not, like English, 'over-stock'd with Consonants' (K3 1046; W2 235). Equally 'Roman' was the *Aeneid*'s celebration of the key concept of *pietas* which is concentrated in the figure of its hero Aeneas. Aeneas's *pietas* (a word very inadequately translated by the English 'piety') is marked by a rigorously self-denying devotion to the will of the gods, in the service of the appointed destiny of the Roman people: to govern the world under the rule of law.

Partly as a consequence of its extreme Romanness, the *Aeneid* was, in Dryden's day, for all the high esteem in which it was held, a highly controversial work. This fact is reflected in Dryden's *Dedication*, where much of the space is taken up in rehearsing arguments put forward by contemporary critics (particularly the French translator, Jean Regnauld de Segrais) to defend the Roman poet against his detractors. In particular, Dryden is anxious to summarise the arguments designed to defend the character of Aeneas against the charges of spinelessness (he frequently weeps, and often seems to have little heart for his destined task) and falseness in love (in obedience to the gods, he deserts Dido, Queen of Carthage, who has befriended the shipwrecked Trojans and fallen in love with him), and the poet against accusations of anachronism (the events of the poem don't tally with known historical facts) and derivativeness (many features of the *Aeneid* are modelled on aspects of the Homeric epics). As in much of the *Discourse Concerning . . . Satire*, these sections of the *Aeneis* Dedication often seem like strategic (and sometimes not wholly ingenuous) contributions to contemporary academic and literary debates rather than reflections directly emerging from Dryden's engagement with Virgil's text. Like the *Discourse*, therefore, the *Aeneis* Dedication has to be used with caution if one is looking for clues as to Dryden's more intimate responses to his original.

Anchises's speech: a vision of human life

Though its sheer size and the peculiar problems involved in its execution make Dryden's *Aeneis* less consistently successful than the best of his shorter translations, it would be quite mistaken to take the words of the *Postscript* at face value, and to regard the poem as a task undertaken and effected in a spirit of dutiful dejection. For the *Aeneis* contains many passages which far transcend the level of competent craftsmanship, and whose qualities show that Dryden's deepest interests had been engaged by his original.

It is not surprising that, coming to translate the *Aeneid* via Lucretius and the *Georgics*, Dryden should have been particularly drawn to the body of philosophico-religious reflections which lie at the heart of Virgil's epic. In the speech which Anchises makes to his son Aeneas in Book VI of the *Aeneid*, it has been often felt that we are afforded a glimpse into the more intimate depths of Virgil's own religious feeling.[16] After the sack of Troy, Aeneas and his Trojan companions have wandered the Mediterranean in search of the new kingdom which has been promised them by the gods. Dispirited after many calamities, Aeneas is conducted by the Sibyl to the Underworld, where he meets the shade of his dead father, who offers him a vision of the future glories of the city which he is destined to found. This vision is prefaced by a description of the ways in which the souls of the dead are purged of their earthly dross before being returned to mortal life. Anchises begins by celebrating the great spirit which links the whole of nature together. His hymn to nature's grand continuum has clear affinities (both in the Latin original[17] and in Dryden's English) with two of the passages from the *Georgics* discussed earlier in this chapter: the description of Spring as an act of divine 'infusion' and 'mingling', and the godly 'inspiring' of 'the whole Created Mass' which accounts for the sparks of 'Etherial Thought' observable in the behaviour of the bees:

Know first, that Heav'n, and Earth's compacted Frame,
And flowing Waters, and the starry Flame,
And both the Radiant Lights, one Common Soul
Inspires, and feeds, and animates the whole.
This Active Mind infus'd through all the Space,
Unites and mingles with the mighty Mass.
Hence Men and Beasts the Breath of Life obtain;
And Birds of Air, and Monsters of the Main.
Th'Etherial Vigour is in all the same,
And every Soul is fill'd with equal Flame:

(980–9; K3 1226)

This exalted vision of nature's fundamental unity and divinity is accompanied by a gloomily acute awareness of the agonising fears and disturbing emotions which disrupt the tranquillity and equanimity of mortal man, and which prevent him from ever attaining, in this world, his godlike potential:

From this course Mixture of Terrestrial parts,
Desire, and Fear, by turns possess their Hearts:
And Grief, and Joy: Nor can the groveling Mind, ⎤
In the dark Dungeon of the Limbs confin'd, ⎬
Assert the Native Skies; or own its heav'nly Kind. ⎦

(993–7; K3 1226–7)

Even death cannot remove the 'long contracted Filth' (999; K3 1227) which mortal life has deposited on the soul, so the individual must endure 'Penances' (1002; K3 1227). Eventually, having taken 'large forgetful draughts to steep the Cares / Of their past Labours, and their Irksome Years' (1017–18; K3 1227), the purified souls are allowed to return to life, but their re-entry is seen as a renewed torture, a 'suffering' of 'mortal Flesh' (1020; K3 1227).

Dryden has, in the majestic march of his verse, responded warmly to Anchises's grand vision of an active universe, inspired by a single soul. He has also recreated with pungent emphasis Anchises's delineation of the pains and torments of mortal existence. That such a vision of life – infinitely painful for the individual sufferer, but governed by large processes of immense grandeur and dignity – was seen by Dryden as lying at the inspirational centre of Virgil's epic may go some way towards explaining what might otherwise seem puzzling or offputting features of his rendering of other parts of the *Aeneid*.

Suffering man: the death of Priam

Dryden's *Aeneis* has been criticised for its inadequacy in rendering the beautifully haunting pathos, the melancholy sympathy for suffering humanity which has often been thought to make Virgil's *Aeneid* unique among the world's epics.[18] Commentators have taken Dryden to task for what they see as a certain heartless matter-of-factness in his treatment of the painful events in the narrative. And, taking their cue from remarks in the *Dedication*, they have suggested that Dryden had a more simple-minded admiration for the hero of the *Aeneid* than Virgil himself.[19] Virgil, it is said, had a more ambiguous and ambivalent attitude to Roman *pietas* and *imperium* than Dryden was prepared to allow himself in his rendering.

Several points can be made in Dryden's defence. First, it is becoming apparent that the conception of Virgil as a poet 'majestic in [his] sadness / at the doubtful doom of human kind'[20] has sometimes itself been seriously over-played, at times even resting on straightforward misreadings of the Latin text.[21] Second, Dryden's remarks on the perfection of Aeneas in the *Dedication* cannot be taken as an adequate guide to his conception of the hero as it emerges in the translation itself. For there Dryden has not obscured Aeneas's moments of fury, melancholy and despair in the way that the *Dedication* might lead one to expect. Nor has he deprived the opponents of Roman destiny of the dignity and stature which they have in the original.

Third, Dryden's warm response to Anchises's speech might suggest that he regarded Virgil's whole conception of his theme and characters in the *Aeneid* as being informed by an altogether larger and more inclusive vision of the processes which govern human life than would be easily compatible with inviting the reader to weep in simple empathy for the sufferings of his fellow men and women.

This can be seen in his handling of one of the most 'pathetic' incidents in the whole poem, the death of Priam, King of Troy in Book II. Priam meets his end at the hands of Pyrrhus, son of Achilles, who first commits the unpardonably barbaric crime of slaughtering the aged king's son, Polites, before his very eyes. The scene is thus one of the most extreme violence and suffering. However, the description of the aged Priam arming for battle amidst the destruction of his city is not one which is merely concerned to emphasise the pathos of the old man's plight. We are also allowed to contemplate the unheroic futility of his action:

His feeble shoulders scarce the weight sustain: ⎤
Loaded, not arm'd, he creeps along, with pain; ⎬
Despairing of Success; ambitious to be slain! ⎦

(697–9; K3 1110)

Priam's queen, Hecuba, upbraids him with almost shrewish sharpness for the sheer madness ('Rage') of what he is attempting:

What Rage, she cry'd, has seiz'd my Husband's mind;
What Arms are these, and to what use design'd?

(710–11; K3 1110)

And when Priam eventually attacks Pyrrhus, the comic feebleness of his action (looked at from one point of view) is again impressed upon us:

his feeble hand a Javelin threw,
Which flutt'ring, seem'd to loiter as it flew:
Just, and but barely, to the Mark it held,
And faintly tinckl'd on the Brazen Shield.

(742–5; K3 111)

Yet these details, written from and encouraging a certain detachment from Priam, do not cause us merely to despise or sneer at the old man. Nor do they diminish our sense of the horrendousness of what is happening. Priam's slaughter is depicted as a hideous parody of a sacrificial killing (748–57; K3 1111), and at one point we are required to forget the feebleness and futility of the old king, when, having witnessed the death of his son, Priam is roused to a vehement instinctive passion, which is, the poet makes quite clear, nothing short of nature's own protest against Pyrrhus's barbarity:

The Fear of Death gave place to Nature's Law.
And shaking more with Anger, than with Age,
The Gods, said He, requite thy brutal Rage:
As sure they will, Barbarian, sure they must,
If there be Gods in Heav'n, and Gods be just:
Who tak'st in Wrongs an insolent delight;
With a Son's death t'infect a Father's sight.

(727–33; K3 1110)

But the same nature deals harshly with the grandeur that was Troy:

He, who the Scepter of all *Asia* sway'd,
Whom Monarchs like domestick Slaves obey'd.
On the bleak Shoar now lies th'abandon'd King,
A headless Carcass, and a nameless thing.

(760–3; K3 1111)

The situation is thus seen in a greater diversity of lights than would have been possible if the reader were empathising more completely with Priam. But the effect is to evince in the reader more, not less, respect for Priam's humanity. Rather than inviting us to weep and suffer with an individual fellow-human (an invitation which could so easily be an exhortation to *self*-pity), the poet requires us, as we observe Priam's plight, to contemplate the awesome and glorious laws whose inexorable operation affects all mankind.

Love and piety: Dido and Aeneas

Similar thoughts arise when considering Dryden's handling of the story of Dido in Book IV of his *Aeneis*. This episode is often thought to have been the most conspicuous failure of Dryden's whole translation. Dryden, it is said, has debased the love of Dido and Aeneas to the level of sordid lust, and has coarsened his portrayal of Dido herself with a degraded 'Restoration' knowingness and misogynism.[22]

Such criticisms, when they do not merely derive from received ideas about the Age of Dryden, seem to rest ultimately on the conviction that Book IV of the *Aeneid* presents a love for which, in the eyes of the poet, the world might have been well lost. Virgil, it is thought, had told the story of a man and woman equally torn between a noble and attractively presented love, and the demands of a duty which is presented as a harsh necessity, and in following which the hero does violation to his deeper human feelings.

But, a close inspection of the Latin reveals, this is not quite the story which Virgil did tell. Dido is indeed presented in the *Aeneid* as a woman of beauty, dignity, resource and generosity. But she is infected by the gods (for their own purposes, and quite without regard for her well-being) with a passion which she and the poet regularly refer to as a *furious madness*. Again and again in Virgil's text, Dido's love for Aeneas is described as a 'furor' ('madness'), a 'vulnus' ('wound') and a 'flamma' ('fire'), and Dido herself is described as 'furens' ('raving'). She roams like a stricken deer and rages like a Bacchante. Her love brings her agony and shame at having abandoned her 'pudor', the sense of shame which is bound up with the pledge of loyalty which she has sworn to the ghost of her former husband Sichaeus.

Virgil also shows Aeneas to obey without question or hesitation when Jupiter commands him to leave Dido. Only one line after receiving the divine command from Mercury he 'burns to be off' ('ardet abire'), his immediate worry being how he might break the news to Dido. Later he tells Dido that he had never promised to marry her or to stay at Carthage. Left to his own devices, he says, he would have returned to rebuild Troy on its old site, rather than following the gods' instructions to seek his destined kingdom in Italy.

The story of Dido and Aeneas, as Virgil tells it, cannot therefore be easily regarded as the heart-rending tale of a love-affair which, had it not been countermanded by the commands of the gods, might have resulted in fulfilment and happiness for both parties. Virgil tells of a woman consumed by a frenzied passion, which results in madness and self-destructive fury, and of a hero who, whatever his private feelings might be, is absolutely and unquestioningly resolute in his adherence to the demands of *pietas*. The situation is one which admits of no possibility of resolution or compromise. Virgil's story certainly does not prevent us from sympathising with Dido. But his handling requires us to see her behaviour in more lights than that of simple pathos. He does not balk the judgement that, in her love, and particularly in her final suicide, she has acted in a way detrimental to the precarious community which is so dependent upon her protection. And it is no accident that the vocabulary used to describe Dido's passion is often strikingly similar to that used by Lucretius of the frenzied lovers in *De Rerum Natura*, and by Virgil himself to depict the furious 'amor' of animals in Book III of the *Georgics*.[23]

In all these respects, Dryden's version is clear-sightedly faithful to its original. For though he was on occasion content, in the *Dedication to the Aeneis*, to adopt what appears to be a condescendingly flippant tone about Dido ('*Dido* was not only amorous, but a Widow', K3 1032), his translation fully endorses his judgement that, in Book IV, 'the whole passion of Love is more exactly describ'd than in any other Poet . . . he has given its beginning, its progress, its traverses, and its conclusion' (K3 1028).

Dryden's version of Book IV stresses the power and force of Dido's developing passion and the equally forceful resoluteness of Aeneas's pious resolve. The conflict between the two stands, for him, at the centre of the drama. We thus behold the events as awed spectators rather than weeping as empathising participants. Like Virgil, Dryden seees Dido's love as a 'Flame' (2,3,5), a 'Fire' (91), a 'venom' (131), a 'wound' (434), a 'rage' (724) which makes her 'furious' (824, 921) and undermines her sense of 'Shame' (132, 250, 324). His own vocabulary is close to that which he employed in his version from Lucretius's Fourth Book and *The Third Book of the Georgics* to describe the inexorable force of love in the human and animal worlds.²⁴ It is the conviction with which Dryden conveys the power of Dido's passion which ensures that she seems far removed from the 'amorous Widow' referred to in the *Dedication*. The Dido of Dryden's Book IV is a *formidable* force:

> Go seek thy promis'd Kingdom through the Main:
> Yet if the Heav'ns will hear my Pious Vow,
> The faithless Waves, nor half so false as thou,
> Or secret Sands, shall Sepulchers afford
> To thy proud Vessels, and their perjur'd Lord.
> Then shalt thou call on injur'd *Dido*'s Name;
> *Dido* shall come, in a black Sulph'ry flame;
> When death has once dissolv'd her Mortal frame.
> Shall smile to see the Traitor vainly weep,
> Her angry Ghost arising from the Deep,
> Shall haunt thee waking, and disturb thy Sleep.
> At least my Shade thy Punishment shall know;
> And Fame shall spread the pleasing News below.
>
> (549–61; K3 1159)

Heroines are not thus presented by poets blinded by masculine complacency.

But if Dryden portrays Dido as a figure of intensity and passion, he also makes it clear that her values are not the only ones in the poem with a claim on our attention. From Jove's point of view, Dido and Aeneas, each neglecting their respective duties to their people, are a

> lustful Pair, in lawless pleasure drown'd
> Lost in their Loves, insensible of Shame;
> And both forgetful of their better Fame.
>
> (323–5; K3 1153)

These lines, substantially Dryden's addition, are not prompted by gratuitous coarseness or callousness. They bring home sharply what it is difficult to deny are clear indications in Virgil's text: that (as both Dido and Aeneas come to admit) their relationship *is* incompatible with both their duties; that they have *not* been legitimately married (despite Dido's claims and the presence of Juno in the cave); and that in Jupiter's eyes their relationship *is* 'lawless pleasure'.

It is to Jupiter's law that Aeneas steels himself to be resolutely obedient. His resoluteness is given the monumental impressiveness of a mighty oak tree, majestically weathering the blast of a great storm:

Unmov'd, the Royal Plant their Fury mocks;
Or shaken, clings more closely to the Rocks:
Far as he shoots his tow'ring Head on high,
So deep in Earth his fix'd Foundations lye.
No less a Storm the *Trojan* Heroe bears;
Thick Messages and loud Complaints he hears; }
And bandy'd Words, still beating on his Ears. }
Sighs, Groans and Tears, proclaim his inward Pains,
But the firm purpose of his Heart remains.

(638–52; K3 1161)

Dryden's rendering of Book IV of the *Aeneid* shows him to have thought that Virgil's purpose in that Book was not, at least in the first instance, to make us feel straightforward sympathy with or admiration for, either of the chief figures (though neither reaction is excluded), but to display something of the nature of violent passion and steadfast piety when both are embodied in two remarkable people. Virgil's episode, as Dryden read it, was not a story of two lovers each torn apart by the equal claims of love and duty, but one in which irreconcilable moral worlds meet in irreducible conflict. This is a purpose which would square well with Anchises's conception of human life as a perpetual strife and anguish which never allows its possessors rest, happiness, or tranquillity. The poet can contemplate the sad tale of Dido and Aeneas with such untroubled precision not because he is callous or indifferent but because he sees the progress of individual human lives from the more inclusive perspective of one who has contemplated the implications of nature's laws. Dryden's reading of Book IV, though it makes for a love story quite unlike those we are more accustomed to, gives the episode a coherence and point which it lacks in most other interpretations.

My account of Dryden's *Aeneis* has had, for reasons of space, to concentrate (and even then, all too sketchily) on a few central issues. Even the triumphs of Books II, IV and VI give little sense of the variety of the whole poem. Elsewhere, Dryden shows himself equally at home in moments of great sensuous beauty (see the description of Souls in Hades, Book VI, 953–63; K3 1225–6), in sexual comedy among the gods (see the Venus and Vulcan episode, Book VIII, 484–538; K3 1275–6), in poetry of imperial dignity (see the prophecy of Rome's future in Book VI, 1168–77; K3 1231),[25] in the exhibition of straightforward pathos (see Mezentius's lament in Book X, 1206–22; K3 1352), and in episodes of well-paced action-narrative (see, for example, Book XI, 684–702; K3 1372–3 and Book XII, 691–706; K3 1406). His central sympathy with the philosophical core of Virgil's epic, along with his mastery in rendering so many of the poem's subsidiary elements, make his *Aeneis* by far the most coherent and consistently readable version of Virgil's *Aeneid* ever made in English, and a fine English poem in its own right.

Comparing Dryden's *Aeneis* with the eighteenth-century version of Virgil's poem by Christopher Pitt, Dr Johnson was prompted to comment that, whereas 'Pitt's beauties are neglected in the languor of a cold and listless perusal', 'Dryden's faults are forgotten in the hurry of delight.' Whereas Pitt often causes one to pause and 'contemplate the excellence of a single couplet', Dryden, wrote Johnson, 'leads the reader forward by his general vigour and sprightliness' (H3 279). In the Preface to his own translation of *The Iliad of Homer*, Alexander Pope referred to Dryden's *Aeneis* as 'the most noble and spirited Translation I know in any Language'.[26]

6

'An improving writer to his last': the *Fables*

Translation and flux

Dryden's last collection of verse, the *Fables Ancient and Modern*, was published in early March 1700, two months before the poet's death at the age of sixty-eight. It consists for the most part of a series of tales or narrative episodes in verse translated from two classical poets, Homer and Ovid, and two medieval writers, the English poet Chaucer, and the Italian author of *novelle*, Giovanni Boccaccio.[1]

Though the *Fables* are nowadays sadly neglected by general readers, they were widely admired in the century-and-a-half after the poet's death, and were frequently cited as conclusive proof that Dryden's creative powers were increasing right to the end of his life.[2] Dryden's friend, William Congreve, declared that the older poet had been 'an improving Writer to his last; improving even in Fire and Imagination, as well as in Judgement'.[3] The young Alexander Pope judged that Dryden's 'fire, like the Sun's, shin'd clearest towards its setting'.[4] Keats, Byron and Tennyson were all admirers of the *Fables*. Wordsworth thought the Boccaccio versions the 'most poetical' of all Dryden's works,[5] and his friend the critic and journalist John Wilson spoke of the 'skilled ease, the flow as of original composition, the sustained spirit, and force, and fervour' of the poems, and observed that 'youthful fire and accomplished skill have the air of being met in these remarkable pieces'.[6] Wilson was not the only reader to feel that Dryden had miraculously combined in this last volume the vitality, exuberance, and unsentimental acuteness of youth, with the sober wisdom, sympathy, and geniality of mellow maturity.

'The "Fables" of Dryden', noted Scott, 'are the best examples of his talents as a narrative poet'.[7] One of the most immediately noticeable qualities of the volume (and one of the hardest to bring out in discursive commentary) is Dryden's sheer virtuosity as a story-teller. The best of the tales are shaped and 'paced' with an unerring deftness, so that the reader is guided surely and pleasurably – pausing where necessary to reflect or observe, and moving onwards rapidly where excessive detail would distract – to the story's culmination and resolution.

In the Preface to *Fables*, Dryden explains how the volume came to be written. Once begun, he suggests, the book almost grew of its own accord. He had started, he tells us, by compiling a little collection of stories about the Trojan War. The main item was a version of the First Book of Homer's *Iliad* which, if it proved a success, Dryden planned to extend into a rendering of the whole epic. But for the time being he decided to fill out his volume with versions of the sections of Ovid's *Metamorphoses* which retell those parts of the Trojan War story omitted by Homer. Once he had begun on Ovid, he says, he began to think of other parts of the *Metamorphoses* which he liked, and to make versions of them. Then, in thinking about Ovid, he had been reminded of Chaucer, whose poetry he thought resembled Ovid's in certain respects. So he resolved to translate some of the *Canterbury Tales* into modern English verse. These then reminded him in turn of some of the stories in Boccaccio's *Decameron*, so he decided to make verse translations of some of these Italian prose stories. Finally, to top the collection up to a good sized volume, he added some of his recent short 'original' poems.

It is clear from his account of the genesis of *Fables* that Dryden saw numerous connections, both in manner and matter, existing between the various tales and authors he included in the volume, and that, while certainly not being compiled according to any rigid scheme, the collection was nevertheless much more than a random assemblage of the old man's favourite snippets.

It is also clear that Dryden's mind was flowing backwards and forwards from the tales themselves to the reasons he had selected them for telling in the first place, and why he felt uniquely equipped to render these particular authors in English. One of the translations in *Fables* which called out from Dryden some of his finest verse of general philosophical reflection was the rendering of Ovid's episode in Book XV of the *Metamorphoses* in which the Greek thinker Pythagoras gives his account of the constant decay and rebirth of matter, and of the transmigration of souls from man to man and from man to animal. Out of Pythagoras's speech (which has clear affinities with the speech of Anchises discussed in the last chapter), Dryden has made a discourse of impressive dignity which celebrates the apparently infinite interconnectedness and interpenetration of different aspects of nature and the ways in which, though everything is constantly changing, nature can also be seen as a glorious whole in which nothing is ever entirely or permanently lost.

In the Preface to *Fables*, Dryden wrote of his own state of mind when composing the volume:

Thoughts . . . come crowding in so fast upon me, that my only Difficulty is to chuse or to reject; to run them into Verse, or to give them the other Harmony of Prose.

(K4 1446; W2 272)

Close similarities of phrasing between the speech in verse made by Ovid's Pythagoras and the prose of Dryden's Preface make it clear that in the very act of composing the *Fables* Dryden saw himself as participating in the same processes of flux and transformation which the Greek philosopher was describing. He has selected for translation writers of the past with whom he feels he has a 'Soul congenial' (K4 1457; W2 287) or who are 'according to [his] Genius' (K4 1448; W2 274). In rendering them for his own times and in his own idiom, he is giving them what amounts to nothing short of a *reincarnation* in the present. This is possible, he believes, because poetical perceptions, while they must find expression in one particular set of words in one particular language at one particular historical moment, can be transmitted, or to use his own term 'transfused' (K4 1458; W2 288) between kindred spirits across the barriers of time and language, and given new expression at a different historical moment. That this can be so depends on a belief that while the passing of time changes everything there is also, paradoxically, an essential continuity in the nature which is the poet's subject. Both halves of this crucial paradox are believed by Dryden with equal force. Here is how the thought is formulated in his rendering of the words of Ovid's Pythagoras:

All Things are alter'd, nothing is destroy'd,
The shifted Scene, for some new Show employ'd.
   Then to be born, is to begin to be
Some other Thing we were not formerly:
And what we call to Die, is not t'appear,
Or be the Thing that formerly we were.
Those very Elements which we partake,
Alive, when Dead some other Bodies make:
Translated grow, have Sense, or can Discourse,
But Death on deathless Substance has no force.

(388–97; K4 1727–8)

'Translation', the activity by which the volume we are reading has been composed, is a living example of the process of rebirth and passing-into-immortality which Pythagoras is celebrating. In the

Preface, Dryden comments on the reasons why Chaucer's portrayal of his Canterbury Pilgrims seems as essentially true in his own day as it had in Chaucer's fourteenth century. The continuities between Dryden's thoughts and those of the Ovidian Pythagoras will be immediately apparent:

> We have our Fore-fathers and Great Grand-dames all before us, as they were in *Chaucer*'s Days; their general Characters are still remaining in Mankind, and even in *England*, though they are call'd by other Names than those of *Moncks*, and *Fryars*, and *Chanons*, and *Lady Abbesses*, and *Nuns*: For Mankind is ever the same, and nothing lost out of Nature, though every thing is alter'd.
>
> (K4 1455; W2 284–5)

Dryden's conviction that he was engaged in a kind of communion with the essential spirit of his originals across the boundaries of time and space explains why the *Fables*, like the other translations, deserve their reputation as integral parts of Dryden's oeuvre rather than as mere renderings (however accomplished) of other men's poems. It is beyond the scope of this book to examine the precise ways in which Dryden reshaped each of his originals in his versions. Such an examination would reveal that his reshapings sometimes take the form of inserted passages which clearly reflect existing preoccupations of his own. But his touch is equally apparent in passages which keep very close to the original in substance, yet are unmistakably Drydenian in diction, tone and movement. In Dryden's communings with his originals, 'his' contributions and 'theirs' mingle and merge with infinite variety and subtlety. In particular, the poems and episodes selected for reworking in *Fables* afforded Dryden the opportunity to develop and extend what had always been one of his characteristic tendencies – to treat matters of serious human concern and philosophical gravity in a way which incorporates comedy, wit, and daring tonal transitions. Dryden's wit-in-seriousness serves, as before, not to evade or trivialise important matters, but to attain a more comprehensive, and thus more truthful, recognition of their implications.

The power of Venus

The imaginative world of the *Fables* is presided over by a series of powerful gods – figures who embody or concentrate the (often competing) forces or principles or laws which hold sway both within the breast and mind of man and in the outside world. The gods of

the *Fables* are extensions of the same divine personages of classical
antiquity which had made their appearance in earlier works of
Dryden. As before, they are given human passions and susceptibilities which make them seem close to humanity, but their power
is far larger than any man's, and their purpose and motives often
seem baffling and contradictory. They have the power to make life
seem wonderful, comic, ordered, random, frightening or blissful as
they please. They often make it seem several of these things at once.
They can invest life with grandeur and dignity, or divest it of all
apparent meaning, purpose or coherence. They can inspire man, or
confound him.

The greatest and most potent of the deities of the *Fables* is the love-
goddess Venus, and nowhere is her power more evident than in the
first story in the volume, Dryden's version of Chaucer's *Knight's
Tale*, *Palamon and Arcite*. This poem tells how Theseus, Duke of
Athens, having besieged the city of Thebes, finds two young
knights, Palamon and Arcite, half dead among the corpses on the
battlefield. He takes the two friends back to Athens where they are
imprisoned in a tower overlooking the palace garden. One May
morning, Emily, Theseus's young sister-in-law, goes out into the
garden and is seen from the tower by Palamon, who is immediately
smitten with an overwhelming passion for her. Arcite, going to
assist his friend in his distress, sees her too and also falls immediately
in love.

Dryden's handling of this opening section of the narrative enables
him both to convey the painful reality of the lovers' feelings, and,
simultaneously, to hold the reader at a certain distance from them,
so that the absurdity of their behaviour, as well as its potentially
tragic dimension, is recognised. Palamon's initial attraction to Emily
is expressed in a sharply physical reaction:

> Scarce had he seen, but seiz'd with sudden Smart,
> Stung to the Quick, he felt it at his Heart;
> Struck blind with overpowering Light he stood,
> Then started back amaz'd, and cry'd aloud.

(I. 233–6; K4 1474)

But later, when Arcite too is smitten, Dryden's exploitation of stock
love-vocabulary, plus an obtrusively matter-of-fact manner of
exposition, encourages the reader if not quite to smile, to raise an
eyebrow at such symmetrical unanimity in the two lovers:

> The fatal Dart a ready Passage found,
> And deep within his Heart infix'd the Wound:

> So that if *Palamon* were wounded sore,
> *Arcite* was hurt as much as he, or more.
>
> (I. 272–5; K4 1474–5)

A little later, when rivalry has caused a breach between the friends, their conduct is described in a way that borders on the tongue-in-cheek:

> Now Friends no more, nor walking Hand in Hand;
> But when they met, they made a surly Stand;
> And glar'd like angry Lions as they pass'd,
> And wish'd that ev'ry Look might be their last.
>
> (I. 354–7; K4 1477)

Arcite is subsequently freed from prison, through the agency of a friend. Palamon's ensuing grief is depicted with a degree of over-stylisation which seems deliberately designed to prevent the reader from straightforwardly sympathising with him, and to draw attention to the grotesque dimension of his behaviour:

> He swells with Wrath; he makes outrageous Moan:
> He frets, he fumes, he stares, he stamps the Ground;
> The hollow Tow'r with Clamours rings around:
> With briny Tears he bath'd his fetter'd Feet,
> And dropp'd all o'er with Agony of Sweat.
>
> (I. 445–9; K4 1479)

Yet the first half of *Palamon and Arcite* does not allow us merely to despise the two lovers as pathetic fools, reduced to childish idiocy by a passion whose genesis has been depicted in the most sketchy and schematic manner. For when Arcite is proclaiming that he has a right to love Emily, even though Palamon may have been the first to fall victim to her charms, his argument – that love is a mightier and more fundamental power than any of the ties or bonds by which men normally think human society is held together – is expressed with a vigour and powerful conviction which (even though we recognise that Arcite is an interested party) it is difficult simply to shrug off:

> know'st thou not, no Law is made for Love?
> Law is to Things which to free Choice relate;
> Love is not in our Choice, but in our Fate:
> Laws are but positive: Love's Pow'r we see
> Is Natures Sanction, and her first Decree.
> Each Day we break the Bond of Humane Laws
> For Love, and vindicate the Common Cause.
> Laws for Defence of Civil Rights are plac'd,
> Love throws the Fences down, and makes a general Waste:

173

> Maids, Widows, Wives, without distinction fall;
> The sweeping Deluge, Love, comes on, and covers all.
>
> (I. 326–36; K4 1476)

Apart from their intrinsic force, Arcite's words are given additional credibility by being later confirmed from the lips of Theseus. In Book II of the tale, Palamon escapes from prison and hides in a grove near Athens to which, by chance, Arcite (who has returned from exile imposed upon him after his release) has also come. The two meet and pledge to fight one another for Emily's love on the following day. They are in the midst of their combat when Theseus, who is out hunting, chances upon them. Enraged at their conduct, he at first resolves that they must die, but later relents and declares that they must return in a year's time to fight in the lists for Emily's hand.

Theseus's words to the young men on this occasion confirm the various impressions we have been forming of them during the tale so far. He is well aware of their folly:

> The Proverb holds, That to be wise and love,
> Is hardly granted to the Gods above.
> See how the Madmen bleed: Behold the Gains
> With which their Master, Love, rewards their Pains.
>
> (II. 364–7; K4 1492)

The object of their love, he points out, isn't even aware of their passion! Yet, at the same time, he does not underestimate the power which has reduced them to such folly:

> The Pow'r of Love,
> In Earth, and Seas, and Air, and Heav'n above,
> Rules, unresisted, with an awful Nod;
> By daily Miracles declar'd a God:
> He blinds the Wise, gives Eye-sight to the Blind;
> And moulds and stamps anew the Lover's Mind.
>
> (II. 350–5; K4 1492)

Theseus knows this not merely on a notional level, but because he has in the past felt the same power at work within him which is now humbling Palamon and Arcite:

> sure a gen'ral Doom on Man is past,
> And all are Fools and Lovers, first or last:
> This both by others and my self I know,
> For I have serv'd their Sovereign, long ago.

Oft have been caught within the winding Train
Of Female Snares, and felt the Lovers Pain, ⎱
And learn'd how far the God can Humane Hearts constrain. ⎰

(II. 378–84; K4 1493)

When the time appointed for Palamon and Arcite's combat arrives, we are given further opportunities of appreciating the devastating effects of Venus's power. Over one gate of the amphitheatre where the two young men are to meet is the goddess's temple. On its walls are carved portrayals of the destructive and disruptive depths of Venus's power which we have only glimpsed in the tale. Venus is shown in these pictures to be a goddess who can convert Man's life into nothing short of a Hell-on-Earth:

> In *Venus* Temple, on the Sides were seen
> The broken Slumbers of inamour'd Men:
> Pray'rs that ev'n spoke, and Pity seem'd to call,
> And issuing Sighs that smoak'd along the Wall.
> Complaints, and hot Desires, the Lover's Hell,
> And scalding Tears, that wore a Channel where they fell:
> And all around were Nuptial Bonds, the Ties ⎱
> Of Loves Assurance, and a Train of Lies,
> That, made in Lust, conclude in Perjuries . . . ⎰
> Expence, and After-thought, and idle Care,
> And Doubts of motley Hue, and dark Despair:
> Suspicions, and fantastical Surmise,
> And Jealousie suffus'd, with Jaundice in her Eyes . . .
> Here might be seen, that Beauty, Wealth, and Wit,
> And Prowess, to the Pow'r of Love submit:
> The spreading Snare for all Mankind is laid;
> And Lovers all betray, and are betray'd.

(II. 471–9, 484–7, 507–10; K4 1495–6)

Venus creatrix

But when Palamon prays to Venus to assist him in the ensuing fight, he ignores, or forgets, these darker manifestations of her power, and concentrates on the forces of fecund creation which also come within her jurisdiction. His prayer is imbued with that vivid consciousness of love as a force of vigorously delightful sexual renewal with which we are by now thoroughly familiar in Dryden's work. Venus is seen as the power who creates the active joy and smiling warmth of Spring:

> For thee the Winds their Eastern Blasts forbear,
> Thy Month reveals the Spring, and opens all the Year.

175

> Thee, Goddess, thee the Storms of Winter fly,
> Earth smiles with Flow'rs renewing; laughs the Sky,
> And Birds to Lays of Love their tuneful Notes apply.
>
> (III. 133–7; K4 1503–4)

She is also the goddess who can inspire the wild and sometimes comic abandon of the animal world:

> For thee the Lion loaths the Taste of Blood,
> And roaring hunts his Female through the Wood:
> For thee the Bulls rebellow through the Groves,
> And tempt the Stream, and snuff their absent Loves.
>
> (III. 138–41; K4 1504)

If Venus, in the carvings on her temple walls, can seem a goddess who is regularly the death of man, her power is now seen (as it was by Lucretius and Virgil) as the force which makes the world go round:

> 'Tis thine, whate'er is pleasant, good, or fair:
> All Nature is thy Province, Life thy Care;
> Thou mad'st the World, and dost the World repair.
>
> (III. 142–4; K4 1504)

This conception of Venus as a delightful renovative force is given vivid expression elsewhere in the *Fables*, in the opening passage of the pseudo-Chaucerian dream poem, *The Flower and the Leaf*. Here Dryden describes the warming and moistening activity of the goddess in the world of plants and flowers. His verse is full of daring metaphorical fusions which allow the mind to bring together with effortless delight the normally separate realms of human and plant life. Spring is the season

> When first the tender Blades of Grass appear,
> And Buds that yet the blast of *Eurus* fear,
> Stand at the door of Life; and doubt to cloath the Year.
>
> (7–9; K4 1650)

The timid hesitancy of the young plants is like that of a group of children waiting to pluck up courage before dancing in a hall full of adult spectators. The young plants/dancers find their confidence when

> gentle Heat, and soft repeated Rains,
> Make the green Blood to dance within their Veins.
>
> (10–11; K4 1650)

The sap rising in the young plants is like the life pulsing in the body of the young human who joys in his or her vitality. The

plants/dancers then appear in joyful procession, swelling with youth
and beauty's pride, and giving off in their dance the scents which are
the bounteous product of the wonderful life which throbs within
them:

> Then, at their Call, embolden'd out they come,
> And swell the Gems, and burst the narrow Room;
> Broader and broader yet, their Blooms display,
> Salute the welcome Sun, and entertain the Day.
> Then from their breathing Souls the Sweets repair
> To scent the Skies, and purge th'unwholsome Air:
> Joy spreads the Heart, and with a general Song,
> Spring issues out, and leads the jolly Months along.
>
> (12–19; K4 1650)

Love and natural law

The power of Venus, it is suggested in *Palamon and Arcite* and *The
Flower and the Leaf*, regularly transcends what Dryden calls 'humane
Law' – the bonds of friendship, loyalty, family, obligation and
order by which human societies are held together – either by over-
riding it, or by making it seem of secondary importance beside the
powerful natural ties which link humanity to the non-human world.

But to argue thus, another poem in the *Fables* suggests, is to
simplify the complex relations which can be seen to exist between
the 'humane' and the irrational 'natural' impulses at work within
the human heart. The story of *Cinyras and Myrrha*, translated from
Book X of Ovid's *Metamorphoses*, tells how Myrrha, daughter of
Cinyras, King of Cyprus, is consumed with an incestuous passion
for her father. Tormented by guilt, she resolves on suicide, but is
prevented at the last minute by her nurse, who eventually worms
out of her the secret of her misery. The nurse agrees to help her
desires, and arranges for Myrrha (disguised and under cover of
darkness) to visit her father's bed. Eventually he discovers the true
identity of his young mistress. She flees, and after wandering
distraught to the deserts of Arabia is granted release by being
metamorphosed into a myrrh tree, a form which preserves (in its
appearance and sweet balm) both the beauty, and (in the resinous
gum which appears to weep from its bark) the sorrow which had
been characteristic of the girl in life.

The mind of Myrrha can be seen as a battlefield for two conflic-
ting sets of impulses each of which seems to have a good claim to be
regarded as 'Natural'.[8] In her opening speech Dryden's heroine

reflects on the predicament in which she finds herself: why, she asks, should incest be a crime for humans when in the animal world it is so widespread? Her argument is in many ways similar to those offered by Montaigne, or, closer to our time, by Freud – that many of the laws and prohibitions which human societies view as absolutes and call natural law are merely the improper imputation of universal validity to the system of practices to which those societies are most accustomed. In submitting to her incestuous feelings, Myrrha suggests, she would be doing something which is quite commonplace in nature:

> The Father-Bull his Daughter may bestride,
> The Horse may make his Mother-Mare a Bride;
> What Piety forbids the lusty Ram
> Or more salacious Goat, to rut their Dam?
> The Hen is free to wed the Chick she bore,
> And make a Husband, whom she hatch'd before.
>
> (43–8; K4 1574)

Indeed, even among human communities, there are some who have no laws against incest of the kind which obtain in Cyprus:

> some wise Nations break their cruel Chains,
> And own no Laws, but those which Love ordains:
> Where happy Daughters with their Sires are join'd,
> And Piety is doubly paid in Kind.
> O that I had been born in such a Clime,
> Not here, where 'tis the Country makes the Crime!
>
> (58–63; K4 1575)

Myrrha's vision of a world in which laws against unbridled sexuality are merely a spiteful and malicious constraint on man's natural impulses is partly confirmed by the events of the poem. When the eagerly complicit nurse goes to tell Cinyras that she can procure him a beautiful young mistress, she finds the king

> Easie with Wine, and deep in Pleasures drown'd
> Prepar'd for Love.
>
> (249–50; K4 1579)

And Cinyras pricks up his ears all the more when he is told explicitly that the girl is the same age as his own daughter. Moreover, at the moment of the incestuous act itself, Dryden reminds us, delicately but definitely, of the crypto-incestuous suggestions which are latent in the very terms of human love-language:

> He found she trembl'd, but believ'd she strove
> With Maiden-Modesty, against her Love,
> And sought with flatt'ring Words vain Fancies to remove. }

Perhaps he said, My Daughter, cease thy Fears,
(Because the Title suited with her Years;)
And Father, she might whisper him agen,
That Names might not be wanting to the Sin.

(297–303; K4 1581)

Yet at the same time as giving due weight to the power of incestuous feelings within and outside the human realm and rehearsing the arguments which suggest that many of the usual objections to incest rest on cant and convention, Dryden's tale also impresses upon us the mysterious and deep resistance of the human mind to incestuous feelings, and its compulsion to recognise certain sanctions, distinctions and categories, and to recoil in revulsion when those sanctions are threatened or abandoned.

In Myrrha's opening speech the poet's manner of presentation prevents us from going along whole-heartedly with what the girl is saying. The audaciously witty mingling of human and animal terms in such lines as

> The Hen is free to wed the Chick she bore,
> And make a Husband, whom she hatch'd before

forces us to see more implications in Myrrha's words than she herself realises. It is, after all, only humans who make the distinction between 'marriage' and 'rutting', and it is only human language which differentiates between a 'mate' and a 'bride'. The poet's mind is playing out, beyond, and around, his character's. In the very act of being invited to recognise the continuities between human and animal sexuality, we are forced to register the profound differences.

And, moreover, Myrrha herself recognises that, whatever she might say to the contrary, she will be violating something which she is compelled to call 'sacred', and something which (paradoxically) can also be thought of as profoundly 'natural', if she succumbs. The animals, she realises, have no 'thoughts of sin' to 'disturb' their 'peace of mind', of the kind which are troubling her. At the end of her speech, her doubts well up into a powerful expression:

> But thou in time th'increasing Ill controul,
> Nor first debauch the Body by the Soul;
> Secure the sacred Quiet of thy Mind,
> And keep the Sanctions Nature has design'd.

(94–7; K4 1575–6)

Such passages suggest that Dryden saw this Ovidian episode as an exploration of the deeply contradictory impulses working away in the mysterious regions of the human mind. It is therefore entirely appropriate, given the complexity of Myrrha's situation, that her final fantastic metamorphosis takes the form which it does. In fairness to the demands of those 'natural' impulses which link her with the freely indulged incestuous sexuality of the animal world, she is not simply punished by her transformation. This is no straightforward cautionary tale of sin and retribution. Yet, at the same time, in fairness to those alternative and perhaps even more 'natural' promptings which suggest that her feelings are profoundly contrary to natural law, she cannot, and does not wish to, be allowed to continue in this life. Myrrha is therefore reassimilated into the nature of which she is so completely a part, and retains in the painless suspended animation of her transformed state indelible marks of the conflict which has so tormented her when alive.

Heroic love

If the power of love is often seen in the *Fables* as disruptive of man's rational powers and civilised impulses, there is one poem which describes a set of circumstances in which the service of Venus works in profound consonance with, and directly inspires, the operation of good sense and reason.

The story of *Sigismonda and Guiscardo* from Boccaccio's *Decameron* tells of a young widow, Sigismonda, living at the court of her possessive father, Prince Tancred of Salerno. She falls in love with a poor but honourable young man named Guiscardo, who is employed as her father's squire. They meet secretly, Guiscardo having entered Sigismonda's room by a secret tunnel leading from a cave outside the palace, and are married. They continue to hold secret assignations until one day Tancred observes them, has Guiscardo arrested, and rebukes his daughter for consorting with a man of such ignoble birth. The culmination of the tale comes when Sigismonda defends her conduct in a boldly defiant and consummately argued speech.

She has, she proclaims, committed no crime. Guiscardo and she were properly married. Having once tasted the joys of marriage, she was no longer prepared to endure the loneliness of a celibate life. The desires which prompted her love were natural, and in attempting to thwart them, Tancred is sinning both against nature and against reason:

Blame then thy self, as Reason's Law requires,
(Since Nature gave, and thou foment'st my Fires;)
If still those Appetites continue strong,
Thou maist consider, I am yet but young:
Consider too, that having been a Wife,
I must have tasted of a better Life,
And am not to be blam'd, if I renew,
By lawful Means, the Joys which then I knew.
Where was the Crime, if Pleasure I procur'd,
Young, and a Woman, and to Bliss inur'd?
That was my Case, and this is my Defence;
I pleas'd my self, I shunn'd Incontinence,
And, urg'd by strong Desires, indulg'd my Sense.

(443–55; K4 1557)

In making this claim, Sigismonda aligns herself boldly in protest
with all those women throughout history whose needs and
promptings have been frustrated by laws and customs in the
formation of which they have been allowed no hand:

What have I done in this, deserving Blame?
State-Laws may alter; Nature's are the same;
Those are usurp'd on helpless Woman-kind,
Made without our Consent, and wanting Pow'r to bind.

(417–20; K4 1556)

Sigismonda's role as nature's spokeswoman in a world of male
malice and cant is, moreover, shown as something far more than an
example of heady youth defying crabbed old age. In her proclama-
tion of Guiscardo's virtue (the reason for which, she claims, she
selected him as a lover in the first place), she now aligns herself with
the finest traditions of Christian and pagan writing (Ovid,
Lucretius, Chaucer, Milton, the Gospels) on the subject of true
nobility.[9] A long quotation is here necessary to convey the full
sweep, dignity, and cogency of her argument:

. . . Search we the secret Springs,
And backward trace the Principles of Things;
There shall we find, that when the World began,
One common Mass compos'd the Mould of Man;
One Paste of Flesh on all Degrees bestow'd,
And kneaded up alike with moistning Blood.
The same Almighty Pow'r inspir'd the Frame
With kindl'd Life, and form'd the Souls the same:
The Faculties of Intellect, and Will,
Dispens'd with equal Hand, dispos'd with equal Skill,
Like Liberty indulg'd with Choice of Good or Ill.

Thus born alike, from Vertue first began
The Diff'rence that distinguish'd Man from Man:
He claim'd no Title from Descent of Blood,
But that which made him Noble, made him Good:
Warm'd with more Particles of Heav'nly Flame. ⎫
He wing'd his upward Flight, and soar'd to Fame; ⎬
The rest remain'd below, a Tribe without a Name. ⎭
    This Law, though Custom now diverts the Course,
As Natures Institute, is yet in force;
Uncancell'd, tho disus'd: And he whose Mind
Is Vertuous, is alone of Noble Kind.
Though poor in Fortune, of Celestial Race;
And he commits the Crime, who calls him Base.

(499–522; K4 1558–9)

Some readers have felt that the impression of stature and passionate dignity which Sigismonda gives in her speech is undercut
by, or incompatible with, the boisterous comedy with which
Dryden had earlier portrayed her courtship and marriage. When
Sigismonda proudly proclaims to Tancred

Before the Holy Priest my Vows were ty'd,
So came I not a Strumpet, but a Bride;

(406–7; K4 1556)

the force of her words, it is thought, is uncomfortably subverted
when we remember the actual incident being referred to:

On either Side the Kisses flew so thick,
That neither he nor she had Breath to speak.
The holy Man amaz'd at what he saw,
Made haste to sanctifie the Bliss by Law;
And mutter'd fast the Matrimony o're,
For fear committed Sin should get before.
His work perform'd, he left the Pair alone, ⎫
Because he knew he could not go too soon; ⎬
His Presence odious, when his Task was done. ⎭
What Thoughts he had, beseems not me to say; ⎫
Though some surmise he went to fast and pray, ⎬
And needed both, to drive the tempting Thoughts away. ⎭
    The Foe once gone, they took their full Delight;
'Twas restless Rage, and Tempest all the Night:
For greedy Love each Moment would employ,
And grudg'd the shortest Pauses of their Joy.

(161–76; K4 1549–50)

Wordsworth objected to this scene, on the grounds that Dryden had 'degraded Sigismonda's character by it'.[10] C. S. Lewis thought that Dryden was offering 'a ribald picture of his heroine as the lascivious widow of conventional comedy' and was 'winking and tittering' to his readers 'over these time-honoured salacities'.[11] But though Dryden's depiction of Sigismonda and Guiscardo's wedding is certainly breathtaking in its daring, it could only, I think, be properly considered 'degrading' by someone who (like Wordsworth) thought that such situations were inherently 'unpleasing subjects', or 'salacious' by someone who (like Lewis) ignored the conspicuous *absence* of the protective Restoration male snigger in the way the scene is portrayed. The breakneck comedy of the episode depends, I would suggest, on the reader's feeling of something approaching awe at the mutual delight and apparently unweariable energy of the lovers, a natural force which the solemnities of the Church can, it appears, only very precariously contain. The poet's delight and wonder is conveyed in the throwaway *élan* of his couplets and triplets.

So while I think a reader may legitimately smile at Sigismonda's claim that she has come to Guiscardo 'not a Strumpet, but a Bride', the smile is one of appreciative admiration rather than ironic condescension. We do not reject her claim, or regard it as her (or Dryden's) hypocrisy. Her frank enjoyment of her wedding-night is, as she rightly points out, far removed from the harlot's calculating professionalism. And her healthy sensuality combines with a strict observance of the letter of the law. Her passionate and rational defence of her conduct is not incompatible with the boisterous sexuality of her earlier behaviour, or antithetical to it, but grows directly out of it. Her defence of her sexual rights derives its force precisely from the buoyant enjoyment with which we have seen her partaking of them. The challenging power of her speech, and of the poem as a whole, is attributable to its frank alignment of unashamed sexual passion and impressively sustained cogency of reason. Mind and body speak as one.

The comedy of love

In those poems discussed so far, Dryden had touched on the power of Venus to destroy, to render absurd, to animate with new life, to confuse, and to inspire with heroic defiance. Elsewhere in the volume he was able to fuse his sense of the exalting and debasing powers of the love-goddess into a single vision by subjecting his thoughts to the distinctive transforming chemistry of pure comedy.

The Cock and the Fox is Dryden's version of Chaucer's *Nun's Priest's Tale*. The setting is a farmyard. Chanticleer the cock awakes one morning in a panic, having had a dream in which a 'murd'rous Beast' had tried to kill him. Partlet, Chanticleer's favourite wife, pooh-poohs his suggestion that the dream is a portent of future disaster and insists that it has been caused by something he has eaten. Chanticleer, however, is adamant and tells his wife several lengthy cautionary tales proving the presaging power of dreams. However, as soon as he looks into Partlet's face he is so struck by her beauty that he forgets his worries and struts out into the yard to join his wife in amatory delights. Then a fox enters the farmyard. Taken in by Reynard's flattery, Chanticleer agrees to sing for him and is, of course, immediately carted off to the fox's lair. But in the nick of time he hits on an inspired ruse to get away: he admits defeat, and begs the fox to finish him off there and then. Reynard agrees, but this gives Chanticleer the opportunity to escape, determined not to be caught a second time.

Every reader of Dryden's tale (as of Chaucer's original) is struck by the extent to which the poet has captured in his portrayal of the cock and hen so many of the traits, gambits and tones of voice of human married couples. Chanticleer's ponderous husbandly insistence on the truth of his point of view, his cocksure smugness and lecturing tone – as well as Partlet's sharp rebukes – are all captured with disconcerting accuracy. It is clear that in this tale of domestic poultry the poet, while not writing allegory, is making some kind of comment on human affairs.

But Chanticleer and Partlet are granted privileges, especially in the sexual sphere, which do not obtain in the human world – unless, that is, it be at Court:

> This gentle Cock for solace of his Life,
> Six Misses had beside his lawful Wife;
> Scandal that spares no King, tho' ne're so good,
> Says, they were all of his own Flesh and Blood:
> His Sisters both by Sire, and Mother's side,
> And sure their likeness show'd them near ally'd.
> But make the worst, the Monarch did no more,
> Than all the *Ptolomeys* had done before:
> When Incest is for Int'rest of a Nation,
> 'Tis made no Sin by Holy Dispensation.
> Some Lines have been maintain'd by this alone,
> Which by their common Ugliness are known.

(55–66; K4 1606)

Chanticleer's incestuous fornication, it seems, is matched only by that practised by the crowned heads of the world. Dryden has incorporated in his version sly allusions not only to the (named) Ptolemys but also, as commentators have pointed out, to Henry VIII, the Habsburgs, Charles II, James II and Louis XIV.[12] Many subversive thoughts are set in motion. Incest and fornication are, we reflect, practised both for the maintenance of farmyard stock and in royal houses. Kings and cocks, the reflections go on, can both indulge in the 'natural' behaviour discussed by Myrrha, but without any of her feelings of guilt or worry. Chanticleer is an even more perfect servant of Venus than David at the beginning of *Absalom and Achitophel*. Not only are his powers of endurance more highly developed:

> Ardent in Love, outrageous in his Play,
> He feather'd her a hundred times a Day:
>
> (69–70; K4 1606)

but also his performance is even more purely centred on pleasure. As the narrator puts it just after Reynard has carted off the cock:

> Ah blissful *Venus*, Goddess of Delight,
> How cou'd'st thou suffer thy devoted Knight,
> On thy own Day to fall by Foe oppress'd,
> The wight of all the World who serv'd thee best?
> Who true to Love, was all for Recreation,
> And minded not the Work of Propagation.
>
> (687–92; K4 1622)

It is in his service to Venus, however, that Chanticleer appears at his most ludicrously cocksure and at his most hubristically deluded. After having spent over two hundred lines of the poem insisting that his dream is indeed prophetic of some disaster that will ensue, one look at the 'Scarlet Red' about Partlet's 'Partridge Eye' is enough to make him forget everything, and, having joined with her in mutual pleasure 'twenty times e'er prime of Day', he turns to deliver her a speech of the utmost complacency, in which he imagines himself occupying the central place in creation which, Milton tells us, God had reserved for man:

> See, my Dear,
> How lavish Nature has adorn'd the Year;
> How the pale Primrose, and blue Violet spring,
> And Birds essay their Throats disus'd to sing:
> All these are ours; and I with pleasure see
> Man strutting on two Legs, and aping me!

An unfledg'd Creature, of a lumpish frame,
Indew'd with fewer Particles of Flame:
Our Dame sits couring o'er a Kitchin-fire,
I draw fresh Air, and Nature's Works admire:
And ev'n this Day, in more delight abound,
Than since I was an Egg, I ever found.

(455–66; K4 1616)

This Miltonic allusion is not alone in the poem. For Dryden's Reynard does not, like Chaucer's, crawl surreptitiously through the hedge, but enters the farmyard boldly:

proudly with a bound
He lept the Fence of the forbidden Ground.

(493–4; K4 1617)

It was in just this manner, we remember, that Milton's Satan had entered Eden:

One Gate there only was, and that look'd East
On th'other side: which when th'arch-fellon saw
Due entrance he disdaind, and in contempt,
At one slight bound high over leap'd all bound
Of Hill or highest Wall, and sheer within
Lights on his feet.

(*Paradise Lost*, IV. 178–83)

The echo might at first suggest that here we have a simple piece of comic inversion – a sly fox playing the village Satan to the anti-Eden of the farmyard. Yet, as in the earlier passage about the incest of kings, the humour is, on consideration, more complex. For just as, in the earlier passage, it would be difficult to say (so finely poised is the wit) whether the lines were intended to condemn or to celebrate the sexual licence of monarchs, so here the Miltonic parallel does not seem intended merely or simply to deflate or denigrate the farmyard paradise, and to deride the absurd pretensions of the deluded fowl. After all, Chanticleer's sentiments were thought by Dryden's admired Montaigne to be no more absurd than those perpetually entertained by man:

Let him make me understand by the force of his reason, upon what foundations he has built those great advantages he thinks he has over other creatures; what has made him believe, that this admirable movement of the celestial arch, the eternal light of those planets and stars that roll so proudly over his head, the fearful motions of that infinite ocean, were established, and continue so many ages, for his service and convenience? Can anything be imagined to be so ridiculous that this miserable and wretched creature, who is not so much as master of himself, but subject to the injuries of all things, should call himself master and emperor of the world, of which he has not power to know the least part, much less to command it . . . For why may not a goose say thus: 'All parts of the universe have I an interest in; the earth serves me to walk upon, the sun to light me, the stars to spread their influence upon me; I have such an advantage by the winds, such conveniences by the waters: there is nothing that yon heavenly roof looks upon so favourably as me; I am the darling of nature. Is it not man that feeds, lodges, and serves me?'[13]

Such thoughts do not lead Dryden (any more than they had Montaigne) to despise Man. Few readers of *The Cock and the Fox*, I would guess, would wish the poem to end by Chanticleer getting eaten – which it strictly ought to, if its true 'moral' were identical with its ostensible one: to teach the evils of Pride and the need to resist succumbing to false flatterers. And most readers, I suspect, are delighted, when, by an exercise of opportunistic and improvised ingenuity, or simple peasant cunning, Chanticleer gets himself out of trouble.

For while the unnerving similarity of Chanticleer's behaviour to human folly forces us to consider the supreme absurdity of much that *we* do, and to wonder whether man's claims to be regarded as God's specially favoured creature ('the end of all yet done') aren't just as silly as Chanticleer's, Dryden's comedy constitutes what we might call a celebration of human folly, rather than merely an attack or a satire upon it. Without relaxing any of the devastating sharpness of its anatomy of human delusion, the poem invites us to love Chanticleer as well as to laugh at him. Its affirmation of man's greatness in his folly is thus a comic counterpart to the solemn Miltonic celebration of humanity, rather than a simple inversion of it.

Surprising as it might at first seem, similar thoughts to those which lie behind *The Cock and the Fox* are visible in another, ostensibly very different, poem in the *Fables* collection. Dryden included in the volume one poem which had appeared before as a separate publication. In 1697 he had been invited by a musical society to write an Ode which was to be set to music and performed on the feast day (22 November) of Cecilia, patron saint of music. The result was *Alexander's Feast: Or the Power of Musique*. This poem, which long remained Dryden's most famous and popular single work, bears all the surface marks of the typical 'baroque' formal ode: refrains, mythological references, elaborately patterned stanza-forms. But it is also a miniature narrative poem and thus is admirably suited for inclusion in the same volume as the other tales we have been considering.

The setting is the feast at which Alexander the Great is celebrating his victory over the Persian king, Darius. Alexander's court musician, Timotheus, begins to sing. Such is his skill that he can manipulate his listeners into whatever mood he chooses. He begins by hymning his monarch. Among the many legends surrounding the career of Alexander was the story that his birth was semi-divine, Jove having come to his mother Olympias (the 'Olympia' of the poem) in the form of a serpent:

> *Timotheus* plac'd on high
>   Amid the tuneful Quire,
>   With flying fingers touch'd the Lyre:
> The trembling Notes ascend the Sky,
>   And Heav'nly Joys inspire.
> The Song began from *Jove*;
> Who left his blissful Seats above,
> (Such is the Pow'r of mighty Love.)
> A Dragon's fiery Form bely'd the God:
> Sublime on Radiant Spires He rode,
>   When He to fair *Olympia* press'd:
>   And while He sought her snowy Breast:
> Then, round her slender Waste he curl'd,
> And stamp'd an Image of himself, a Sovraign of the World.
> The list'ning Crowd admire the lofty Sound,
> A present Deity, they shout around:
> A present Deity the vaulted Roofs rebound.
>   With ravish'd Ears
>   The Monarch hears,
>   Assumes the God,
>   Affects to nod,
>   And seems to shake the Spheres.

(20–41; K3 1428–9)

Many readers have used the word 'sublime' to describe *Alexander's Feast*, and it may be presumed that such readers have found something that they would wish to call genuinely godlike about this moment in the poem where Alexander gestures to acknowledge his subjects' applause, thereby acknowledging his own divine parentage. This is the moment in the poem, it may be felt, where Dryden's claim that Timotheus 'rais'd a Mortal to the Skies' (179; K3 1433) is most fully justified. And the sublimity of *Alexander's Feast* has always been felt to be bound up with the poet's own effortless mastery of the musical effects which he is celebrating: Horace

188

Walpole once remarked that the poem, in his opinion, was more harmonious *before* Handel set it to music. The poem's daring wit, it was felt, found its perfect expression in Dryden's apparently artless manipulation of an elaborate and complex form, and of the most intricate patterns of rhyme and alliteration.

'Sublime', though, might seem on the face of it an unlikely epithet for a poem which tells of a man who, though conqueror of the world, is an arrant fool who is tricked by his own court musician into jingoistic bravado, maudlin sentimentality, amorous pining, and finally an act of pointless and savage mass-destruction, when, egged on by his mistress Thais, he sets light to the city of Persepolis. It is here that the connection between *Alexander's Feast* and *The Cock and the Fox* becomes apparent.

Though love can inspire humans to great achievements, it is in his submission to the power of Venus (so the comic logic seems to go), and to the equally divine power of music, that man often appears at his most foolish, irrational and absurd. Yet, the argument goes on, so pervasive and irresistible are the force of Venus and the concord of sweet sounds that, in submitting to the rule of the love-goddess and to the sway of music, man is cooperating with two of the grandest principles of the universe – the love that makes the world go round, and the music of the spheres. So while, looked at from one point of view, the man under the influence of love or music is a fool, no longer master of himself, and deserving nothing better than derision, in another sense the fool-lover is the incarnation or living agent of a god, the embodiment of a principle of the greatest grandeur and beauty. Chanticleer, in the infinite stupidity and self-delusion of his uxoriousness, becomes an emblem of lovable man. Alexander, conjured into a sequence of abandoned moods by his court musician and mistress becomes transformed, by the connecting powers of Dryden's comic wit and the sublime music of his versification into a more credible figure of a demi-god than all the strutting grandees of the 'heroic' plays.

The realm of Mars

In his firing of Persepolis, Alexander also becomes the servant of another of the presiding deities of the *Fables*, Mars. Mars, in Dryden's imaginings, is not just the classical war god but the deity responsible for most of the destructive or calamitous activities to be found in nature.

At another gate of Theseus's amphitheatre from that occupied by

Venus's temple stands the temple of Mars. It too has carvings on its walls illustrating its god's sphere of influence. The pictures show acts of felony, treason, murder, wrath, hypocrisy, false friendship and sacrilege. They depict madness, riot, arson, and disasters which are normally ascribed to the operation of mere chance. Mars, in Dryden's conception, is the embodiment of all the murderous and malign human impulses which he had both observed in the events of his own lifetime (in the carnage of the Civil War, the unruliness of the London mob, the treachery and malice of the court, the dangerous ambition of politicians) and read about in his favourite literature. The god is also the deity responsible for storms, fires, plagues, shipwrecks, earthquakes. Like the other deities in the *Fables*, then, Mars is at work both within and outside the breast of man.

In attributing the calamities of life to the workings of a god, Dryden makes them seem in one sense more horrific than they do ordinarily, since they are prompted by a figure whose susceptibilities and motives seem frighteningly close to our own. But the conception of Mars as a godly personage also has something of the opposite effect. For, in submitting to Mars's influence, man can be seen (just as with Venus) to be collaborating in one of the grand processes which govern the world, and thus to be exalted rather than demeaned in his service to the god. It is for reasons of this kind that Dryden is able (as in *Alexander's Feast*) to write of carnage, blood-lust and destruction with a breathtakingly light and uncensorious touch, with awed appreciation, and even, on occasions, with frank *delight*, without, at the same time, seeming merely facile or callous.

Dryden's most vivid celebration of the power of Mars comes, perhaps, in his imaginative recreation of the impetuous fury of the Homeric Achilles in his version of the First Book of the *Iliad*. Something of the zestful relish with which Achilles's powerful passions are evoked was suggested in Chapter 2. This poem certainly proves that Dryden saw far more in the Homeric heroes than the 'Athletick Brutes' and 'Man-killing Ideots' to whom he refers in the Dedication to *Fables*. In his translation of *The First Book of Homer's Ilias*, Dryden was able to cut through the cordon of decorum-bound academicism which had so inhibited appreciation of Homer during the Renaissance, and to make vital contact with the fiery energy and comedy of the original.[14]

The story of *Ceyx and Alcyone*, from the Eleventh Book of the *Metamorphoses* presents a very different side of Mars's operations. In the Preface to *Fables* (as on several previous occasions) Dryden had criticised Ovid's habit of deploying verbal wit in grave and harrowing situations. 'On these Occasions', he had written, 'the Poet shou'd endeavour to raise Pity: But instead of this, *Ovid* is tickling you to laugh' (K4 1451; W2 279). But the translation of *Ceyx and Alcyone* shows him to have had no such reservations about this kind of Ovidian wit in the act of rendering it. Shortly after the beginning of the poem, Ceyx's ship is caught in a storm. The waves buffeting the boat are imagined as soldiers besieging a city:

> Now all the Waves, their scatter'd Force unite,
> And as a Soldier, foremost in the Fight
> Makes way for others: And an Host alone
> Still presses on, and urging gains the Town;
> So while th'invading Billows come a-brest,
> The Hero tenth advanc'd before the rest,
> Sweeps all before him with impetuous Sway,
> And from the Walls descends upon the Prey;
> Part following enter, part remain without,
> With Envy hear their Fellows conqu'ring Shout:
> And mount on others Backs, in hope to share
> The City thus become the Seat of War.
>
> (161–72; K4 1641)

The passage is saved from callous frivolity by the inventive but sustained precision with which the behaviour of waves and soldiers is mutually assimilated. The fanciful play of mind is similar to, but less miscellaneous than that of the description of the Great Fire in *Annus Mirabilis*. The gleeful malice, the zestful onrush of the leading wave/commanding officer, the undifferentiated mass of water/troops eagerly finding its/their way through every aperture of the breached ship/city all impress upon us the curiously similar spirit of utterly amoral joy which seems to imbue those who bring about each disaster. The poet looks on in tranquillity but without indifference, imaginatively involved in the scene, yet in a way that allows him to attend appreciatively to aspects of the situation which could probably not be perceived, and certainly not enjoyed, by any actual victim of a natural disaster. A large part of the pleasure of the episode for a reader is that he is here afforded a set of circumstances in which he can appreciate the vitality and beauty of a situation which, in virtually any other presentation imaginable, would appear almost unbearably painful.

The goods of life

Man, in the *Fables*, does not always and inevitably live his life as the helpless victim of the gods. He can occasionally, whether by inherent disposition or by the strenuous exercise of his distinctively human faculty of reason, attain that 'content of mind' which alone can allow him to lay hold on the goods of life and attain peace in his soul.

In the story of *Baucis and Philemon* from the Eighth Book of Ovid's *Metamorphoses*, Dryden shows us a human couple whose capacity to find contentment in the humblest circumstances and through basic attachments and values is evoked with the most loving precision and detail. The poem tells how Jupiter and Mercury, on a visit to the earth, are refused hospitality by all the inhabitants of a particular region except for Baucis and Philemon, an old married couple who live in a humble cottage – 'A homely Shed; the Roof, not far from Ground, / Was thatch'd with Reeds, and Straw together bound' (30–1; K4 1566). The old couple entertain the gods warmly and provide them with a rich selection from their humble but plenteous home-grown fare. The evening is passing agreeably when the couple suddenly realise that the wine-bowls are being replenished of their own accord. They immediately recognise that they are in the presence of gods and go to sacrifice their single goose (which acts as a 'watch-dog' over their smallholding) in reparation for the humbleness of the meal. But the goose is spared and the gods command the couple to leave the neighbourhood immediately for the mountains, since they intend to destroy all those who had denied them hospitality, in a flood. Baucis and Philemon's cottage is the only dwelling in the region to be preserved and it is transformed into a temple. The old couple are granted the privilege of serving in the temple until the appointed hour, when they are simultaneously metamorphosed into trees which remain as a memorial to their piety and marital fidelity.

Ovid's episode had been widely allegorised by commentators as an illustration of the Christian virtues of humility, piety and hospitality. In particular the story had been seen as an analogue of the episode in the book of Genesis where angels rescue Lot from the impending destruction of Sodom. Dryden's rendering shows that he had read such interpretations and he incorporates details from them in his own text.[15] But, interestingly, he makes no sustained attempt to bring out a 'Christian message' in Ovid's tale. The setting remains firmly pagan, and rather than attempting to impose an explicit moral interpretation on the tale Dryden has lavished most of his art (drawing on his Elizabethan and Caroline predecessors, and mingling English rural customs with the Italian details of his original) on evoking the precise details of cottage life which are then left to carry an implicit charge of religious significance. Baucis and Philemon's life is to be revered not because it can be conscripted into any explicit doctrinal scheme, but because of the values which are *embodied* in what might seem its merely circumstantial details:

> By this the boiling Kettle had prepar'd,
> And to the Table sent the smoking Lard;
> On which with eager Appetite they dine,
> A sav'ry Bit, that serv'd to rellish Wine:
> The Wine it self was suiting to the rest,
> Still working in the Must, and lately press'd.
> The Second Course succeeds like that before,
> Plums, Apples, Nuts, and of their Wintry Store,
> Dry Figs, and Grapes, and wrinkl'd Dates were set
> In Canisters, t'enlarge the little Treat:
> All these a Milk-white Honey-comb surround,
> Which in the midst the Country-Banquet crown'd:
> But the kind Hosts their Entertainment grace
> With hearty Welcom, and an open Face:
> In all they did, you might discern with ease,
> A willing Mind, and a Desire to please.
>
> (106–21; K4 1568)

But the tale is not merely a sentimental idyll of rustic bliss. The gusto with which Philemon hauls down a side of bacon with a prong to cut a frugally measured piece off for their guests, the 'officious' Baucis, busily bustling round the cottage, sticking a piece of pottery under one of the table-legs to stop it wobbling – these details, and others, allow the reader to smile at the couple's earnestness as well as appreciating their goodness. Particularly telling in this respect is the behaviour of the goose:

> One Goose they had, ('twas all they cou'd allow) ⎫
> A wakeful Cent'ry, and on Duty now,   ⎬
> Whom to the Gods for Sacrifice they vow: ⎭
> Her, with malicious Zeal, the Couple view'd;
> She ran for Life, and limping they pursu'd:
> Full well the Fowl perceiv'd their bad intent,
> And wou'd not make her Masters Compliment;
> But persecuted, to the Pow'rs she flies,
> And close between the Legs of *Jove* she lies.
>
> (130–8; K4 1568)

The goose makes its desperate supplication to the gods, not inspired by any human notions of reverence, but because it's afraid of being eaten!

Nevertheless our smiles at the old couple's expense do not under-mine our sense of their worthiness, not do they prevent us being touched when we are reminded of the happy married mutuality which stands at the centre of their contentment, and which the gods are pleased to honour:

> since not any Action of our Life
> Has been polluted with Domestick Strife,
> We beg one Hour of Death; that neither she
> With Widows Tears may live to bury me,
> Nor weeping I, with wither'd Arms may bear
> My breathless *Baucis* to the Sepulcher.
>
> (167–76; K4 1569)

Nature's processes

For those not gifted with Baucis and Philemon's natural disposition to be contented with the true goods of life, 'content of mind' must come by means of a more strenuous exertion of the mind and soul. Such exertion, the *Fables* suggest, is most properly exercised in the way with which we are now familiar from Dryden's poems – by 'studying Nature's Laws', contemplating and taking the full measure of the principles and processes which govern the course of sublunary nature.

We saw at the beginning of this chapter how Dryden had seen a special significance for his own current activities in the speech from Book XV of Ovid's *Metamorphoses* in which Pythagoras surveys the processes of perpetual decay, flux and renewal which can be observed throughout nature. Dryden saw the same speech as bear-ing equally directly on the public events of his own century:

> Nature knows
> No stedfast Station, but, or Ebbs, or Flows:
> Ever in motion; she destroys her old,
> And casts new figures in another Mold.
> Ev'n Times are in perpetual Flux; and run
> Like Rivers from their Fountain rowling on;
> For Time no more than Streams, is at a stay:
> The flying Hour is ever on her way;
> And as the Fountain still supplies her store,
> The Wave behind impels the Wave before;
> Thus in successive Course the Minutes run,
> And urge their Predecessor Minutes on,
> Still moving, ever new: For former Things

Are set aside, like abdicated Kings:
And every moment alters what is done,
And innovates some Act till then unknown.

(262–77; K4 1724–5)

The allusions here to Marvell's Cromwell (who, we remember, had sought 'To ruine the great Work of Time / And cast the Kingdom old / Into another Mold'), to the book of Revelation ('for the former things are passed away'),[16] to the alleged 'abdication' of James II and the Acts of William's reign, combine with the dignified and stately march of the verse to give a sense of the inexorability and inclusiveness of mutability.

But nature's processes are simultaneously destructive and creative. If everything is fated to pass away, essential continuities are preserved, and the spirit of life is constantly and mysteriously renewed:

Then, Death, so call'd, is but old Matter dress'd
In some new Figure, and a vary'd Vest:
Thus all Things are but alter'd, nothing dies . . .
So Death, so call'd, can but the Form deface,
Th'immortal Soul flies out in empty space;
To seek her Fortune in some other Place.

(237–9; 251–3; K4 1724)

For the Ovidian Pythagoras, the flux of nature is visible not only in the march of time, but also synchronically, in the overlaps and resemblances between various facets of existence. His account of the seasons (296–323) is imbued with a sense of the delightful resemblances between the phases of the year and those of a man's life. Here, for example, is Spring:

Spring first, like Infancy, shoots out her Head,
With milky Juice requiring to be fed:
Helpless, tho' fresh, and wanting to be led.
The green Stem grows in Stature and in Size,
But only feeds with hope the Farmer's Eyes;
Then laughs the childish Year with Flourets crown'd,
And lavishly perfumes the Fields around,
But no substantial Nourishment receives,
Infirm the Stalks, unsolid are the Leaves.

(299–307; K4 1725)

Similar resemblances, Dryden wryly observes, can be divined in the time of life in which he writes:

Autumn succeeds, a sober tepid Age,
Not froze with Fear, nor boiling into Rage;
More than mature, and tending to decay,
When our brown Locks repine to mix with odious Grey.

(312–15; K4 1726)

The consolations of philosophy

From what has been said so far it can be seen that the ultimate purpose of much of Dryden's best verse in the *Fables* can, like that of the best poems in *Sylvae*, be described as *consolatory*. Here is a volume of tales which help the reader to recognise and enjoy forces at work in himself and in his world which might otherwise serve to baffle and confuse. Recognition is itself consolatory. To have lived through in the imagination the follies of Chanticleer and Alexander, the bloodlust of Achilles, the sexual defiance of Sigismonda, the insoluble dilemma of Myrrha, and the married goodness of Baucis and Philemon is, however indirectly, to have come to a fuller relish of the pleasures of one's own life and a fuller understanding of its pains.

One passage in the *Fables* besides Pythagoras's speech is designed to offer explicit consolation to those beleaguered and perplexed by the vicissitudes of life. Since the speech which Theseus makes to the gathered assembly at the end of *Palamon and Arcite* draws on, and in some ways epitomises, many of the consoling thoughts to be found both in the *Fables* and elsewhere in Dryden, it makes a fitting culmination and conclusion to a consideration of his last volume and of his life's work.

Palamon and Arcite have returned to fight in the lists for Emily's hand. At first Arcite is victorious, but by the intervention of Saturn on Venus's behalf he is then thrown from his horse and mortally wounded. On his death bed he commends Emily to Palamon's protection. He dies and is buried with great pomp. A year later, Theseus summons Palamon to Athens. At the same time Emily is brought before him, and in a long speech Theseus lays out the reasons why it is fitting that Palamon should now marry Emily and that both should put their sorrow aside.

It is important, as we attend to Theseus's speech, that we remember how the figure of the Duke has been established for us during the course of the tale. Theseus is a man of great dignity and authority. But he is no saint, and has achieved his stature by attaining a strenuous mastery of the irrational and uncivilised impulses within him. We have already witnessed how he admitted, in his words to the two youths in the grove, that in his youth he was under the sway of Venus. He has served Mars too. Near the beginning of the tale we are told how at the siege of Thebes he

> The Country wasted, and the Hamlets burn'd;
> And left the Pillagers, to Rapine bred,
> Without Controul to strip and spoil the Dead.
>
> (I. 138–40; K4 1471)

And when he came upon the youths in the grove, it was only after a period of intense inner debate that 'Reason resum'd her Place, and Passion fled' (II. 349; K4 1492), and that he was then prepared to rescind his initial decision that Palamon and Arcite must die.

Theseus's speech, then, does not come from the lips of a man untainted by the irrational passions of the world. Nor does it rely on the reassuring backing of any systematic theological or philosophical system for its message of consolation. It offers no hope of personal afterlife or world-denying metaphysic. It requires the audience (and by extension, the reader) to be impressed by its intrinsic force and truth, rather than resting its case on dogma or faith.

Theseus seeks to console his audience by reminding them of certain fundamental facts of existence. He surveys the inexorable conditions under which life on this planet must be lived, and the way in which man, like all other parts of creation, must inevitably pass away. He does not blind himself to the pains and miseries of mortal existence. But, he argues, there is no alternative for the reasonable man but to seize the goods of life when he can. Life is to be lived.

Such a speech could easily seem (as it does in the foregoing summary) merely platitudinous. All depends on the speaker's power to convince the reader that he has taken the full measure, and contemplated the full vastness of the natural processes he is describing. His sense of nature must seem grand rather than merely matter-of-fact. We must be convinced that his apprehension of nature's laws has been felt on his pulses, not merely as an intellectual abstraction. Nothing must seem facile or glib. The portentous and the prosaic note must equally be avoided. The consoling words, if they are to have the proper effect, must have the ring of ungainsayable *truth*.

Theseus begins by affirming the ultimate beneficence which can be divined in the scheme of things. Beyond the capricious contending deities whose activities we have witnessed in the poem there can be deduced the presence of a 'First Mover', a shadowy divine

197

force, quite unlike the personal God of Christianity, who keeps the whole grand system of life in motion, a system in which any individual human life constitutes an infinitessimally small and transient part:

> Parts of the Whole are we; but God the Whole;
> Who gives us Life, and animating Soul.
> For Nature cannot from a Part derive
> That Being, which the Whole can only give:
> He perfect, stable; but imperfect We,
> Subject to Change, and diff'rent in Degree.
>
> (III. 1042–7; K4 1526)

The peculiar beneficence of the First Mover is to ensure that nature's forms continue, even when its individual parts are in constant and continual decay. The 'long majestic march' of Theseus's words, and the sense they convey of a mind surveying vast tracts of time and space in a single sober conspectus lends a grandeur to what might, in another handling, have seemed merely commonplace observations:

> That Individuals die, his Will ordains;
> The propagated Species still remains.
> The Monarch Oak, the Patriarch of the Trees,
> Shoots rising up, and spreads by slow Degrees:
> Three Centuries he grows, and three he stays,
> Supreme in State; and in three more decays:
> So wears the paving Pebble in the Street,
> And Towns and Tow'rs their fatal Periods meet.
> So Rivers, rapid once, now naked lie,
> Forsaken of their Springs; and leave their Channels dry.
>
> (III. 1056–65; K4 1527)

But Theseus does not merely survey the processes of existence from a lofty and stately height. He can also dwell with minute precision on the tiniest and most intimate regions of life's workings:

> So Man, at first a Drop, dilates with Heat,
> Then form'd, the little Heart begins to beat;
> Secret he feeds, unknowing in the Cell;
> At length, for Hatching ripe, he breaks the Shell,
> And struggles into Breath, and cries for Aid.
>
> (III. 1066–70; K4 1527)

As well as an Ovidian (or Blakeian)[17] sense of the wonder of biological processes, Theseus also shows a Lucretian awareness of Man's capacity to alienate himself very soon from the nature of which he is part:

> He creeps, he walks, and issuing into Man,
> Grudges their Life, from whence his own began.
> Retchless of Laws, affects to rule alone,
> Anxious to reign, and restless on the Throne:
> First vegetive, then feels, and reasons last;
> Rich of Three Souls, and lives all three to waste.
>
> (III. 1072–7; K4 1527)

Yet such a perception does not lead Theseus to despair of life or (like his father Egeus earlier in Book III) to advocate a passive quietism as the only way of enduring the miseries of existence. What he offers is not simply making the best of a bad job, but a vigorous Horatian relish (in which Dryden boldly echoes his own translation of *Odes* III. 29) of the good things of life while they are in our grasp:

> Then 'tis our best, since thus ordain'd to die,
> To make a Vertue of Necessity.
> Take what he gives, since to rebel is vain,
> The Bad grows better, which we well sustain:
> And cou'd we chuse the Time, and chuse aright,
> 'Tis best to die, our Honour at the height.
> When we have done our Ancestors no Shame,
> But serv'd our Friends, and well secur'd our Fame;
> Then should we wish our happy Life to close,
> And leave no more for Fortune to dispose:
> So should we make our Death a glad Relief,
> From future Shame, from Sickness, and from Grief:
> Enjoying while we live the present Hour,
> And dying in our Excellence, and Flow'r.
>
> (III. 1084–97; K4 1527–8)

Theseus ends with a further defiant affirmation. What, he asks, can a reasonable man do, faced with the facts of life as presented in this speech and in the poem as a whole, but be thankful for what he has, and live on:

> What then remains, but after past Annoy,
> To take the good Vicissitude of Joy?
> To thank the gracious Gods for what they give,
> Possess our Souls, and while we live, to live?
>
> (III. 1111–14; K4 1528)

The energy of the lines derives from the fact that, in full recognition of all that might lead one to nihilism or despair, Theseus finds deep within him by sustained exercise of passionate reasonableness not merely the capacity to go on living, but to grasp life and live it to the full in a spirit of profound gratitude.

In the grandeur and inclusiveness and philosophical dignity of his vision of nature, in his capacity to subsume and transcend attitudes to life which we normally call 'optimistic' and 'pessimistic', in his ability to dwell with equal attentiveness on the tiniest details and the largest cycles of existence, in his command of a manner of speech which is both general and precise, cogent and moving, in his ability to fuse the delighted appreciativeness of youth with the mature reflection of old age, it is difficult to avoid seeing profound resemblances between Duke Theseus and his creator, the sixty-eight-year-old poet, John Dryden.

Notes

Introduction

1. Though Wordsworth criticised Dryden (see pp. 127, 183 of this book), he also remarked on another occasion to his nephew and biographer: 'I have been charged by some with disparaging Pope and Dryden. This is not so. I have committed much of both to memory.' See *Wordsworth's Literary Criticism*, ed. Nowell C. Smith (London, 1905), p. 256.

2. For an excellent short account of the Restoration theatre, see Peter Holland's article in vol. X (*Companion*) of *The Diary of Samuel Pepys*, ed. R. Latham and W. Matthews (11 vols., London, 1970–83), pp. 431–45.

3. See Richard Luckett, 'Music', in *The Diary of Samuel Pepys*, X, pp. 258–82.

4. See Chapter 2 of Dale Underwood's *Etherege and the Seventeenth-Century Comedy of Manners* (New Haven and London, 1957).

5. J. P. Kenyon, *Stuart England* (Harmondsworth, 1978), p. 8. See also John Miller, *The Glorious Revolution* (London, 1983), pp. vi–3.

6. Kenyon, *Stuart England*, p. 7.

7. Kenyon, *Stuart England*, pp. 9–11. See also J. R. Jones, *Country and Court: England, 1658–1714* (London, 1978) and J. R. Jones, ed., *The Restored Monarchy, 1660–1688* (London, 1979).

8. See John Miller, *Popery and Politics in England, 1660–1688* (Cambridge, 1973).

9. Kenyon, *Stuart England*, p. 10.

10. See John Miller, 'The Later Stuart Monarchy' in J. R. Jones, ed., *The Restored Monarchy*, pp. 30–47, and the same author's *James II: A Study in Kingship* (Hove, 1978).

11. Gilbert Burnet, *Some Passages in the Life and Death of John, Earl of Rochester* (London, 1680), p. 12.

12. *The Life and Times of Anthony à Wood*, abridged and ed. L. Powys (reprinted Oxford, 1961), p. 132.

13. *The Diary of Samuel Pepys*, VIII, p. 355.

14. *The Diary of Samuel Pepys*, VIII, p. 356.

15. John Wilmot, Earl of Rochester, *Selected Poems*, ed. Paul Hammond (Bristol, 1982), p. 26.

16. H. W. Smith, 'Nature, Correctness and Decorum', *Scrutiny*, 18 (1951–2), 289.

17. Patrick Cruttwell, *The Shakespearean Moment, and its Place in the Poetry of the 17th Century* (reprinted New York, 1960), p. 186.

18. Sir Anthony Weldon, quoted in Robert Ashton, ed., *James I by his Contemporaries* (London, 1969), p. 12.

19. H. A. Mason, *Humanism and Poetry in the Early Tudor Period* (London, 1959), pp. 86–7. See also G. K. Hunter, *John Lyly: The Humanist as Courtier* (London, 1962), pp. 13–35.

20. Thomas Sprat, *History of the Royal Society*, ed. J. I. Cope and H. W. Jones (St Louis and London, 1959), p. 113.

21. Michael Hunter, *Science and Society in Restoration England* (Cambridge, 1981), especially Chapters 1, 2 and 7.

22. Margery Purver, *The Royal Society: Concept and Creation* (London, 1967), pp. 99–100.

23. S. I. Mintz, *The Hunting of Leviathan: Seventeenth-Century Reactions to the Materialism and Moral Philosophy of Thomas Hobbes* (Cambridge, 1962); Hunter, *Science and Society*, pp. 138, 149, 151–2, 181.

24. See John A. Winterbottom, 'The Place of Hobbesian Ideas in Dryden's Tragedies', *Journal of English and Germanic Philology*, 57 (1958), 665–83.

25. Donald Greene, *The Age of Exuberance: Backgrounds to Eighteenth-Century English Literature* (New York, 1970), p. 90.

26. Sir Walter Scott, ed., *The Works of John Dryden*, 2nd edn (18 vols., Edinburgh, 1821), I, p. 406.

27. Greene, *Age of Exuberance*, p. 91.

28. See Howard Erskine-Hill, *The Augustan Idea in English Literature* (London, 1983).

29. See P. J. Smallwood's Introduction to the facsimile reprint (London, 1979) of René Rapin's *Reflections on Aristotle's Treatise of Poesie*, and Paul Hammond, *John Oldham and the Renewal of Classical Culture* (Cambridge, 1983).

1 Dryden's verse

1. In this chapter, since the main focus is on versification, no references are given for individual quotations and all italics in quotations are mine.

2. *Sleep and Poetry*, lines 186–7.

3. See, for example, Edward Bysshe, *The Art of English Poetry* (London, 1702), pp. 3–8.

4. This was first pointed out by J. Sargeaunt in his edition of *The Poems of John Dryden* (Oxford, 1910), p. xviii.

5. 'The Metaphysical Poets', *Selected Essays*, 2nd edn 1934 (reprinted London, 1944), p. 287.

6. See Tom Mason, 'Dryden's Chaucer' (Ph.D. Dissertation, University of Cambridge, 1977), pp. 146–7.

7. Mason, 'Dryden's Chaucer', p. 199.

8. *The Progress of Poesy*, line 110.
9. 'Christopher North' (John Wilson), *Specimens of the British Critics* (Philadelphia, 1846), p. 311.

2 Disappointment and promise: Dryden's early career

1. According to Dryden's friend, Charles Blount. See J. and H. Kinsley, eds., *Dryden: The Critical Heritage* (London, 1971), p. 160. For Rochester's tribute of the mid 1670s, see Chapter 4.
2. See Paul Hammond, 'Dryden's Employment by Cromwell's Government', *Transactions of the Cambridge Bibliographical Society*, 8 (1981), 130–6.
3. In *Dryden: The Public Writer, 1660–1685* (Princeton, N. J., 1978), George McFadden offers a biographico-critical account of the whole of Dryden's earlier career, with particular emphasis on the poet's relations with his courtly patrons and associates. Not all scholars, however, have been convinced by Professor McFadden's interpretation of the complex evidence. See Ken Robinson's review in *Modern Language Review*, 75 (1980), 847–9.
4. Robert D. Hume, *The Development of English Drama in the Late Seventeenth Century* (Oxford, 1976), p. 17. I am indebted to Professor Hume's research throughout my account of Dryden's theatrical career.
5. In this section, all dates given are of first performances, rather than, as elsewhere in the book, of publication.
6. *On Poetry: a Rhapsody*, lines 269–70. See also *A Tale of a Tub*, ed. A. C. Guthkelch and D. Nichol Smith, 2nd edn (Oxford, 1958), p. 131.
7. See John Barnard, 'Dryden, History and "The Mighty Government of the Nine" ', *English*, Summer 1983, 129–53; James D. Garrison, *Dryden and the Tradition of Panegyric* (Berkeley, Los Angeles, London, 1975).
8. See, for example, L. C. Knights, *Explorations* (reprinted Harmondsworth, 1964), p. 142.
9. *Dryden: The Critical Heritage*, p. 177.
10. *Dryden: The Critical Heritage*, p. 50. For an attempt to defend *The Conquest of Granada* by reference to the performance conventions of the Restoration theatre, see Jocelyn Powell, *Restoration Theatre Production* (London, 1984), pp. 106–26.
11. In a series of interesting articles, Professor D. W. Jefferson has drawn attention to the comic, grotesque and exaggerated elements in the plays. See 'The Significance of Dryden's Heroic Plays', *Proceedings of the Leeds Philosophical and Literary Society*, 5 (1940), 125–39 (reprinted in Earl Miner, ed., *Restoration Dramatists: A Collection of Critical Essays* (Englewood Cliffs, N.J., 1966), pp. 19–35); 'Aspects of Dryden's Imagery', *Essays in Criticism*, 4 (1954), 20–41 (reprinted in Bruce King, ed., *Dryden's Mind and Art* (Edinburgh, 1969), pp. 24–42);

' "All, All of Piece Throughout"'; Thoughts on Dryden's Dramatic Poetry'; *Restoration Theatre*, ed. J. R. Brown and B. Harris, Stratford-upon-Avon Studies: 6 (London, 1965), pp. 159–76; 'Dryden's Style in *The State of Innocence*', *Essays in Criticism*, 32 (1982), 361–81. Professor Jefferson sees the comedy and extravagance as part of Dryden's conscious artistic intention, but never, to my mind, makes it quite clear how satisfactorily he thinks Dryden has integrated these elements with the more 'serious' sides of the plays to make coherent wholes.

12. *The Plays of William Shakespeare*, ed. S. Johnson and G. Steevens, 2nd edn (10 vols., London, 1778), I, pp. 9–11.

13. *The Plays of William Shakespeare*, X, p. 166.

3 Poems of controversy: *Mac Flecknoe* and *Absalom and Achitophel*

1. David M. Veith, 'The Discovery of the Date of *Mac Flecknoe*', *Evidence in Literary Scholarship: Essays in Memory of James Marshall Osborn*, ed. René Wellek and Alvaro Ribiero (Oxford, 1979), pp. 63–87.

2. C. E. Ward, 'Shadwell, 1658–1668', *The Times Literary Supplement*, 3 April 1937, p. 256; Dryden's literary relations with Shadwell are surveyed, and the relevant documents reproduced in facsimile, in Richard L. Oden, ed., *Dryden and Shadwell: The Literary Controversy and Mac Flecknoe (1669–1679)* (Delmar, New York, 1977).

3. See, for example C3 209–30; David Ogg, *England in the Reign of Charles II*, 2nd edn (reprinted Oxford, 1967), Chapters XV–XVII; J. P. Kenyon, *The Popish Plot* (London, 1972).

4. Phillip Harth, 'Legends No Histories: The Case of *Absalom and Achitophel*', *Studies in Eighteenth-Century Culture*, 4, ed. D. E. Pagliaro (Madison, 1975), pp. 13–29.

5. The views summarised here draw on a number of studies, of which perhaps the most influential has been Bernard Schilling, *Dryden and the Conservative Myth: A Reading of 'Absalom and Achitophel'* (New Haven, 1961).

6. See K4 1877–1903, C2 209–85 (on *Absalom*), K4 1913–22, C2 299–327 (on *Mac Flecknoe*). On *Absalom* see also Leonora L. Brodwin, 'Miltonic Allusion in *Absalom and Achitophel*: its Function in the Political Satire', *Journal of English and Germanic Philology*, 68 (1969), 24–44; E. S. de Beer, '*Absalom and Achitophel*: Literary and Historical Notes', *Review of English Studies*, 27 (1941), 298–309; R. F. Jones, 'The Originality of *Absalom and Achitophel*', *Modern Language Notes*, 46 (1931), 211–18; Barbara K. Lewalski, 'The Scope and Function of Biblical Allusion in *Absalom and Achitophel*', *English Language Notes*, 3 (1965), 29–35; R. G. Peterson, 'Larger Manners and Events: Sallust and Virgil in *Absalom and Achitophel*', *PMLA*, 82 (1967), 236–44; W. K. Thomas, *The Crafting of 'Absalom and Achitophel': Dryden's 'Pen for a Party'* (Waterloo, Ontario, 1978). On *Mac Flecknoe*, see note 7 below.

7. The topical references and literary allusions in *Mac Flecknoe* are noted

by various commentators; particularly full commentaries are found in C2 311–27, Oden, *Dryden and Shadwell*, pp. 231–46 and Philip Roberts, ed., *John Dryden: 'Absalom and Achitophel' and Other Poems* (London, 1973), pp. 107–19.

8. *The Dunciad*, I, lines 59–68, *The Poems of Alexander Pope*, ed. John Butt, 2nd edn (London, 1965), p. 723.

9. *The Dunciad*, IV, lines 13–16, *The Poems of Alexander Pope*, p. 766.

10. *The Virtuoso* (London, 1676), Sig. A2r.

11. Ben Jonson, *The Complete Poems*, ed. G. Parfitt (Harmondsworth, 1975), p. 448.

12. P. Roberts, ed., *Absalom and Achitophel*, p. 114.

13. *The Dunciad*, II, lines 1–5, *The Poems of Alexander Pope*, p. 736.

14. I am grateful to Dr Felicity Rosslyn for drawing my attention to the nature and interest of this echo.

15. *Essay on the Genius and Writings of Pope*, 4th edn, 2 vols. (London, 1782), II, p. 383.

16. 'Monarch-oak' is, of course, the technical term for an oak tree 'superior to the rest of the same kind' (Johnson, *Dictionary*).

17. Boileau, *Oeuvres Complètes*, ed. A. Adam and F. Escal (Paris, 1966), p. 200; *The Works of Monsieur Boileau, Made English . . . by Several Hands*, 3 vols. (London, 1712–13), I, pp. 26–7.

18. A modern commentator who has attempted to account for the qualitative discrepancy between the various parts of *Absalom and Achitophel* is A. L. French in 'Dryden, Marvell and Political Poetry', *Studies in English Literature*, 8 (1968), 397–413.

19. See also Philip Hobsbaum, *Tradition and Experiment in English Poetry* (London, 1979), pp. 162–5.

20. See C2 276–7.

21. See Isabel Rivers, *The Poetry of Conservatism, 1600–1745: A Study of Poets and Public Affairs from Jonson to Pope* (Cambridge, 1973), pp. 157–8.

22. Godfrey Davies, in 'The Conclusion of Dryden's *Absalom and Achitophel*', *Huntington Library Quarterly*, 10 (1946), 69–82, showed that *Absalom and Achitophel* does not draw on the king's Oxford speech, but on Charles's *Declaration*. Subsequent commentators have also shown resemblances between the poem and Dryden's prose pamphlet, *His Majesties Declaration Defended*.

23. See Edwin Morgan, 'Dryden's Drudging', *Cambridge Journal*, 6 (1958), 414–29 (reprinted in Bernard N. Schilling, ed., *Dryden: a Collection of Critical Essays* (Englewood Cliffs, N.J.,1963), pp. 55–70 (p.67)); Ian Jack, *Augustan Satire: Intention and Idiom in English Poetry, 1660–1750* (Oxford, 1952), p. 63, fn. 3.

24. *The Spectator*, ed. G. Gregory Smith, 8 vols. (London, 1906), II, pp. 292–3.

25. Michael Wilding, 'Dryden and Satire: "Mac Flecknoe, Absalom and Achitophel, the Medall"', and Juvenal', *Writers and their Background:*

John Dryden, ed. Earl Miner (London, 1972), pp. 191–233 (pp. 213–14).

26. *Dryden: The Critical Heritage*, p. 236.
27. *Dryden: The Critical Heritage*, p. 132.
28. John Aikin, ed., *Fables from Boccaccio and Chaucer: by John Dryden* (London, 1806), p. iii.

4 New directions: religion and translation in the 1680s

1. Aphra Behn, *Works*, ed. M. Summers, 6 vols. (reprinted New York, 1967), IV, pp. 8–9.
2. Rochester, *Selected Poems*, p. 43. The staple of the pamphlet attacks on Dryden can be sampled in the *Critical Heritage* volume, and (at greater length) in the fourteen-volume collection of *Drydeniana* published (1974–5) by Garland Publishing as part of their facsimile series *The Life and Times of Seven Major British Writers: Dryden, Pope, Swift, Richardson, Sterne, Johnson, Gibbon*. See also Hugh Macdonald, 'The Attacks on Dryden', *Essays and Studies*, 21 (1936), 41–74.
3. Rochester, *Selected Poems*, p. 46.
4. J. Richardson, father and son, *Explanatory Notes and Remarks on Milton's Paradise Lost* (London, 1734), pp. cxix–cxx.
5. John Dennis, 'To Judas Iscariot, Esq.,; On the Degeneracy of the Publick Taste', *Critical Works*, ed. E. N. Hooker, 2 vols. (Baltimore, 1939–43), II, p. 169.
6. In a forthcoming study, Mr J. R. Mason will document the many hundreds of borrowings from *Paradise Lost* which are to be found in Dryden's poetry and which increase markedly in frequency in Dryden's later years.
7. See Paul Hammond, *John Oldham and the Renewal of Classical Culture* (Cambridge, 1983), especially pp. 212–16.
8. For a good modern study of Tonson's career, see K. M. Lynch, *Jacob Tonson, Kit-Cat Publisher* (Knoxville, 1971). See also S. L. C. Clapp, ed., *Jacob Tonson in Ten Letters by and about him* (Austin, 1948).
9. See Arthur Sherbo, 'The Dryden-Cambridge Translation of Plutarch's *Lives*', *Etudes Anglaises*, 32 (1979), 177–84. Discussions of Dryden's relations with Roscommon in the early 1680s must start with a consideration of Knightley Chetwood's 'A Short Account of some Passages of the Life & Death of Wentworth late Earle of Roscommon, To the Right Honorable My Lord Cartaret' (Cambridge University Library, Baker MSS. Mm. 1. 47).
10. See, for example, the correspondence between Dryden and Walsh (L 25, 30–7) and T. and E. Swedenberg, eds., *George Stepney's Translation of the Eighth Satire of Juvenal* (Berkeley and Los Angeles, 1948). The Swedenbergs reprint (pp. 9–10) a handwritten remark of Pope's preserved on Stepney's manuscript: 'Who compares this Original of Mr. Stepney's with that printed in Dryden's Juvenal, will see ye vast

advantages it receiv'd by passing under his hands. I question not, the same w^d appear of ye other translations there, if ye originals were extant to make the same comparison. This was what That great Man did for almost all his acquaintance.'

11. See the lists of Tonson publications printed in G. F. Papali, *Jacob Tonson, Publisher: His Life and Work (1656–1736)* (Auckland, 1968). The reader should be warned that these lists contain some inaccuracies.

12. *The Works of John Dryden*, I, pp. 306–7.

13. See T. A. Birrell, 'James Maurus Corker and Dryden's Conversion', *English Studies*, 54 (1973), 461–9; Phillip Harth, *Contexts of Dryden's Thought* (Chicago, 1968), Chapters 7 and 8.

14. These are discussed by Earl Miner in C3 340–8.

15. On the theological background to this subject, see Harth, *Contexts*, Chapter 5.

16. On the philosophical background and sources of Dryden's poem and its relation to 'epicurean' thought of the Restoration, see Paul Hammond, 'The Integrity of Dryden's Lucretius', *Modern Language Review*, 78 (1983), 1–23.

17. Montaigne, *Essays*, trans. C. Cotton, rev. W. C. Hazlitt, 5 vols. (London, 1923), I, pp. 98–100.

18. On this poem, see H. A. Mason, 'Living in the Present: Is Dryden's "Horat. Ode 29. Book 3" an example of "creative translation"?', *Cambridge Quarterly*, 10 (1981), 91–129. On the rendering of Epode II, see H. A. Mason, 'Dryden's Dream of Happiness', *Cambridge Quarterly*, 8 (1978), 11–55, and 9 (1980), 218–71. On the *Beatus Ille* tradition, see Maren-Sofie Røstvig, *The Happy Man: Studies in the Metamorphoses of a Classical Ideal*, 2nd edn, 2 vols. (Oslo, 1962), I.

19. *Dryden: The Critical Heritage*, p. 324; Lord Macaulay, *The History of England*, ed. C. H. Firth, 6 vols. (London, 1913–5), II, p. 852.

20. See Fredson Bowers, 'Dryden as Laureate: the Cancel Leaf in "King Arthur"', *The Times Literary Supplement*, 10 April 1954, p. 244.

5 'Studying Nature's Laws': the *Juvenal* and *Virgil*

1. See Alexandre Beljame, *Men of Letters and the English Public in the Eighteenth Century, 1660–1744: Dryden, Addison, Pope*, 1881, trans. E. O. Lorimer (London, 1948), pp. 354–66; John Barnard, 'Dryden, Tonson, and Subscriptions for the 1697 *Virgil*', *Papers of the Bibliographical Society of America*, 57 (1963), 129–51; Pat Rogers, 'Books, Readers and Patrons', *The New Pelican Guide to English Literature, 4: From Dryden to Johnson*, ed. Boris Ford (Harmondsworth, 1982), pp. 214–77.

2. See J. R. Moore, 'Political Allusions in Dryden's Later Plays', *PMLA*, 73 (1958), 36–42; William Myers, *Dryden* (London, 1973), pp. 129–33; Howard Erskine-Hill, review of C15, *The Times Literary Supplement*, 12 August 1977, p. 998.

3. Earl Miner, 'On Reading Dryden', *Writers and their Background: John Dryden*, pp. 1–26 (p.17).

4. The allusion is to Judges 8. 2.

5. See C4 514–86 *passim*, and Alex Lindsay, 'Dryden and Juvenal' (Ph.D. Dissertation, University of Dublin, Trinity College, 1982), Chapter 1 ('Dryden and the Scholars').

6. See Niall Rudd, *The Satires of Horace* (Cambridge, 1966), pp. 258–73.

7. See H. A. Mason, 'Is Juvenal a Classic?', *Critical Essays on Roman Literature: Satire*, ed. J. P. Sullivan (London, 1963), pp. 93–176.

8. See Johnson's *Dictionary*, under 'buxom': 'In an old form of marriage, used before the reformation, the bride promised to be *obedient and* buxom *in bed and at board*'.

9. Here and elsewhere in this section I am indebted to a forthcoming study of Dryden's *Georgics* by Katy Koralek.

10. See John Chalker, *The English Georgic* (London, 1969), Chapter 1 ('Dryden and Addison').

11. On the political allusions in the later work, see particularly W. J. Cameron, 'John Dryden's Jacobitism', *Restoration Literature: Critical Approaches*, ed. H. Love (London, 1972), pp. 277–308; William Myers, *Dryden* (London, 1973), Chapters 8–10; George Watson, 'Dryden and the Jacobites', *The Times Literary Supplement*, 16 March 1973, p. 301; Alan Roper, *Dryden's Poetic Kingdoms* (London, 1965), pp. 113–35, 165–84; James Kinsley, 'Dryden's "Character of a Good Parson" and Bishop Ken', *Review of English Studies*, 3 (1952), 155–8; Jay Arnold Levine, 'John Dryden's Epistle to John Driden', *Journal of English and Germanic Philology*, 63 (1964), 450–74 (reprinted in Bruce King, ed., *Dryden's Mind and Art*, pp. 114–42); William Frost, 'Dryden's Virgil', *Comparative Literature*, 36 (1984), 193–208 (pp. 195–8).

12. *The Works of John Dryden*, VIII, p. 451.

13. As suggested to me by Katy Koralek.

14. T. S. Eliot, 'Introduction' to *The Selected Poems of Ezra Pound* (London, 1928), p. 13.

15. The evidence which supports this statement – an advertisement in *The Gentleman's Journal* for November 1692 and two early letters of Joseph Addison – is presented and discussed in my unpublished Ph.D. dissertation, 'Dryden's Translations from Ovid' (University of Leicester, 1979), pp. 171–7.

16. See *P. Vergilii Maronis Aeneidos Liber Sextus*, ed. R. G. Austin (Oxford, 1977), p. 221; R. D. Williams, 'The Sixth Book of the Aeneid', *Greece and Rome*, 2nd series, 11 (1964), 48–63.

17. See *P. Vergilii Maronis Aeneidos Liber Sextus*, pp. 222–3 (on Virgil, lines 726–7).

18. See, for example, E. M. W. Tillyard, *The English Epic and its Background* (London, 1954), p. 480.

19. See, especially, T. W. Harrison, 'Dryden's *Aeneid*', *Dryden's Mind and Art*, ed. Bruce King (Edinburgh, 1969), pp. 143–67.

20. Alfred, Lord Tennyson, 'To Virgil', stanza VI.

21. Most notably of the famous *sunt lacrimae rerum* passage (*Aen.* i. 462). See William Frost, *Dryden and the Art of Translation* (New Haven, 1955), pp. 34–6 and T. W. Harrison, 'English Virgil: the *Aeneid* in the XVIII Century', *Philologica Pragensia*, 10 (1967), 1–11, 80–91 (pp. 88–90).

22. See L. Proudfoot, *Dryden's 'Aeneid' and its Seventeenth Century Predecessors* (Manchester, 1960), especially Chapter 14 ('The Coarsening of Tone'), and Mark O'Connor, 'John Dryden, Gavin Douglas and Virgil', *Restoration Literature: Critical Approaches*, ed. H. Love (London, 1972), pp. 247–74 (p. 251).

23. Compare *Aen.* iv. 1–2 with Lucr. i. 34, iv. 1048–9, 1060, 1120, 1139, 1153, and with *Geor.* iii. 210, 244, 258–9. Compare *Aen.* iv. 66–7 with Lucr. iv. 1087, and with *Geor.* iii. 271. See *Publi Vergili Maronis Aeneidos Liber Quartus*, ed. A. S. Pease (Cambridge, Mass., 1935), and W. A. Merrill, 'Parallels and Coincidences in Lucretius and Virgil', *University of California Publications in Classical Philology*, 3 (1918), 135–247.

24. Compare AE4 2–4 with L4 18–9, 50–1. Compare AE4 73–4 with G3 106–7. Compare AE4 99–100 with G3 403–4 and with L4 1–2. Compare AE4 108 with L1 50. Compare AE4 129–31 with L1 63–4, and with L4 23–4, 80–1, 197–8. Compare AE4 769–70 with G3 419–20. (AE4: *The Fourth Book of the Aeneis*, G3: *The Third Book of the Georgics*, L1: *Lucretius, The Beginning of the first Book*, L4: *Lucretius, The Fourth Book, Concerning the Nature of Love*.)

25. An appreciative account of this passage will be found in R. G. Austin, *Some English Translations of Virgil* (Liverpool, 1956), pp. 14–15.

26. *The Twickenham Edition of the Poems of Alexander Pope*, ed. John Butt *et al.*, 11 vols. (London, 1939–67), VII, p. 22.

6 'An improving writer to his last': the *Fables*

1. Much of the most detailed recent work on the *Fables* remains unpublished. I am particularly indebted, in what follows, to two Cambridge doctoral dissertations: Tom Mason's 'Dryden's Chaucer' (1977), and Richard Bates's 'Dryden's Translations from "The Decameron" ' (1982).

2. See Mason, 'Dryden's Chaucer', Chapter 2, and H. G. Wright, 'Some Sidelights on the Reputation and Influence of Dryden's *Fables*', *Review of English Studies*, 21 (1945), 23–37.

3. *Dryden: The Critical Heritage*, p. 265.

4. *The Correspondence of Alexander Pope*, ed. G. Sherburn, 5 vols. (Oxford, 1959), I, p. 2.

5. *Dryden: The Critical Heritage*, p. 324.

6. *Specimens of the British Critics*, p. 206.

7. *The Works of John Dryden*, I, p. 493.

8. For a fuller discussion of this poem, see my article, 'Nature's Laws and Man's: the Story of Cinyras and Myrrha in Dryden and Ovid', *Modern Language Review* 80 (1985), 786–801.

9. For a full discussion of the sources of this passage, see Bates, *Dryden's Translations from 'The Decameron'*, pp. 190–5.

10. *Dryden: The Critical Heritage*, p. 324.

11. C. S. Lewis, 'Shelley, Dryden and Mr Eliot', *Selected Literary Essays*, ed. Walter Hooper (Cambridge, 1969), p. 192. A good rebuttal of many of Lewis's points is provided by Emrys Jones, 'Dryden's Sigismonda', *English Renaissance Studies: Presented to Dame Helen Gardner in Honour of her Seventieth Birthday* (Oxford, 1980), pp. 279–90 (pp. 287–9).

12. See K4 2075; Earl Miner, 'Chaucer in Dryden's *Fables*', *Studies in Criticism and Aesthetics, 1660–1800: Essays in Honor of S. H. Monk* (Minneapolis, 1967), p. 64; Charles Hinnant, 'Dryden's Gallic rooster', *Studies in Philology*, 65 (1968), 647–56; G. R. Noyes, ed., *The Poetical Works of John Dryden*, 2nd edn (Cambridge, Mass., 1950), p. 1032 (citing G. Saintsbury).

13. See Montaigne, *Essays*, III, pp. 40, 169. For further discussion of the Montaignian and Miltonic connections in the poem, see Mason, 'Dryden's Chaucer', pp. 197–245 *passim*.

14. See H. A. Mason, *To Homer through Pope* (London, 1972), Chapter 3; R. E. Sowerby, 'Dryden and Homer' (Ph.D. Dissertation, University of Cambridge, 1975).

15. For details, see Hopkins, *Dryden's Translations from Ovid*, pp. 342–56.

16. See Mason, 'Dryden's Chaucer', pp. 117–19.

17. Blake drew upon this very passage when supplying the captions to his set of engravings *The Gates of Paradise*. See Mason, 'Dryden's Chaucer', pp. 396–7. I am generally indebted to Dr Mason's account of Theseus's speech.

A note on further reading

What follows is not intended as a complete Dryden bibliography, but is, rather, a very brief series of suggestions for those wishing to pursue the lines of enquiry sketched in the present book. More specialised suggestions on particular points will be found in my notes. Those wanting fuller bibliographical information should consult (in the case of 'primary' material) Hugh Macdonald, *John Dryden: A Bibliography of Early Editions and of Drydeniana* (Oxford, 1939) and (in the case of 'secondary' material) David J. Latt and Samuel Holt Monk, *John Dryden: A Survey and Bibliography of Critical Studies* (Minneapolis, 1976). The latter can be updated by referring to the lists and surveys of recent scholarship published in the periodicals *Philological Quarterly*, *Restoration*, and *The Scriblerian*.

Much useful information on Dryden's works and their context will be found in the annotation in the California, Oxford, and Everyman editions (see p. ix above) and in the edition of the *Poetical Works* by George R. Noyes (2nd edn, Cambridge, Mass., 1950). Philip Roberts's edition of *Absalom and Achitophel and Other Poems* (London, 1973) has full and useful notes, as does James Boulton's edition of the *Essay of Dramatick Poesie* (Oxford, 1964). In *The Beauties of Dryden* (Bristol, 1982), Tom Mason and the present writer offer an ordered sequence of passages from the full range of Dryden's work (with Introduction, Life and Notes) which attempts to arrange and juxtapose extracts so as to reveal the creative interests which recur throughout the Dryden *corpus*.

The standard scholarly *Life* of Dryden is that by Charles E. Ward (Oxford, 1961), but a livelier and more imaginative biography which, though marred by inaccuracies and a tendency to conflate gossip with hard fact, radiates an infectious enthusiasm and sympathy for the poet, is Kenneth Young's *John Dryden: A Critical Biography* (London, 1954; reprinted New York, 1969). David Wykes's *A Preface to Dryden* (London, 1977) has an attractive chapter on 'Dryden the Man'.

Perhaps the best short modern book on the historical, social and intellectual contexts of Dryden's work is Donald Greene's *The Age of Exuberance* (New York, 1970). The new edition of *The Diary of Samuel Pepys*, edited by Robert Latham and William Matthews, 11 vols. (London, 1970–83), well annotated and fully indexed, gives invaluable insight into Dryden's world, its tenth volume (*Companion*) virtually comprising an encyclopedia of Restoration England, with excellent concise articles on such subjects as science, the Royal Society (by A. Rupert Hall), music (by Richard Luckett) and the theatre (by Peter Holland).

The best critical account of Dryden's work which there has ever been (or is ever likely to be) is contained in the writings of Samuel Johnson, not only in the *Life of Dryden* but also in relevant passages in the *Life of Pope* and elsewhere. Beginners sometimes find Johnson's critical idiom difficult, and it is from their point of view unfortunate that the *Life of Dryden* lacks the judicious inclusiveness of the *Life of Pope*, being avowedly more miscellaneous in its emphases. But the reader who persists with Johnson's various writings on Dryden will find his remarks a perpetual source of insight and wisdom. Dryden's next best critic after Johnson is Sir Walter Scott, in the headnotes included in his edition of Dryden's *Works*, 2nd edn, 18 vols. (Edinburgh, 1821) and in the *Life of Dryden* which forms the first volume of that edition. Two attractive later nineteenth-century accounts of Dryden are to be found in *Specimens of the British Critics* by 'Christopher North' (John Wilson) (1846; reprinted Delmar, New York, 1979) and George Saintsbury's volume on Dryden in the English Men of Letters series (1881). Extracts from Dryden's early critics (to c. 1810) are collected by James and Helen Kinsley in *Dryden: The Critical Heritage* (London, 1971). Upali Amarasinghe's *Dryden and Pope in the Early Nineteenth Century* (Cambridge, 1962) is a critically illuminating study of Dryden's reputation between 1800 and 1830.

Three recent articles on Dryden will be of particular interest to readers of the present book: H. A. Mason's 'Living in the Present: Is Dryden's "Horat. Ode 29. Book 3" an example of "creative translation"?', *The Cambridge Quarterly*, 10 (1981), 91–129, Tom Mason's 'Dryden's version of *The Wife of Bath's Tale*', *The Cambridge Quarterly*, 6 (1975), 240–56, and Paul Hammond's 'The Integrity of Dryden's Lucretius', *Modern Language Review*, 78 (1983), 1–23. In the Introduction to *The Oxford Book of Verse in English Translation* (Oxford, 1980) and *Poetry and Metamorphosis* (Cambridge, 1983), Charles Tomlinson discusses Dryden's translations as part of a larger treatment of questions of poetic metamorphosis and renewal.

Index of works

References to works and volumes composed, edited or translated by Dryden
(The more substantial references are indicated in bold type.)

General index

Persons referred to or quoted in the text